## PUBLISHER'S NOTE

The original publication date of this book was August 1, 1977 fifteen days prior to the unfortunate and untimely death of Elvis Presley. **ELVIS: WHAT HAPPENED?** is based on reminiscences of three longtime friends and bodyguards of Presley as told to journalist Steve Dunleavy.

This book was to be, in their minds, a desperate effort to communicate to Elvis one last time: "He will read and he will get hopping mad at us because he will know that every word is the truth," said Sonny West, ". . . but maybe, just maybe, it will do some good." It is too late for Elvis, but perhaps not too late for those who believe that every life contains a painful but instructive truth worthy of recording and understanding.

# ELVIS:
# What Happened?

Red West, Sonny West,
Dave Hebler

As Told To
Steve Dunleavy

BALLANTINE BOOKS • NEW YORK

Library of Congress Catalog Card Number: 77-6127

ISBN 0-345-30635-X

Manufactured in the United States of America

First Edition: August 1977
Thirteenth Printing: July 1988

Las Vegas. It is February and the air is so crisp and clean, it almost crackles. The temperature is below freezing in New York. It is raining in Los Angeles. But in Vegas it is party time as usual. On the ground floor of that monument to human indulgence called the Las Vegas Hilton, the salesmen from New Jersey and Ohio are lurching over blackjack tables, whiskey glasses in their hands. Their wives are addictively pushing quarters into the slots of the one-armed bandits.

High above the casino, on the thirtieth floor of this giant hotel, in the Imperial Suite, the mood is somber, silent and tense. Two husky men, their custom-made shoes sunk deep in the plush carpet, grimly survey the toyland spread four hundred feet below them. Like a giant explosion in a paint factory, the lights flash convulsively, stitching a patchwork of madness that seems fitting in this Mecca of insanity.

Normally, the one-night-standers below them in the casino would have given their eyeteeth to be in that lavish suite. There is champagne in the refrigerator, Dom Perignon chilled to perfection. Exotic foods are on call every minute of the day and night in a town that pays no attention to what time it is when you want to eat, whether breakfast or a five-course feast. A few casual telephone calls can jam the suite with a who's who of the celebrity register and some of the most beautiful women in the country.

But right now Robert "Red" West, thirty-seven, and Delbert "Sonny" West, thirty-five, would have done anything to be far from that suite. Anywhere. A hundred times before in that same suite, it had been different. They had enjoyed the parties, the celebrities, the pretty women, the booze, the laughs. From time to time, they allowed themselves a rare feeling of smug self-satisfaction. It wasn't a bad life for a pair of hicks from Memphis, Tennessee, whose only ambition when they left school had been to land a steady job. It hadn't been bad at all going to opening nights, rubbing shoulders with millionaires and movie stars, men who slapped them on the back, bought them drinks, called them by their first names.

It is different now. Very different. It is 3:00 A.M., February 19, 1973, and the party is over. The champagne stays in the refrigerator. Sonny and Red settle for beer. There are no calls to pretty girls or movie stars. As the two lift the cans of beer to their lips, their casual jackets hang open, and the tool of their trade peeks out from the leather holster each wears on the left side of his chest—a .38 caliber Smith and Wesson revolver. They are crack shots. They are bodyguards to one of the most valuable human properties of the twentieth century. They stand silent, avoiding each other's eyes. Talk will only make it worse. It has been a bad night. The adrenaline pumps through their temples. Red and Sonny, who know too well the man propped up in a king-size bed in the master bedroom, realize the silence will end very soon, and the night is going to get a lot worse. Minutes, normally irrelevant in a town where the casinos ban clocks, tick away painfully. Then the summons comes. The voice bellows from the bedroom.

"Sonny? Red? Sonny? Red? Y'all there?" Sonny clangs the beer can down on the custom-made bar. "Yes, boss, here." Red chimes in, "Coming, coming in." They move quickly.

In the massive bedroom, which is carpeted in lush

green, stands a split-level platform. On the platform is a huge bed, covered in dark green corduroy. It is a regal room. Kings, queens, presidents and prime ministers have slept in this bed. The occupant can survey the domain of the bedroom and the panoramic view of the city below. A man lies in this bed, propped up by four puffy pillows. Soft lights from the ceiling bathe the bed in an aura reserved only for supreme beings.

The man is dressed in expensive, hand-made white silk pajamas. Draped across the chairs are glistening, gem-studded jumpsuits. A long-limbed honey blonde sits on the corner of the bed. Her clothes speak of classy boutiques where the patrons ignore price tags. She is very beautiful. But there the elegance ends. The man in bed is disturbed, very disturbed. His eyes are heavy lidded and bloodshot. Sweat glistens from the pores of his face and forehead, as if he were suffering a cruel attack of malaria. The blonde darts her beautiful eyes nervously, first to Red, then to Sonny. Red avoids her look and stares at the ceiling, only to realize the scene is reflected there in a large mirror.

Sluggishly, the man pulls himself up from the pillows. He leans forward and crosses his legs, yoga fashion. When he speaks, the words are thick, merging into one another. "Come here, Sonny," the man says softly. "Come here, Sonny."

Sonny mounts the platform and kneels at the bedside. The Smith and Wesson prods into his left breast as he leans across the bed to be closer to the man. The man extends his hands to Sonny, and Sonny reaches out to hold them. The man's grip is clammy, the nails sink into Sonny's palms. "Look into my eyes, Sonny, look into my eyes." The words tumble out in a quiet, tired monotone.

"The man has to die. You know the man has to die, the sonofabitch must go. You know it, Sonny, you know it. There is too much pain in me and he did it. Do you hear me? I am right. You know I'm right. Mike Stone has to die. You will do it for me

3

—kill the sonofabitch, Sonny, I can count on you. I know I can."

The beads of perspiration are now rolling down the man's face and into the white silk pajamas. The voice is striking the edge of hysteria. Tears flash in the eyes of Sonny West, a six-foot two-inch ox of a man who has never said no to a fight in his life and never lost one he has said yes to. Sonny is pleading, "No, boss, let's forget that talk, boss. I know he has caused you pain, but you can't talk like that. It ain't right, it just ain't right."

The man is repeating over and over, "Mike Stone must die, he must die. You will do it for me, you must, he has no right to live."

There are books on religion and the occult spread on the bed in front of the man. He sweeps back the covers and they fall on the floor. He rolls out of bed and lurches past the chairs where the beautiful clothes of a star are draped. He brushes past them, and they fall on the floor. He is a driven man now, muttering to himself, "He's gotta go." Carelessly he swings open a giant closet door. Inside more outfits glisten.

The beautiful honey blond is losing her cool. There is desperation on her face. "What's the matter with him? Can't somebody do something? Will somebody tell me what's happened? Calm him down, for God's sake. What's wrong? Oh, my God. Oh, my God."

Sonny looks like a little boy pleading with someone he loves dearly not to jump off a cliff. The man stumbles into the closet, knocking aside the finery inside. He is looking for something. He grabs at a long bulky object. Sonny West knows what it is, and he can feel his heart hit his stomach. Red West feels the back of his neck crawl. "Oh, Lordy," he whispers to himself. "Oh, Lordy."

The man staggers back from inside the closet gripping a gray-green M 16 rifle. Sonny springs to his feet and backs toward the door. The man moves toward him and presses the gun into his hand. Sonny looks at it as if he were holding a rattlesnake. "Jesus Christ, boss, no, not that. Please don't."

The man in pajamas abandons his insistent monotone. "Doesn't anyone understand? Oh, God, why can't anyone understand? Why can't you all understand why this man must die?" He leaps drunkenly on the bed. He is now jumping up and down. He turns to face the wall.

He tries literally to climb the wall, his nails digging into the surface to get a hold, his legs trying to get an impossible grip. "He has hurt me so much, you all know that. He has broken up my family. He has taken my wife away from me. He has destroyed everything and hurt me so much and nobody cares. He is the one who has done it all."

Sonny backs away gripping the M 16. There are tears glistening in his eyes. Big Red is choked with emotion.

The man continues to try to negotiate the bedroom wall. The honey blonde is pleading, "Baby, don't, honey, don't, please don't."

Sonny slowly walks backwards out of the room, holding the M 16. Tears stream down his face. The man in pajamas doesn't know he's gone. Sonny turns and throws the M 16 into a wastebasket in the hallway, then walks into the sitting room. Another man has just come into the suite. His name is Lamar Fike, a normally jolly, three hundred-pound Texan who is now looking worried. He collapses into a chair and hefts his cowboy-booted feet onto a table. Lamar Fike is like a member of the family to Red and Sonny. He knows there is a bad scene inside.

Sonny answers before the question is asked, "Lamar, it's awful. You know what he wants me to do? He wants me to kill Mike Stone. He was in there trying to hypnotize me. He put that M 16 in my hands and told me to go out and waste Mike Stone, just blow him away."

Lamar looks up, his face full of sympathy, and

addresses Sonny with his rarely used Christian name: "Delbert, Cousin, it's gonna be a long, awful night."

Sonny replies solemnly, "No, it's gonna last longer than a night. Not just one night. This is gonna last for a long time . . . And I don't know what to do."

Elvis Presley was long past caring about Sonny's rare show of disobedience. He was not in this world. As Sonny and Lamar glumly reviewed the seriousness of what they were faced with, Red West and the long-limbed blond, Linda Thompson, a former Miss Tennessee beauty queen, Southern belle and girl friend to Presley, tried to calm him in the bedroom. Their attempts were useless.

Red remembers: "There was just Linda, me and 'E,' which we called him, in there alone. I was damned if I knew what to do. I had seen him like this before but never as bad. Linda was as nervous as a cat. I must confess I was pretty emotional too. It's very difficult to see someone you love flip out like that."

Linda was the first to act. She called one of Presley's doctors, Elias Ghanem, a genial, soft-spoken Lebanese who was on twenty-four-hour call whenever Presley was in Las Vegas. Dr. Ghanem told Linda he was on his way. He would give Presley a shot to calm him down.

Sonny had had the presence of mind to walk out of the bedroom. Red was scared to leave, in case Presley did something drastic. "There was no telling what he might do in this state," he said.

Presley turned to Red and weaved across the room toward him. He repeated the chant, "Goddamnit, *you* know he has to die. Red, find someone, somebody to wipe him out. I want the sonofabitch dead. . . . Make some calls. . . . Find someone. . . . I could find a hit man in ten seconds. . . . You can do it, just do it. This man, Mike Stone, has caused me too much suffering." Those words had frightened everyone in the room, but they lay especially heavy on Red's mind.

Red and Sonny are in many ways very much alike. Both are tough, Southern boys. But in other ways they are different. "Sonny and I are closer than most cousins," says Red. "We grew up like brothers. His daddy bought my daddy off a farm where he worked. My grand-daddy used to whip up on my dad, and Sonny's dad just got him away from there. They were both a pair of wild men and we sort of grew up in their shadow, so we are very close. But when it came to our reactions to 'E' there was a difference. Sonny sure as hell loved the man very much. But when it came to me, it was even more than that. Elvis had a kind of hold over me, a hold that I even feel today, even after all that has happened.

"Elvis could bring out the best in me, and he sure as hell could bring out the worst in me. He could really change my moods. If he gave me a hard time, I would get angry and then take it out on someone else. It was something I find difficult to explain, but it's there."

Sonny rejected Presley's pleas to kill Mike Stone with horror, but they lay like a festering sore on Red's mind. Red's love for Elvis Presley was close to being obsessive, and his obedience matched. Red relates: "Man, I got to thinking, 'E' was suffering. And, well, maybe it was just this one man who was causing the suffering. It happens like that. And I got to thinking maybe it just ain't right that any one human should be responsible for another human being's suffering.

"I guess, what I'm saying is this. When he told me to get a hold of someone to wipe out Mike Stone, I gotta tell the truth: I was listening and, like a damn fool, I was listening hard."

That night Red watched Dr. Ghanem give Presley a sedative to calm him down. As Presley slipped away into sleep, Red drew a deep sigh of relief. Maybe, he thought, the talk of killing is over. Maybe tomorrow when he is calmed down, he will forget all about it.

Red had seen Presley get these "attacks" before. Often, the next day not a word would be said, and everything of the previous night would be forgotten.

But Elvis Presley did not forget. The next day when he saw Red, he was calm, but he wanted to know what Red had done about his order. "Red, you made that call yet? Are you working on that thing I asked you about last night? I want it done."

Red shuddered. "I'm working on it, boss. I've made some calls. It's gonna take a little time. I'm working on it." Red was confused, torn between a blind loyalty to Elvis Presley and the gravity of the request. Red West had sure punched a lot of men out, but getting a hit man—that wasn't his scene.

Red turned to his close friend, actor Robert Conrad. "He was the only guy I could open up to," says Red.

Conrad, the handsome, nuggety star of *Hawaiian Eye*, *Wild, Wild West* and *Baa Baa Black Sheep*, is a Hollywood veteran who has been around the track and doesn't shock easy.

Red recalls: "I was scared but I didn't want to let Elvis down and I didn't want to go around hiring anyone for a hit either. Listening to myself now, I must sound like a crazy man. It was crazy to even talk to Elvis about it, but I did and, well, I'm telling the truth."

Conrad spoke to Red with the calm expected of him. "Look, man, don't get into it. Don't go near it. Stay well away. I've seen guys act like that before, just flip out. I've seen it as a reaction to pills or shots. Just go along with what they say and just keep putting them off until they calm down and realize what they are asking. He will come to his senses and will forget all about it . . . we hope."

Red listened quietly to Conrad and came to his senses. "Yeah, you're right, Bob. Thanks a lot and let's forget all about it."

But Elvis still had not forgotten about it. He had become obsessed with this man Mike Stone. Presley would say to Red, "Hey, are you working on that thing? You made any calls?"

Red would always stall for time and put him off. "Yeah, I'm making some calls. Sure am." Red was lying, of course. He hadn't made any calls about the hit—yet.

"Now at that time, Elvis was playing the Hilton," Red continues, "and I guess there were about six or maybe seven days left of his show there. About every second day, Elvis would come on me again. He would ask what am I doing about the hit. I would just keep putting him off. Now what I did, I'm not going to make a whole lot of excuses, apart from the fact that I loved the guy and just couldn't stand seeing him hurt so bad. And let me tell you he was hurting." So Red made some calls—this time for real.

In Las Vegas, you can get a telephone number for a strong-arm man fairly easily. The town was founded on that sort of thing. A mob hit can be organized from there for five thousand dollars, although no hits are to take place in Vegas itself. That's Mafia policy.

Red relates: "Look, man, believe me, anyone, a Baptist minister, can get a telephone number for that sort of thing, anywhere, anytime. Well, like a big dumb ass, I got a telephone number for a hit." The price he was quoted was ten thousand dollars. "Now, I didn't give anyone's name to anyone. I just called this guy and asked how much it was going to cost to be looked after. Then I told them I would call them back."

On the last night of the show, Red went to Elvis with the information. "I guess it must have been around February 25 or 26. I went to him just before he was going on stage. I said to him, 'Well "E," I made that call. I didn't do anything about it. But do you want me to call the guy back?' "

Red was going to make the call from a pay telephone. He wanted Elvis to know that he hadn't let him down, but he also wanted to face Presley with just what he was doing.

It was about twenty minutes before Presley was to go on stage. He pondered Red's question for several seconds and said, "Aw, hell, just let's leave it for now. Maybe it's a bit heavy. Just let's leave it off for now."

Red to this day can remember the feeling of sheer relief. That night he was so happy he went out and got drunk. "Now, the point was, when Elvis asked me to do this, I wanted 'E' to realize what he was saying. That's why I strung him along. At the same time I went as far as making a telephone call, which was just plain, dumb-ass crazy, but Elvis had that thing with me.

"But there is something here. I know some crazy asses, crazier than me, who as soon as 'E' had asked for Mike Stone to get hit, they woulda gone right out and got themselves a hit man and before anyone realized what was going on Mike Stone woulda been dead. Now, there were guys like that around him from time to time. Real strung out. Nutty people."

What would Red have done if Presley had said, "Make the call"? It's a question Red doesn't like to ask himself.

Dave Hebler was thirty-five at the time. He was a fifth-degree black-belt karate champion. He had not yet started to work for Elvis; that trip was yet to come. But he was one of the many of the karate fraternity that always had a place among Presley's circle of friends. He was driving Presley in a Mercedes up to his mansion on Monovale Road in Beverly Hills. They were talking. Hebler had just split with his wife.

He recalls: "Elvis had just come back from the Vegas trip, so I guess it must have been about March of 1973. I had heard a lot of talk among the boys about the night Elvis had asked to have Mike Stone hit. Elvis and I had built up a rapport. We both shared the experience of having split with our wives. We sort of talked about it on a common ground—the problems you go through, the way you miss the kids, all that sort of stuff. But I got the distinct impression that the conversation was leading up to something about Mike Stone."

Dave Hebler is one of the most dedicated karate talents in the country. From his involvement in the art, Dave knew Mike Stone very well. Stone, for his 180 pounds, is one of the most furious karate experts in the United States. He is a quiet, good-looking young man from Hawaii. Of ninety top-class karate matches, he had not lost a single fight. He looked after his body at all times and was well liked in the Los Angeles karate circle. He made a modest living as an instructor, which suited his modest habits. Elvis knew that Mike Stone and Dave Hebler knew each other well.

Dave recalls: "That talk about hitting Mike Stone was pretty disturbing. I did not know Elvis then like I do now, and I was sort of disappointed that he could think in those terms.

"First up, knowing Red and Sonny, I knew they had quite a bit of respect for Mike Stone. They didn't want to get mixed up in that rubbish. From what they knew of Stone, they liked the guy.

"Secondly, let's face it, that kind of talk is pretty heavy stuff, even for guys like us who have been around a bit. Just because things don't fall your way, you don't go asking about hiring a hit man, for God's sake.

"And thirdly, the whole thing could have got very nasty. Mike Stone is a pretty quiet guy, but, believe me, if he had heard a word about this shit going around, he could have turned into a very bad dude. He is the kind of guy who would say, 'Man, if you're looking for me, well here I am.' And if that happened, there is no question in my mind that Mike Stone could have ripped Elvis apart."

Of course, Dave Hebler had known the problem.

He knew that Mike Stone was the man who took Priscilla Presley from Elvis Presley. She had been a caged canary for too long. She had longed for a normal life, around normal people doing normal things. She had found it in a darkly handsome karate instructor. Dave knew the situation very well.

In fact, a few days before Elvis tried to draw him into this conversation about Mike Stone, Dave had been talking to Mike Stone and Priscilla at Orange Coast College in Westminster, Orange County, at a karate tournament.

Priscilla, the beautiful little army brat who for more than a decade had one of the world's most glamorous fortunes at her fingertips, was dressed simply in a pair of jeans and a blouse. She was giggling and laughing like a cheerleader at her first football game. "She was standing at the door of the tournament stamping the hands of paying customers who came in. She was very sweet and so was Mike. Very, very natural," Dave recalls. "So this was Priscilla Presley and here she is stamping hands at her boyfriend's tournament. She was just helping out her struggling karate instructor boyfriend, who I guess in those days in a good week would have been making two hundred and fifty dollars. Maybe that was what bugged Elvis so much. If she had run off with someone like Frank Sinatra maybe, somehow that would have erased the hurt ego. I don't know. But a two-hundred-and-fifty-buck-a-week karate instructor, that must have hurt."

Red West believes that Dave is only partly right: "There is no doubt that his ego was very badly hurt. It happened right before our eyes. We knew it was going on when he didn't even know. Now I don't blame her for leaving Elvis. She had a life that no normal woman could put up with. But I do know he loved that woman. Even today he would never have a word said against her. He always told me, 'I will always have a love for Priscilla.' In fact, deep down,

I believe that Priscilla was only one of two people he *ever* really did love in his whole life. He didn't love us. We thought he did. But he did love that woman Priscilla."

2

Humes High School was one of those drab, three-story relics of the South's nineteenth-century past. A dull, brown brick building, it stood forbiddingly on Manasas Street, Memphis, Tennessee, a monument to all that was strict, Southern and no nonsense. The only good thing about Humes High School on that hot, summer day in 1952 was that the 3:15 P.M. bell had rung, and the kids were pouring out of classrooms like frothy beer from a bottle.

Sixteen-year-old Red West, having been bent into a classroom desk all day, suddenly got a little spring into his lanky gait as he headed for one of the really important things in life—football practice. To Red, school hours spent in the classroom were just pesky interruption to his teenage life of raising hell or playing football or baseball. Red, naturally enough, got his name from a defiant thatch of carrot-colored hair, which he wore in the fashionable crew cut of the era. When time or money was short, the crew cut would often grow out, giving Red the appearance of an overused toothbrush. He was a good-natured kid, dreadfully shy at times and easy to embarrass, not very much different from the Red West of today. Quick to go into battle with his fists if someone took too many liberties with his shyness, he had a reputation of being easy to get along with if left alone, but a sheer terror if rubbed the wrong way.

Red was hardly every girl's idea of a school heart-throb. He was freckle-faced and painfully skinny as a legacy of childhood rickets triggered by a dirt-poor Southern diet as a baby. But what he lacked in glamor, he made up for in his handling of muscle, footballs and baseballs. Despite his spare build, he was one of the best centers Humes High School had ever produced.

Red stopped off at his locker to pick up his football gear. It was not yet 3:30, but the school halls were silent, empty of children. Red clattered eagerly down the polished brown asphalt hallway. His eye was caught by a solitary figure leaning desolately against the wall. Red was struck by the boy's apparent loneliness. He recognized him as a kid in the year ahead of him, Elvis Aron Presley. Red knew him to say hello to but nothing more.

Seventeen-year-old Presley was a nice kid, even if he looked a little out of place in the sea of kids with crew cuts and pink scalps. He was pasty-faced with a virulent case of acne. He had long brown hair cut in a ducktail fashion. The handfuls of Vaseline he put on it made it look much darker than it was. Long sideburns intruded into the acne. He had a preference for leather jackets and would often tie a red bandanna around his neck in the fashion popular with interstate truck drivers of the era.

Despite the fact that Presley was a year senior to Red, in fact in his graduation year, he broke with teenage protocol and addressed Red first. He muttered a shy "Hi, Red."

Red West's eyes mist a little these days when he recalls that moment: "Even just looking at him, I knew something was wrong, something was bugging him."

Red stopped his charge toward football practice and simply said, "Hi, Elvis, what's the matter? Something wrong?"

Young Presley shuffled uncomfortably and said,

"There's three guys outside who are going to beat me up."

Red was never slow to lift his dukes to anyone, but he was particularly prone to go into action against bullies. Without looking to see how many were waiting outside, Red nodded his head and said quietly, "Let's go check on it and see what it's about."

Red led the way along the hallway, down some steps and onto the sidewalk of Manasas Street. There stood three boys, high school seniors, like Elvis. It seemed they had some objection about the way Elvis wore his hair. Now, there is no real way of telling when Red West is angry if you go by his voice. It's the same slow Tennessee country drawl that seems to take hours to complete a sentence.

Red looked at the biggest boy there. "I understand you three fat asses are gonna whip this little guy's ass."

The big guy stuttered out an explanation: "Hey, man, it ain't your business. We were just gonna talk to him, that's all."

Red nodded. "Well, that's just fine. I tell you what: you and I will talk here for a while, while he just walks home in peace." Elvis turned quickly on his heels and sprinted home. The confrontation seemed to have ended.

The next day, Elvis sidled up to Red after class and said gratefully, "Gee, Red, thanks a lot for yesterday."

Red smiled, just as shy. "Forget it, man."

Red has perfect recall for those days: "It seems that the way I remember it, someone was always picking on him. Don't know why. He was easygoing enough, quiet, well mannered, was always respectful of his elders, and he never wised off at anyone. In many ways he was a very good kid, a lot nicer than some of the others around."

But if Presley's mouth wasn't arrogant, his appearance was. He would spend hours in the school washroom combing his ducktail to perfection. When he wasn't wearing a leather jacket and jeans, it was some outrageously colored pair of pegged pants. In the sea of 1,600 pink-scalped kids at school, Elvis stood out like a camel in the Arctic. Intentionally or not, his appearance expressed a defiance that his demeanor did not match.

Red relates: "It was that hair, man—it got him into all kinds of trouble. If he had a regular haircut like the rest of us, he probably wouldn't have been bothered. But I guess the other kids thought he was trying to show off or something. That hair has always been his crowning glory. I have never known any other human to take more time over his hair. He would spend hours on it, smoothing, mussing it up and combing it and combing it again."

Despite the rescue operation by Red, he and Elvis never really got close. "It was just a warm 'hello' or a 'hi there' and we'd go our separate ways. We were in different classes so we would see each other a little bit on and off. He would always go straight home after school. He never fooled around in the streets, just straight home."

Elvis tried out for the football team but without much success. With a bit more weight and a lot more confidence, he just might have made a good guard, but things didn't seem to work out. "I think," says Red, "that Elvis lasted on the squad about three weeks. The coach, a good old guy called Coach Boyce, just couldn't stand Elvis and his long hair. Coach Boyce could be a real tough sonofagun and he was always onto Elvis to cut his hair. He just shamed 'E' so much, he finally left the squad.

"I really felt sorry for him. He seemed very lonely and had no real friends. He just didn't seem to be able to fit in. But I gotta admire him. All that razzing that the kids and some of the teachers gave him about his hair. Elvis would never cut it. That was his trademark. He went his own way without fighting back but he wouldn't give in, he would have rather died than cut that hair."

In fact, the way Red remembers it, there was a time when Elvis thought his hair was going to be cut, and he had a look on his face that gave the impression he was going to die. It happened not too long after Red's first rescue operation of Elvis. In those days, when children were forbidden to smoke on the school grounds, the school washroom was the smoking gallery. It was there that all the swingers congregated to sneak their clandestine puffs, away from teachers' watchful eyes. Red walked in to take a leak.

"The place was full of smoke, you could hardly see in front of you for all the smoke," Red recounts. "But I could see far enough to notice that old 'E' was in a whole heap of trouble again. About four or five guys had him in there, and they were holding him and pushing him up against the wall and then grabbing him from behind. They were yelling and laughing and wising off at him and his hair. They decided they were gonna cut his hair.

"Now a smart guy usually keeps his nose out of other people's business. I knew the guys who were hassling Elvis. They were on the football squad. I suppose they got this haircutting business from old Coach Boyce. The guys who were giving Elvis a hard time were not really bad guys, just a bit noisy and stuff. But when I saw Elvis's face, it just triggered something inside of me. I mean we were just kids and they weren't gonna kill him or anything, but there was that look of real fear on his face. He was looking like a frightened little animal and I just couldn't stand seeing it. When you're very poor, you tend to let everyone look after their own troubles, but that face of Elvis's, I can see it to this day. And I saw that face like that many times later, and it always had the same effect on me. Just churned something up inside of me. It's a child's face and it asks for help."

Red zipped up and strolled over to the wall where

the mob had Elvis pinned. "Now, look," said Red to the mob, "this ain't gonna do anyone any good. There ain't no need for this. If he likes his hair that way, well, no sense in hassling him. Now, if you cut his hair, you're gonna have to cut my hair too, and that's gonna develop into something else." Once again that lazy, quiet drawl had a dramatic effect. The mob let Elvis go. Before Elvis left, he darted a look at Red that said thanks a million times over.

Dave Hebler, who got to know Red as well as anyone, sums up Red this way: "You know, if a guy hassles me, I walk away. If he follows me and persists, then, okay, I'll hit him. Now with Sonny, if someone hassles him, he will try to talk the guy out of it, and if that doesn't work, then he'll hit him. But with Red, if someone hassles him, he gives you the two-minute warning. If you don't get the message pretty quick, boom, it's all over." In later days, the three of them together were like the Three Musketeers.

Elvis saw Red the next day and gave him a shy thank you. It couldn't have been easy for Elvis, a year older than Red and a year ahead of him at school, to have to thank him twice for getting him out of trouble.

"In later years," says Red, "he remembered those two incidents, although he never mentioned them. Elvis never forgets a damned thing; he has a memory like an elephant. Somehow, you know, that year 1952 put me in a role as Elvis's protector. It wasn't a role I looked for, it just happened that way."

It was a role that Red assumed for the next twenty-four years in one way or another. "Elvis had a way with me. Sometimes he was like a damned spoiled kid who needed to be spanked, and other times he was just so helpless and needing of help it was like he was your own child. It's a job I took on readily and had a lot of fun doing and a lot of heartbreak. And even now, I still feel it's my job, even if I never see him again."

Delbert "Sonny" West ran his hands through his bristly U.S. Air Force regulation haircut and looked at the spectacle before him with amazement. Only half an hour earlier, he had walked through the main gates of the Rodeo Grounds in Tucson, Arizona. With him was a quiet, corn-fed Southwestern girl whose demeanor and looks suggested that when someone invented virginity and apple pie, they must have had her in mind. The dainty face and the Sunday-best dress she was wearing told him immediately to resist cursing in her presence and scrap any thoughts of ever scoring.

Yet only a half-hour later, she was behaving totally out of character—like a sex-starved little nymphet. Perhaps he was wrong after all, and the night would not go unrewarded. The reason for her transformation was up there on the stage—Elvis Aron Presley, the kid from Humes High School, where Sonny West had also gone, four years behind Elvis.

Elvis Presley, his hair shining like sprayed patent leather, was straddling the microphone in the most suggestive of manners. His groin gyrated inches from the upright stand, and he was shaking in convulsive movements as if possessed by an alien spirit. When he sang quietly he sobbed. When he sang loudly, he commanded his worshippers. The women seemed to be beset by alternating emotions, from motherly pity to slavelike obedience. His lips, curling down on the right side of his mouth, arrogantly pouted suggestion and triumph. Then his mouth would twist in pain, and a thousand females screamed in pity and wanted to enclose the poor child in their arms.

"Since mah babeeee left me . . . " The words of "Heartbreak Hotel," already a stupendous seller, had the women crying out in pain for his loss.

My God, thought Sonny West, and this is pimply-faced Elvis Presley, who only four years ago had to look to my cousin Red to get him out of jams. "It was hard for me to believe," he recalls.

Sonny was having considerable trouble keeping Miss Apple Pie in her seat. Sonny was in the air force and had gone along to the Rodeo Ground, which was not far from his base, to see what all the fuss was about this kid he'd gone to school with. "Believe me, this gal changed right before my eyes. I had heard all the publicity and I knew Red was very close to Elvis, but it didn't really seem to make any impression on me. He was just a country and western singer who had got onto the rock 'n' roll bit. But this gal, I'm telling you, if someone had grabbed that lady there and then and dragged her off to bed, it would have happened there and then. Every time he moved, it seemed like a couple of hundred gals were getting it off. Then, after the show, my gal just went back to what she was like before. It was as if all that carrying on was for Elvis and nobody else."

Sonny never did score with the lady, but the incident gave him a preview of the awesome control Elvis had over a female audience, a power that Sonny was to see underlined a thousand times in the years to come. Sonny never knew Elvis at school. "Just saw him in the hallway now and then," he recalls. "I was about four years behind him, so there was no call to know him. Maybe if he had been a big football hero or he had been a bit of a wild man with his fists, I would have made it my business to know more about him, but really he was just an older kid who happened to get noticed because he had this long hair and pretty wild clothes. He was pretty much of a nobody."

But now Elvis Presley was indeed a somebody— who, Sonny now realized, had had something hidden far inside him when he was at Humes High School. Now it was all coming out.

Sonny wanted to go backstage that night and try to see Elvis, but he was too shy, and anyway he probably wouldn't have been able to get near him. The year was 1956, and "Heartbreak Hotel" was setting sales records all over the country. Churchmen were preaching about the evil of Elvis Presley. Even the Communist press of eastern Europe saw Elvis Presley as the main reason why American youth was so degenerate. In fact, they said, Elvis Presley was just about the best reason Communist youths should stay Communists.

In popular appeal, Elvis Presley was surpassing even Valentino. There was Frank Sinatra, too, of course, but Elvis was someone American youth could call its very own. Two more years of worldwide hysteria over Elvis would pass before Sonny West met him.

"I knew my cousin Red was very close to Elvis," Sonny recalls. "They had become like brothers. But when they were teaming up, I was off somewhere else. Then I joined the Air Force, so I was not in on it at the beginning like Red was. By the time I met him, it was 1958. Elvis was getting pretty close to going into the army, and Red had done a stint in the marines.

"When Red came back to Memphis on leave, he would always be with Elvis on his gigs; in fact, just about anywhere he went, Red was with him. I had just got out of the air force, and I told Red I wanted to meet him. I was a pretty typical Southern kid at the time. A crew-cut hellraiser who was easy to impress."

If Sonny was expecting to see a sophisticated, elegantly tailored superstar clinking champagne glasses with other celebrities, he was in for a big disappointment. "Red told me he would introduce me," Sonny recalls. "So he told me to come on down to the Rainbow Roller Skating Rink. Roller skating was big in those days in Memphis. If you didn't go to the movies on a date, then you took your date to the Rainbow." Elvis was twenty-three at the time and the biggest single-recording star in the country.

Today, twenty-three-year-old superstars would go to a roller skating rink with the same enthusiasm they would go to church. But Elvis was a different sort of superstar. Despite his outrageous gyrations on stage, he was very faithful to his Deep South roots.

22

He lived with his parents, whom he adored. He was polite to the point of humility with his elders, and his pleasures were decidedly simple.

"In those days," says Sonny, "Elvis would rent the roller rink for himself and his boys from midnight onwards. There would often still be fans hanging around, and occasionally they would join in. He was always polite and considerate to them." For most twenty-three-year-olds, roller skating would probably have seemed a bit juvenile. But it was as if Elvis was trying to make up for the things he had missed out on as a kid at school. Elvis would keep on visiting that rink right into the early 1960s.

Other nights, he would rent the Memphis fairgrounds from the owner, a local character named Wimpy Adams. He would ride the roller coaster and the Dodgem cars with his Memphis friends until dawn some mornings. "It was just plain, clean fun, but they were among the best days of our lives. Red's life, my life and I know Elvis's life."

Sonny met Elvis on a spring night in 1958. He went to the rink with his brother-in-law, Bill Thorpe, a superb athlete who was Memphis All-Schools Boxing champion. "It was just before midnight, and we just hung around the edge of the rink until Red rolled up with Elvis. He introduced us and Elvis couldn't have been nicer. He shook hands and asked about my time in the air force. We shot the breeze for a while. He seemed genuinely interested in me and what I had to say. He was, despite who he was, a very ordinary kind of guy. He was as good-looking as hell, but he seemed to take all the girls falling all over him as a bit of a joke. It hadn't gone to his head. You just couldn't meet a nicer guy." In the years to come, whenever Red remembered that first impression of Sonny's, he would get a lump in his throat, because Elvis did indeed change; even if it wasn't his fault, he changed.

Elvis turned to get onto the rink, extended a warm

handshake, gave that curled-lip smile of his and started to laugh as he eyed Sonny and Bill Thorpe. He left them with the comment "New meat, huh?"

Red smiled back at Elvis, rubbed his hands together and said, "Yup, Elvis, new meat." And neither Sonny nor Bill understood what they meant, although they soon would.

Elvis, Red and a crowd of insiders, including Elvis's cousins, Bobby and Junior Smith, started to skate around the rink. Sonny recognized the Smith boys. They had another brother, Billy, who would become part of Presley's entourage when Sonny hit the road. Bobby and Junior were not as fortunate. They were the black sheep of the Presley family and were later exiled to the outer limits of the group, but in those days they were about as skillful skaters as one could find in Memphis.

A little after midnight, Sonny and Bill Thorpe noticed that several cardboard boxes had been brought on the scene. Inside was an assortment of pads for the shins, shoulders, elbows and knees.

"Looked a pretty sensible idea," recalls Sonny. "We weren't very good skaters, so we started to put them on. If we fell over we wouldn't get hurt, and seeing most of us played football, it was a good idea to keep the injuries down."

Then Sonny and Bill saw what the pads were really for, and they realized what Elvis's "new meat" remark meant. The group on the floor had divided themselves up into two teams and were playing a game called "war." The game had extremely simple rules. Both teams charged each other, and the object was to knock the opposition off their feet.

Sonny remembers Bill Thorpe looking at this: "We said, 'Are you crazy, I'm not getting in there with that stuff.'" Sonny was not as prudent, particularly as his cousin, Red, dared him to get on the floor.

Sonny relates: "I must have been mad, but it was too late. The next thing I knew I was on the floor.

Junior Smith was the referee. He blew the whistle and the war was on."

Sonny was on the team opposite Red and Elvis. There were no rules, except a gentleman's agreement that there would be no punching. Despite the fact that the toughest guy on the opposition team was Red West, Sonny had no real trouble from him.

"But, Lordy, there was this gal, I'll never forget her . . . she flat-assed killed me," says Sonny. "I would be skating along, then wham, this gal would knock me flat. Elvis would see this and burst out laughing. I would get up and, wham, down I would go again. When I first got in there and saw a woman on the other side, I was ready to go easy on her, but I grew to where I wanted to kill her.

"After about half an hour she had near broken me in half. One time she sent me skidding into the railing and I split my cheek. Elvis always had a first-aid man there. So he patched me up and I went on the floor again.

"In the end, I saw her coming toward me, and I set myself to send her flying.

"Well, man, that was a mistake. When she hit me, she knocked me flatter than a tack. Me, six-foot two-inch me, and a gal knocks me flat on my ass. This time, she hit me so hard that I hit my head on the floor and that was it. I was out cold. When I regained consciousness, there was Elvis standing over me, laughing that boyish laugh. He looked down and said, 'New meat, huh?' Those sonsofbitches knew all along what she could do. But it was great fun and Elvis was fun to be with."

Sonny and Red recall that Elvis played hard and tough on those nights, and he reveled in the rough and tumble. At last, Elvis Aron Presley was one of the boys.

"Well, not quite," corrects Red. "We made sure that he never really got hurt. We were always looking after him. Nobody picked on Elvis. Most of us were very close friends. Occasionally, an outsider would come in and try to show off in front of his girl friends, trying to take Elvis out.

"About a week after Sonny came to the rink there was one guy who was making a real ass of himself. Just going for Elvis and nobody else. Well, we took care of him real good. After the first night, Sonny and I were always on Elvis's team.

"Well, this one guy, Sonny and I taught him a lesson. We hi-lowed him and sent him about fifteen feet through the air. Lucky he didn't hit the railing or we would have killed him. Elvis liked that kind of loyalty."

Elvis was only a few weeks away from going into the army. He took an immediate shine to the big, husky, handsome Sonny. Red knew that Sonny was going to be on the Elvis team for a long time to come. Elvis had told Sonny that when he returned from his stint in the army, he would like to see more of him.

There was only one little note of discord. Elvis told Red a week before leaving for Germany, "He's a heck of a nice guy, your cousin Sonny. But he never stops saying 'sonofabitch.' He calls everyone 'sonofabitch.' I just wished he would stop saying it all the time."

"Elvis thinks you're a great guy," Red told Sonny, "but he figures you cuss too much. Always cussing, saying goddamn and calling everybody a sonofabitch." They both laughed. But as Sonny became closer, much closer, he realized that for Elvis the word *sonofabitch* held a particularly deep insult. If Priscilla Presley was, as Red points out, one of the two people whom Presley ever loved, then the other was his mother, Gladys Presley.

Sonny relates: "It was as if the word was an immediate insult to his mother, and, man, that was treading on dangerous ground with Elvis." It was in 1963 that Sonny saw the word trigger an uncontrollable flash of temper.

By then, Presley was making an estimated three million dollars a year, and his spending habits had reached exotic proportions. His film commitments meant he was spending more time in Hollywood. Along with a mind-boggling fleet of cars, Presley rented, and later bought, some of the best and most stylish houses that Tinseltown had to offer. One in particular that he rented was in Bel Air, on Belagio Road. It was the kind of house that poor Memphis kids dreamed about when they flicked ravenously through movie magazines.

Elvis was particularly generous with his hospitality. His houses were continual halfway stops for his cronies and the ever-faithful band of Southerners who had been dubbed by the press the "Memphis Mafia." If he liked you, you were in, and when Elvis liked you, there were no half measures. Clothes, parties, Cadillacs were all part of the accoutrements of being "a friend." In return, he demanded blind loyalty and a faith that whatever he did was right.

On this particular night, one that is indelibly imprinted in Sonny's mind, Elvis held open house. The place was made for fun and games. Apart from its lavish furnishings, there was a special party room that contained every conceivable kind of pinball game. In the center of the room was a large competition-size pool table. The room was on a lower level. Steps from the games room took you into a gigantic living room. Sonny knew there were going to be a few of the boys around throwing an impromptu party. The final filming for *Fun in Acapulco* was over, and everybody was winding down. "I was at the International House of Pancakes down on the Strip, and I picked up on these two pretty girls. One of the girls later became quite a well-known actress, and the other one—let's call her Judy (which is not her real name)—was a sweet little thing. I think she is probably married now, so I don't want to embarrass her by identifying her.

"Anyway, I took them up to the house, and there is a whole thing going on up there. Depending on what sort of mood he is in, Elvis on one of these nights just might say hullo to everybody and go straight to bed. Other nights he wouldn't even come down at all, but if he was looking around for a little action, he would sweet-talk some gal for a while and then take her upstairs for some action. On this night, Elvis didn't seem to be doing any of those things. He was pretty tired and seemed a bit agitated. I walked in and gave him a big hullo. He wanted me to play pool with him. Now I had these ladies with me, but when Elvis wants you to do something, you do it. So I left these two little gals to all the other vultures up there and started to play pool with Elvis.

"After a while we started playing four-hand pool with two other guys at the party. Elvis's mood was not being helped by the fact that he was muffing about every second shot. As in all these cases, I got a bit tense, knowing that Elvis can flash in these situations. What made me more worried was the fact that there were a lot of people there, lots of chicks, and I was scared he would do something in front of them all." Sonny's intuition was shockingly accurate.

By this time, little Judy had gotten a bit bored with the party. The man she had come in with, Sonny, seemed too busy playing pool to take any notice of her. She decided to leave. "Anyway, Elvis is just about to hit a shot, and little ole Judy comes down the steps into the games room."

She called to him, "I think I'd better be leaving now, Sonny. Could you move your car please? It's blocking mine and I can't get out."

Sonny replied, "Yup, hon, just a minute."

Elvis slowly rose from the table where he was about to hit a shot. "Sonny, what in the hell does she want?"

Sonny shrugged. "Nothing, boss. She just wants me to move my car so she can get out."

That didn't satisfy Elvis. "Whoa, there. Hell, man, you're playing pool. Let her get someone else to move the damn car."

Judy flushed with embarrassment. She had never met Elvis, although she admired him, and now here he was telling her to go to blazes. Judy replied, "Look, I'm sorry, I just don't know anyone else here. That's why I asked Sonny. And, Sonny, if you just move it, I'll leave. I'm sorry to bother you." Judy looked like she wanted to jump into a hole somewhere. Elvis Presley's eyes narrowed, he pulled himself upright and his lips curled back. Sonny knew the signs.

"Goddamnit!" Elvis yelled. "Goddamnit, didn't you hear what I said? Get someone else to move it."

Judy had endured enough embarrassment and she flared in return. "Go to hell, you sonofabitch." That did it. It happened very fast.

"He took that pool cue in his fist," Sonny recalls. "Then, like he was throwing a spear, he just leaned back and threw it right at her across the pool table. She had no time to duck. The sharp end of the pool cue bored right into her body. It hit her just above the nipple of the left breast. She didn't scream. It was more like a sharp little gasp, and she crumpled backwards on the floor."

Sonny dashed around the table to where Judy lay on the ground. "Judy, Judy, you okay, hon?" Sonny was worried. "She was very pale. And she was lying there sobbing very quietly. Her face was whiter than vanilla ice cream. I was scared something bad had happened. It was a helluva blow."

When Sonny yelled out and asked Judy whether she was all right, Presley picked up another cue and replied, "Hell yes, she's all right. It was just one of those dramatic falls. Drag her ass out of here."

Sonny picked up the quietly sobbing Judy in his arms, carried her up the steps to the upper level of the den and laid her gently on a couch. A hush had fallen over the party. Everybody seemed embarrassed. Elvis called for Sonny to get back to the pool table. "She was hurting," Sonny recalled. "Her face was all screwed up with pain. And she was sobbing. Jesus, I felt awful. I talked to her, trying to calm her down. But she was hurting and she was mad, and I didn't blame her for being mad."

She looked up at Sonny and repeated, "That sonofabitch, why did he do that? I never did anything to him. He needn't have done that."

She was holding her breast and sobbing. "Gee, hon," said Sonny, "I'm sorry that happened. I know he didn't mean it. It was just one of those reaction things, you know. It was temper. He didn't mean it. It's gonna be all right." Sonny was angry at himself. Here he was covering for Elvis for what he thought was a particularly brutal act. If any other man had done it in Sonny's presence, he would have dismembered him.

"Then," recalls Sonny, "she started talking about suing Elvis. I was worried about that in the back of my mind. She had every damn right to sue him. I told her not to be silly. She should forget about it. Then I very gently told her that she was in his house, and she did insult him, and there were a lot of his friends around as witnesses and then I said, 'Who do you think they're gonna stand up for?' "

Judy was steaming. "I don't care who they will stand up for. I'm going to sue him. He deserves it." Sonny felt ashamed of himself. That really wasn't his style. Here was this little girl, victim of a sudden, sadistic flash of temper, and he was trying to talk her out of suing.

"I wouldn't have blamed her a bit," he says, "but I was so locked into Elvis. It was second nature for me to stand up for him, even when I knew he was very wrong. We had all brainwashed ourselves into that way of thinking."

Judy got up and left. She never did file a suit.

Sonny went back to the den after Judy left. He was angry at Presley. He scowled across the pool table at his boss, who had now calmed down and was obviously feeling guilty. He was trying to justify his actions. No way would he have said he was wrong, according to Sonny. "Look, Sonny," he said, "if she had hit me or called me a bastard or told me to go fuck myself, it would have been okay."

Sonny scowled. "Hey, man, that little gal is hurting. There was no need to do that. She just wanted me to move the damn car."

Elvis was insistent that he had a right to do what he did. Then he said sheepishly, "Well, man, she shouldn't have called me a sonofabitch. That ain't right."

Doctors report that a particularly severe blow in the sensitive region of the breast can trigger a mass of ailments—a tumor reaction, a cyst or a blood clot. Soon after the pool cue incident, Sonny bumped into Judy on the Strip in Hollywood. She was still very annoyed at what had happened.

"I apologized to her because it was a bad deal and I quite liked her. I felt responsible because I brought her to the place. Anyway, I don't know whether it's true or not, but she told me that the pool cue had damaged some nerves in the left breast. The nipple of her left breast had dropped lower than the right breast nipple. Damn, that made me angry. She was a pretty little thing with a cute little figure. . . . Sonofabitch, that made me angry."

**4**

Dave Hebler was one of the few Yankees who became a member of the inner circle, the Memphis Mafia. Born in Pittsfield, Massachusetts, in 1937, he is of average build and given to a quiet, almost intellectual manner of speech. His distaste for guns set him aside from the Memphis boys, who, following Elvis's lead, always seemed to have an arsenal somewhere on hand.

As a child, a stray BB slug, fired by another child, deprived him of the sight of his right eye. When he got close to Presley, he adopted the habit of wearing a .38 Smith and Wesson revolver, although he was not crazy about the idea.

Despite his mild manner and his distinct distaste for gun sports, he can be one of the most lethal men imaginable. When he first met Elvis he was a fifth-degree black-belt karate master. Today he has a seventh degree. He stays away from street fights, and he is not much of a boozer. But in three seconds—two and a half seconds on a good day—he can deliver a combination of thirteen blows to a man's body that will first cripple and then kill.

In the fall of 1972, Dave had undergone a rather big change in his life. He had left his job and split with his wife, the mother of his two young daughters.

He was now coming out of the tailspin of a broken marriage and working off his frustrations by devoting himself almost around the clock to the art of karate, in which he had been involved for nineteen years. He was particularly close to his instructor, Ed Parker, a man regarded as the doyen of American karate.

Parker comes from a prominent family in Hawaii and is even a shade sharper than Hebler when it comes to delivering killer chops and kicks. Parker's lightning expertise with his feet and hands had drawn him to the attention of Elvis Presley, who had become smitten with the art while in the U.S. Army in Germany. Parker would often tour with Presley and act as his karate mentor.

One fall evening in 1972, Hebler met Elvis Presley for the first time. It was around seven, and Dave was working out at Ed Parker's karate studio in Santa Monica. On the mats that night were fifteen of Los Angeles' top karate exponents swishing the air with deadly chops and kicks. "I remember there was a little activity around the door to Ed's studio," Dave says. "I took a break from training, looked up and saw the rather dramatic entrance of a good-looking, husky guy, a little overweight, with jet black hair, dressed in tight black pants and a white Spanish-style bolero shirt. It was Elvis."

Presley would often drop by the Parker studio, shoot the breeze and sometimes work out. Of course, it wasn't a casual visit. Elvis Presley never moves without several telephone calls to his destination, and then he leaves with an entourage that can number a dozen people. Presley came into the studio at the head of his entourage and shook hands all around. He was accompanied by a beautiful girl who, Dave Hebler later learned, was Linda Thompson.

To Dave's surprise, after a brief conversation, Presley got out on the mats with some of the most deadly karate talent in the country. "I have been an instructor, having had my own studio, so I don't

34

know whether Ed manipulated it, but he paired me off with Elvis, perhaps thinking I could handle any problem that being paired off with Elvis could present.

"In these situations one member of the pair acts as a karate dummy. That is, he takes simulated kicks and blows. He reacts as if the blows were making full contact. Often, of course, they do. But in training, you have to keep that stuff to a minimum or you would have broken bones all over the place. Real karate artists are very controlled both in their movements and their emotions. It's not something to be played at.

"Now I have been in these situations a million times. You are usually working out with someone of similar experience to yourself, someone who knows what he is doing. Within seconds out there on the mats with Elvis it was very obvious to me that one, Elvis didn't know half as much about karate as he thought he did; and two, he hardly knew where he was. He was moving very sluggishly and lurching around like a man who'd had far too much to drink. When I got close to him, I could smell his breath, and it sure didn't seem as if he had been drinking. I mean, he was actually tripping over and damn near falling on his butt.

"Somehow, I got the drift of things, and while I couldn't make him look like an expert, I tried to react to his moves in such a way that he wouldn't look half as bad as he could have. Of course, the entourage, headed by Linda, was fascinated by him. By the looks on their faces, you would have thought he was a world champion. Thankfully, the karate 'demonstration' by Elvis ended. But then some bright spark suggested we have an impromptu tournament with guess who officiating. Elvis."

According to Dave Hebler, officiating, even for an expert, is not an easy task. "You have to really know what you're doing," says Dave. "Those blows are whipping by at a hundred miles an hour, and you have to pick up on them very fast. You also had to know instantly the ones that would connect and the ones that would just float into the air. It is very difficult. You can imagine what it was like for Elvis, who, in fairness, never officiated at a real karate tournament. I mean, I promise you, it was hopeless."

Hebler, seeing the beginning of a very embarrassing situation, took up a position behind Presley, the referee. "I am standing behind him, to help by prompting the action, you know: 'left hand punch, right kick,' and I was giving him the points, so he would know who to appoint as a winner."

At the end of it, Elvis sluggishly shook hands with Dave with a hint of recognition that Dave had helped him through an impossible moment, even for an experienced referee. "Not that Elvis didn't sincerely believe he was in charge of the situation. He did. But, in the back of his mind, he must have recognized that I had helped him." For Dave Hebler, those two hours out there on the mats were some of the most awkward moments he had ever had in a karate studio. Two days later, Hebler was working out in his own small karate studio on Alosta Boulevard in Glendora, outside Los Angeles. It was a modest operation but was netting Dave about two hundred dollars a week, and he had a young and enthusiastic following. It was fun and it was his. "I got a call from Ed Parker, who was with Elvis a lot around that time. Ed said he was calling for Elvis and that Elvis wanted to come out to the studio. I was surprised and very flattered. I said, 'Wow, sure. How about 4:00 P.M.? That will be great.'

"At four that day, a gigantic custom-made blue Mercedes-Benz rolled up. Guys poured out of it like it was a marine invasion. The last one out, of course, was King Elvis.

"It was quite an impressive sight. There were all these members of the palace guard walking in front of him as if they were casing the place and behind them came the king. But what was the most amusing about this spectacle was Elvis's appearance. It was about seventy-four degrees, maybe warmer. Anyway, Elvis was wearing this unbelievably thick overcoat. It was black with red piping. He had a ring on every finger, and a gigantic ram's head necklace, which I learned later the Hilton Hotel had given him as a present and which I was told was worth forty thousand dollars. And then, get this, on top of his head, he was wearing this goddamned turban. So help me, he looked like he had just walked off a set for a Valentino movie.

"Underneath this overcoat, he wore a karate gi, the traditional karate outfit. It was just straight-out bizarre, man. My two little daughters, Lorie, twelve, and Kristie, eleven, were very impressed, however. He looked like an ancient sheik, but all he wanted to do was fool around on the karate mats."

There were some other students at the studio and Elvis must have realized he looked extremely out of place. He offered Dave an explanation: "I'm wearing this damn turban because I didn't wash my hair and it looks bad, man." Dave really didn't care too much. He admits he was impressed that a man like Presley would drive all the way out to Glendora just to see him.

"It was quite a build-up to my ego," says Dave, "even though, thinking back, he did look sort of ridiculous."

That day was the first time Dave saw Sonny West. "He didn't say much," Dave remembers. "He just stood on the side very quietly. His appearance was sort of quietly menacing. He was watching that nobody tagged Elvis one as we fooled around on the mats. Very watchful.

"It's a funny thing when you're into karate, you get to know a lot about how a person moves their body. Just the way he was holding himself, just by the way he was moving, I knew he was wearing a shoulder holster."

"Yeah," Sonny remembers, "I had this special holster on that held the .38 upside down in a spring. I could whip that thing out faster than you could say 'karate.' We were in a strange part of L.A., and we always carried the heat. You never know what can happen when you are around Elvis; there are so many nut cases running around.

"Besides, I see all these crazy mothers leaping around on the floor, doing karate and stuff. I felt a whole lot safer."

Dave had a partner at the karate studio named Jim Thompson (no relation to Linda Thompson), who, Dave recalls, "says to me, 'Watch out for that big fucker in the corner carrying the heat.' It was, of course, Sonny, who between his silence and his gun, looked sort of menacing but who, of course, became a very close friend of mine."

Presley seemed to lap up the atmosphere of karate. He was getting very expansive in his conversation. He was telling the assembly, which included Sonny, Ed Parker, Charlie Hodge, Elvis's rhythm guitarist, and Gerald Peters, his chauffeur, a dry-humored Englishman who once drove for Winston Churchill, what he intended to do for the future of karate. "I'm gonna start my own karate system," Elvis promised. "We will make our own movie about the art and have our own competitions." Presley himself planned to star in the lead role as the boss tough guy.

That day Presley stayed there, under the watchful eye of Sonny, for about an hour. He went through some basic karate kicks and moves. But Dave noticed something about his movements that was very similar to what he saw the first time he met him, at Ed Parker's studio. "You had the idea if Elvis had really dedicated himself to the art, he could be good. But he only played at it. He never really worked hard at it and drove himself. Also he seemed to stumble around a lot, tripping and fumbling moves."

Although the sight of a man wearing a black and red overcoat, turban, necklace and rings, fanning the air with karate chops and kicks, was a curious enough sight, there was something else that seemed a little out of focus. "He was sweating profusely," Dave says. "I mean, he had a right to be with all that clothing on, but, man, it was literally pouring out of him. And his eyes, they were big, red and watery. It was like he had a dreadful case of flu or fever. I just couldn't put my finger on what was wrong with him."

After the brief visit, Elvis Presley led his entourage back to the blue Mercedes. As the impeccable chauffeur, Peters, held the door open for Presley, two of Dave Hebler's students looked at each other. "Man," said one to the other, "I'd like to have half of whatever he's got inside him."

Both were young men who had had brutal experiences with drugs.

# 5

She was a striking-looking girl yet somehow had a quality of innocence. A beautiful mane of hair hung carelessly past her shoulders. She had gorgeous eyes, a petite but well-rounded body, dainty movements and a very quick, shy laugh. Somewhere today this girl—let's call her Jane Robertson (which is not her real name)—is trying to put together a life that was almost ruined.

She was not a model, not a singer, not an actress, just a giggly little girl who didn't smoke, didn't drink. If she had a vice, it was one that she shared with millions of women: a total infatuation with Elvis Presley.

On most occasions when Elvis played the Sahara Club Casino in Lake Tahoe, Jane and her mother would come in to see the show. One night, in the spring of 1971, her fidelity as an Elvis fan paid off beyond her wildest dreams. She was singled out of the audience by Elvis to be his companion. Just as simple and breathtakingly unbelievable as that.

It was Elvis's last number. He looked stunning that night. A thirty-six-year-old Adonis, arrogantly standing in the spotlight, orchestrating the audience with a tiny flicker of his bejeweled fingers. His mouth was sensuously pouting the words of his closing number, "I Can't Help Falling in Love with You," and, as usual, middle-aged women who should have known better were swooning like teenyboppers in front of their portly husbands.

In the second row of the packed audience sat Jane, totally mesmerized, as always, when Presley stood on stage. As Presley got halfway through his number, he whipped the sweat-soaked scarf from around his neck, kissed it and threw it into the audience. Women charged like Oakland Raiders linebackers, knocking over tables to the sound of broken cocktail glasses. Presley added to the pandemonium by reaching back into the band and producing more scarves. He would mop his forehead, kiss the scarf, and float it into the audience.

The pandemonium that followed was unbelievable, as middle-aged ladies waged tug-of-war battles over scarves with "The Man's" perspiration on it.

Jane just sat there in the second row, sighing. She did not get a scarf that night. But she did get something else: some very admiring glances from Elvis Presley. Every time he came to the edge of the stage, he would turn and wink at her. Jane was flabbergasted, but she didn't read too much into it. Why would he be attracted to her, with all his women? As the show ended, Jane almost thought she saw Presley half wave to her. Impossible. She was drained of emotion. The show was over. It had been fantastic. Now for a night sleeping in the car before beginning the long trip home.

Elvis was not the only one giving her the eye that evening. From offstage she received some very admiring glances—from bodyguard Sonny West, a man not unused to the beauty of ladies at an Elvis performance. Also backstage with Sonny was Joe Esposito. Esposito, along with Dave Hebler, was one of the few non-Southerners in Elvis's entourage. Esposito was a fast-witted man from Chicago who had a reputation of being able to get things done quickly and smoothly. A taste for sharp clothes and a passion for diamonds caused the Memphis boys to call him "Diamond Joe," a name that Esposito seemed to revel in. Esposito had met Elvis in the army and had been with him on and off ever since. He had a keen eye for anything that would please his boss and, for his trouble, was the first member of the Presley entourage to be put on the regular payroll. He was Presley's most valued aide-de-camp.

What Joe and Sonny were looking at in Jane Robertson was something that sure would please their boss. She simply oozed beauty and un-self-conscious sex appeal. Not an ounce of makeup or lipstick on her face . . . she was really something else.

As the show finished to thunderous applause and long, loud squeals, Sonny and Joe raced around to where Presley would leave the stage. The three of them got into the elevator that would take them to the master dressing rooms in the basement. Presley was drenched with perspiration and his chest was heaving. He had put every ounce of energy into the show. "Good show, 'E,'" said Sonny. "You really turned 'em on." Elvis nodded thanks, but his mind was somewhere else.

"Goddamn, man, did you see that gal sitting there in the front of the audience? Hell, that was some good-looking piece of woman. Who is she? She was beautiful."

Sonny and Joe were not surprised he had spotted her. Normally it's almost impossible to see an audience from a spotlit stage, but when Elvis had gone to the edge to throw out his scarves, he had been able to see for the first three or so rows. "Yup," said Sonny with a big smile, as he helped his boss off with a gleaming, sequined white jumpsuit, "I know the one you're talking about. A real honey." Sonny didn't need any pictures drawn for him. He dashed upstairs as the dinner crowd was still recovering from their hysteria and zeroed in on Jane Robertson.

"Hi, hon," Sonny said, "do you want to meet Elvis? I'm Sonny West and I work security for Mr. Presley. I would be very happy to introduce you to him." The response was to be expected.

"Oh, come on," replied Jane, not unfamiliar with lines used by men on the make, "you're kidding me."

Sonny flashed a big charming smile. "Nope, hon, here's my identification. I work for Mr. Presley. I would be very happy to introduce you. C'mon, he's upstairs in his room. I'll take y'all right on up."

Elvis was in the inner dressing room changing, so Sonny introduced her around. She exchanged small talk with Sonny and Joe on how much she'd enjoyed the show. She told them she had been an Elvis fan ever since she could remember being able to listen to music. She laughed and giggled shyly. Then Elvis materialized from the inner dressing room, and Sonny thought Jane was going to collapse. "She had this great laugh, a beautiful shy personality. Boy, she was a looker."

When meeting a new girl, Elvis very rarely changes his line. He comes on very quiet, very attentive, very considerate. He turns on the little-ole-country-boy act like a tap, and the girls fall like chopped-down oaks.

"Even if Elvis wasn't who he was, say he was just an old truck driver," says Sonny, "when he turns on that country-boy charm, he could romance the queen of England." Not surprisingly, Jane stayed in Elvis's suite that night. Her mother would make the trip home alone. "Elvis really dug her," says Sonny. "He saw a lot of her during that engagement. Bought her some clothes and stuff. Not that she wanted them. She just wanted to be close to Elvis." But in a short while, Jane began to change in an ever-so-small way. "Elvis started to give her a couple of pills here and there to give her a lift, not that she needed it. But I guess she just didn't want to look like a hick or a square. She was taking things with Elvis. And I know she had never taken anything before," says Sonny.

The night that Sonny would like to forget, Elvis, Sonny, and Charlie Hodge took Jane on a trip to the Presley home in Chino Canyon Road, Palm Springs. When they arrived, Elvis was feeling like getting out of it. He had taken his usual dose of pills during the day, but as bedtime came around, about three in the morning, Elvis produced a bottle of prescription Hycadan. Normally prescribed by doctors for severe cases of coughing and congestion, Hycadan in large quantities is a dangerous narcotic.

"Elvis would get out of his gourd on that stuff," Sonny recalls. "I've tasted it—yuk." That night Jane took a little swig. More giggles. Toward 4:00 A.M., the two of them were nodding off, giggling, stumbling and slurring their words in happy unison. Then they went to bed.

The swigging of the Hycadan continued. The two of them could be heard giggling and laughing inside the master bedroom. The next day, Sonny had planned to force Elvis to take some sun. "He was awful white-looking, so we wanted him to get a tan to make himself look healthier."

The entourage woke around eleven in the morning. Sonny and Charlie read the papers, waiting for their boss to rise from his heavy night. "Noon came and went," recalls Sonny. "Normally someone would have taken up his breakfast, but this day they didn't, and it's now getting on for one o'clock. I casually asked whether anybody had checked on Elvis. The point is that the fear of him taking an overdose is never far from our minds, although he is very skillful when it comes to measuring out drugs. He knows those drugs better than a doctor."

But on this morning he had miscalculated. Sonny wandered back to the master bedroom to check. He went through the first door and then banged on the second door, which opened into Presley's suite. "You gettin' up, boss? What do you want for breakfast? I'll fix it." Silence. "Hey, Elvis, boss, you there?"

No answer. Sonny's heart started to pump. "Jesus." He opened the door. Elvis was sprawled across the bed sideways.

"Inside the bedroom, the temperature is way down. It's freezing. He would keep that room temperature down so low you could hardly stand it," Sonny relates. "I dashed over to Elvis. 'Boss, boss, boss, c'mon snap out of it. Boss, boss.'" Sonny was screaming. He recalls that Elvis was taking long, deep breaths about five seconds apart. Sonny crawled across the bed to where Jane was lying naked under the bedclothes. "Jane, Jane, hon, c'mon let's get up, c'mon."

Sonny will never forget what he felt then. "Oh, man, this was it. The whole trip was over. I was sure that they had both bought it. I opened Jane's eyes. They were staring straight ahead like glass marbles. And there was that terrible gasp. She wasn't breathing properly. It was like a long, strangled half-groan, half-gasp. I then opened her eyelids again, and they were blank. I slapped her across the face, hard, a coupla times, but no reaction. Christ, I was scared. I yelled out to Charlie Hodge, 'Charlie, you better get a doctor here quick. Elvis and his gal here are out of it real bad.'"

Within minutes, a doctor—whom we will call "X"— arrived at the house on Chino Canyon Road. By this time, Elvis had started to come around. Dr. "X" took one look at the girl, checked her pulse, her breathing and her eyes, and said, "We've got to get an ambulance up here. . . . This girl is dying . . . We can't waste any time."

Elvis was still staggering around like a drunken sailor. He told the doctor, "C'mon, doc, she'll be okay, just give her a shot of Ritalin. I'm telling you she'll be okay."

Sonny was getting exasperated. Here they had a girl dying on their hands, and Elvis is telling the doctor what to do. "Man, I was hot. I coulda smacked him right in the mouth. Damn fool telling the doctor his business."

Dr. "X" was obviously extremely concerned. Elvis started to argue with him. "It's just too much Hycadan, that's all. She was drinking the damn stuff like water. Just give her a shot of Ritalin and she's gonna be okay."

Dr. "X" cut him short. "No, we're getting her in an ambulance and straight to emergency." Within minutes the ambulance sped to the house. Charlie Hodge and Sonny followed the ambulance to the hospital.

"They pumped her stomach, hooked her up to machinery and everything," says Sonny.

Charlie Hodge looked at her, glanced back to Sonny and said, "Man, she looks like she ain't gonna make it." Sonny looked at the ground, and for a moment he thought he was going to cry.

Dr. "X" came across to them. "This girl is in bad shape . . . I'll be honest . . . I can't promise anything. Why don't you go back to the house, and I will call you if there is any change."

Sonny and Charlie drove home in silence. Elvis was beginning to snap out of it. He had popped some Ritalin. "Any change?" he said in a flat monotone.

"No," said Sonny gravely.

Charlie chipped in, "The doctor doesn't know if she is gonna live or die."

Elvis frowned. "I told that girl not to drink that much. She was whacked." He then went into the bedroom to make an important telephone call.

Sonny was getting angry. Here was a girl dying on them, and within seconds Elvis was telling everybody it had nothing to do with him.

"I don't care how he cuts it," said Sonny, "it was his bottle of drugs. That little girl had never even touched a glass of champagne, and now because of him, she's battling for her life in the hospital. And all he can do is tell the doctor what to do and then tell us it is all her fault. Goddamn. He is a sonofabitch."

At about seven that night, Charlie Hodge got the call from Dr. "X." "She is starting to come out of it. She just might be okay. I can't promise anything but we're doing our best," he told Charlie. "Why don't you drop by the hospital."

Charlie and Sonny jumped into the car and were there within minutes. "We went into the intensive care unit," Sonny recalls. "There were four or five beds in there. Jane was the only patient. She looked awful. Her eyes were closed."

"I think she is going to be okay," Dr. "X" said. "It looks like she is coming out of it. She is going to live."

Sonny's skin crawls when he thinks of what happened next. He went across to her and touched her arm. "Jane," he whispered softly. She opened her eyes and suddenly, Sonny remembers, "she came off that bed like a wild animal. She was hissing like a goddamn mountain lion. Snarling like a wild beast, *hhhhhshhhh*, like that. Wow, I got scared."

Sonny threw an alarmed glance at Dr. "X," who explained. "She doesn't know where she is."

"Is she okay?" Sonny asked. "Is she gonna be okay?"

"Well," said the doctor, "we don't know how she is affected by it. We don't know how much oxygen was stopped. We can just do our best and hope."

Jesus, thought Sonny, what if this little girl is turned into a vegetable just because of some crazy stunt back there in Chino Canyon? As Sonny and Charlie left the hospital, Sonny remembers that Jane was still having trouble breathing. She needed oxygen.

Elvis was sitting in the lounge room of the Chino Canyon home. "She's gonna be all right, I think," Sonny said sullenly, "but she just might never be the same again. She was hissing at me like a damn cat. She didn't recognize me."

Elvis was off again on his own trip. All he said was "man." Sonny doesn't remember his ever making a telephone call to Jane, ever visiting her or even acknowledging her existence for a long time.

Someone else was doing the worrying. The person to whom Elvis had made the important telephone call was a man he often turned to at a time of trouble.

"Elvis always turned to him when he got involved in something he couldn't handle," Sonny remembers. "The hospital bill was paid for. She was flown back home. There wasn't a whisper about it in the press. The newspapers would have had a party with that one. Later on, someone brought up the fact that there might be a lawsuit brought by the girl or her mother. Joe Esposito was instructed to give her some money. The mother, bless her, wouldn't accept it. I think Joe ended up by giving them something. But the girl and the mother didn't want anything. They didn't sue or anything like that. They were real great people.

"The point was because Elvis had this image of being so anti-drug, the girl and the mother didn't want to destroy that image. That girl, Jane, she loved Elvis, man. Do you know, I believe that even if her daughter had died, the mother still would have kept her mouth shut."

Jane did call Elvis later that year. He spoke to her briefly and he told her, according to Sonny, "Hon, when you get a little bit better, I'll take you on tour." But Sonny relates: "She was out. Elvis didn't want to face the situation."

Sonny saw Jane again. She and her mother had driven to Las Vegas to catch Elvis's show. He met her mother, too. "They were sleeping in their car because they couldn't afford a room in the hotel. Joe Esposito found out about it, picked up the tab, and put them up in a guest room at the Hilton. When I spoke to her, she had tears in her eyes. 'Sonny, don't you know I don't hold that against him. He didn't do anything. It was all my fault.'

"There she was taking the rap for the whole thing.

He did get her to drink it. He was the king. Anyone would do anything to please him." Then Sonny grows sad. "Man, it was all over for that little girl. Her face never lit up any more. Whatever happened back there to her when she overdosed, it had affected her whole personality. She was a different person. There wasn't that shy giggle, that easy laugh any more. She seemed to be deep and quiet and introverted. I'm no doctor, but that experience just turned her completely around. And yet all she could talk about was Elvis. There was a genuine love there.

"I never heard Elvis talk about her again. By 1971, Elvis was a changed guy. He was no longer the shy, fun-loving kid from Memphis. No, he was just living for himself and all that damn junk he took. He was like a walking drugstore."

**6**

Elvis's senior year at Humes High School was not much different from his other school years. Very little about him was particularly noticeable, apart, of course, from his appearance. His teachers remember him as a very average student who, with a little less concentration, might not have graduated.

His life in Memphis had been only marginally better than life in Tupelo, Mississippi, where he was born, the surviving twin in a birth that almost killed his mother, the former Gladys Smith. His earlier life was lived in much the same squalor and poverty experienced by the many destitute blacks in the rigidly segregated South of those days. In 1948, when Elvis was thirteen, his father, Vernon Presley, decided it was time to leave the tiny shotgun home in Tupelo. The big city across the border might afford a chance for higher pay and a shot at the good life. He packed all the household goods into a green Plymouth one night and the family headed for Memphis.

Vernon Presley didn't find the big time in Memphis. He did find a job at the United Paint Company, packing cans for less than fifty dollars a week. Gladys helped out with part-time work first in the sewing mills, then in coffee shops and restaurants and as a nurses' aide at St. Joseph's Hospital.

If living conditions in the tiny white frame in Tupelo were bad, life didn't improve in their next "home," a three-room structure in a dull concrete complex where water and electricity alternated in not working. It was part of a dingy, federally funded housing project called Lauderdale Courts especially designed for poor Southerners. It was eventually discovered that Gladys and Vernon's combined income exceeded the two-hundred-dollar-a-month maximum allowed for tenants in the project, but somehow they escaped eviction.

Red and Sonny West grew up in similar housing projects a mile away, Hurt Village and Lamar Terrace. "It sure had the right name," Red recalls, "because the people living there sure did hurt. If you made more than two hundred bucks a month in any of those projects, you had to move out. It was as if it was considered that two hundred bucks a month was too much money for you to live in a federal housing project. Well, I guess we didn't miss many meals, but we sure postponed a darned lot. We were poor and so was Elvis."

Like most transplanted kids in a new town, Elvis withdrew into a shell of timidity and shyness. Whatever he lacked in friends on the street, Gladys Presley more than made up for with her attention and affection. Presley has said that he often wanted to go down to the local creek with the other little boys from the project, "but Mama wouldn't let me. She just never let me out of her sight. I used to get annoyed when I was little, but I later realized it was all because she loved me so much." It was as if God had told the deeply religious Gladys Presley that the death of Elvis's twin, Jesse Garon, was a sign from heaven to double her love and vigil over Elvis.

Mrs. Faye Harris was a friend of the Presleys when they lived in Tupelo. "Gladys thought Elvis was the greatest thing that ever happened," Mrs. Harris recalls, "and she treated him that way. She worshipped that child from the day he was born until the day she died. She'd always keep him at home or, when she let him go out to play, she was always out looking to see that he was all right. And wherever she went—whether it was out visiting or even down to the grocery store—she always had her little boy along."

Despite the tight dollars, Elvis's parents did everything they could to make Elvis feel he was better off than a lot of the kids he rubbed shoulders with at school. His Christmas and birthday presents were always a shade better or more expensive than his friends'. As a result, Elvis could be considered a spoiled child—certainly by comparison with the kids he grew up with. When Elvis was fourteen, he wanted a bike for Christmas. The Presleys couldn't afford it. But they did manage to scrape up twelve dollars for a guitar. With a few lessons from his uncle, Vester Presley, Elvis was soon able to pluck away at the main chords.

"Elvis doesn't play the guitar, apart from the rhythm chords," says Red West. "Most people think he is an expert guitarist, which he is not. He doesn't read a lick of music, either. Although when he is singing, he knows what he is doing. He has natural music in him. He has never had a lesson on the piano, either, but he can pick up a number with surprising skill. But there are a lot better guitarists than him around, which is kind of funny because that guitar was his trademark, and most people think he is fantastic on it."

While Red West as a young teenager was practicing to become a bone-crusher on the football field, Elvis stayed at home, practiced his guitar and began developing a singing voice at the First Assembly Church of God, a tiny, rickety structure on Adams Street in Tupelo.

Red recalls Presley's telling him on a dozen occasions that his mother remembered three-year-old Elvis slipping off her lap at a church service and running down to the choir. There his little voice would try to follow the singing. It gave him his first contact with music and that stayed with him. "People are always talking about where he got his natural ability from," says Red. "That little sonofabitch was singing his ass off back in that church in Tupelo. And when he was about nine he would sing trios with his mother and father. To this day, old Vernon can throw his head back and sing one helluva song. He's a great singer. Vernon can be walking around a suite singing his ass off, particularly a gospel song like 'Where No One Stands Alone.' Now his voice is so good, sometimes you will stop what you are doing and start listening to him. Then he will get kind of embarrassed and knock it off. But Elvis gets a lot of his ability from the old man . . . and, incidentally, he gets a lot of his good looks from the ole boy, too."

Later, in Memphis, he would wander through the black section of town, the famous Beale Street, and listen to the blacks wail their blues. The influence was so strong that people said Presley's first records sounded like a black voice inside a white body, a reference that never pleased Presley. He had definite ideas about blacks, as he did about Catholics and Jews.

If Elvis was sheltered—Red West recalls that Gladys once threw groceries at a child who was threatening to beat up her son—he was, in the broadest sense, a "good boy." Red puts it this way: "He simply worshipped the ground his mother walked on. To him she was a mother, a friend, a big sister all rolled into one. I mean, she was his whole life. If ever he talked about his family going anywhere, he would never talk about the family as a whole. It would always be Mom and them went to church, or Mom and them went to the movies. It was like she was the only one in the whole family, and the rest just were along for the ride. It was like that even after she died. He still talked about her like she was living."

In Elvis's senior year, Red didn't see much of him—

apart from pulling him out of jams or an occasional hello in the hallways—except for woodshop class, run by a teacher named Mr. Hiltpole. It was there that Red saw Elvis at his wildest. "And that meant," says Red, "he would occasionally get in woodchip-throwing fights with the other kids when Mr. Hiltpole was out of the room. And that was about as wild as he got. He was a pretty quiet kid."

Elvis Presley, save for the long hair, rated as being highly forgettable in a school that measured its respect quotient on whether you were at the top of your class or whether you could pound through a defensive line or whether you could knock a guy on his butt. Elvis really couldn't handle any of that, so there was no place for him to go down in Humes High School history until midway through his final year.

"One of the big events of the year was the school variety concert," Red recalls. "It consisted of about thirty acts. The principal, old T. C. Brindley, was a tough old son of a gun on the outside, but inside he was a good old boy with a soft heart. The idea behind the variety concert was to be able to set up a school fund to raise money. Now, during the year, if some kid didn't have the money to go to a school dance or buy some football gear, you could go to old Brindley and if your hardship was legitimate, he would see that the variety-concert fund would look after it all for you.

"The person who ran the show was a history teacher who taught Elvis. I think she always had a soft spot for Elvis because he was so polite toward her. I put an act in the show. I played the trumpet and I got together a guitar and a bass. It was a heck of a big day and we were all very nervous. I didn't take much notice of all the others because I was so intent on my own."

The rules of the concert were that whoever got the biggest applause would be given the honor of having an encore and would be declared the winner. Red recalls he had finished his act when he got the shock of his life, seeing Elvis come out on the stage with his guitar. "To be honest, I never thought he would have the guts to get out there in front of those people. He just never impressed me as being that brave. I never even knew he sang, but I was to get a surprise."

Elvis shuffled timidly onto the stage. His shyness, however, was offset by his elaborately combed crowning glory—his Vaseline-walled hair—and a bright red shirt. Then it happened. Elvis put one foot up on a chair to act as a prop, and he started to plunk away at the tune "Old Shep." Then he whipped into a fast song, then a ballad. Red West smiles. "Hell, do you know while Elvis was singing the love songs, there was one lady teacher crying?

"And there were other teachers who had tears in their eyes. When he finished his show, the kids went crazy; they applauded and applauded. They just went mad. He was an easy winner. At first Elvis just stood there, surprised as hell. He seemed to be amazed that for the first time in his life someone, other than his family, really liked him. I'll never really know when Elvis got bitten by the bug of loving the applause of the audience, but my guess is that it happened right then in Humes High School. At last, it seemed, he had found a way to make outsiders love him.

"He still to this day craves that live audience yelling and screaming for him. Of course, it's the same with most performers, but with Elvis I think it goes all the way back to the time at school where the only time he made a mark was on stage. I saw it that day. As shy as he was, he had a definite magic on stage. After the show, he just seemed to go back to being ordinary old Elvis. But on stage he had control."

Red continues. "Later on, when he got a little more confidence and he started to feel himself, he really knew how to manipulate an audience. He knew exactly when to hit them with fast tunes that whipped them up, and he knew exactly when to hit them with ballads and love songs. If any audience doesn't warm to him immediately, he uses every trick in the business. I'll even tell you of a time later on when he actually bought an audience that was being too quiet. He bought them, then he whipped them up until they went berserk."

In the final six months of school, Elvis became an instant favorite at school parties. Despite his shyness, he would often arrive with his beaten-up old guitar slung over his shoulder. He would go to a corner of the room, but as soon as the kids pushed him hard enough, he would oblige with a song. After Elvis graduated, however, his ambitions extended only as far as what his appearance suggested—being a truck driver. He got a job at the Crown Electric Company driving a truck for $1.25 an hour. He turned over most of the money to his mother for household bills. With Elvis making almost fifty dollars a week, the Presley family could afford to move out of Lauderdale Courts to a slightly cleaner and bigger apartment on Lamar Avenue. What little money he didn't give to his mother, he would occasionally use on buying sprees at Lansky Brothers, a clothing store on Beale Street. Lansky Brothers specialized in shocking-pink pegged trousers and lemon-yellow suits with shoulders so wide that the wearer would have to slide through doors sideways if he wanted to avoid contact with the door frame.

In later years, Presley was to go to such celebrity tailors as Sy Devore and Nudies, where he would often pay four thousand dollars for one gold lamé suit. And right up until 1974, he would occasionally go to Lansky Brothers and pick out something he liked. "I remember when he was about seventeen or eighteen," one of the owners, Bernard Lansky, recalls. "He would come over and press his nose against the window, like it was a candy store. He didn't have any money then. Now he comes in and buys the place out. He has never forgotten us. No airs about that man. You meet some people and watch them go up the ladder and never come down to say hello. Not Elvis. He has always got a word for you."

In his final year at school, Red kept on playing football, and Elvis kept on driving a truck. Occasionally they would see each other, wave hello, and that was about the size of it. Elvis was happy as a truck driver, extremely well liked, and he had the prospect of a steady job for life before him. But the ambition to perform was never far from his mind.

On Elvis's truck route was the Sun Recording Company, a small outfit run by a genial man named Sam Phillips. Phillips's dream was one day to put his name on the map by getting something "new in a sound."

Among other studio services performed by Sun Recording was a gimmick that offered the public a chance to "cut your own disc." For four dollars anyone could come in and record a birthday message, an anniversary song or anything he or she wanted. One Saturday afternoon, Elvis wandered into Sun Recording carrying his guitar over his shoulder. On that particular afternoon, the office manager, Marion Keisker, was running the office. Miss Keisker, an enthusiastic woman who was always on the lockout to give new talent a helping hand, was a former "Miss Radio Memphis." If Marion Keisker had not been on duty that Saturday afternoon in 1954, Elvis Presley might still be a truck driver today. Perhaps as much as the choir at the First Assembly of God Church in Tupelo and as much as Gladys and Vernon Presley for buying him a twelve-dollar guitar, Marion Keisker must be credited with helping spawn the phenomenon known as Elvis Presley. (Presley himself certainly thought so. Says Red West: "One thing I got to say about Elvis—he never forgot that lady. He would pick up magazines and newspapers all saying about how he got started. And all the stories had Sam Phillips as being the man who discovered Elvis. Well, Elvis told me I don't know how many times that Marion Keisker was the one who really did the job. She was the one who kept his telephone number and she was the one who knew what Sam was looking for, a black sound inside a white body. Now, Elvis had respect for Sam but he would say to me: "If it wasn't for that lady, I would never have got a start. That woman, she was the one who had faith. She was the one who pushed me. Sure, Sam had the studio, but it was that Marion who did it for me.'"

Elvis Presley swaggered in, a broodingly handsome boy of eighteen, not realizing that he was about to step on the first rung of a ladder that would take him to breathless heights—heights where he would be history's highest paid performer. He plunked down his four dollars in front of Marion Keisker and said he wanted to cut a disc for a present. Not surprisingly, the present was for his mother. The first song he recorded was "My Happiness," a number made famous by The Ink Spots. The flip side was a number called "That's When Your Heartaches Begin." For some reason that Miss Keisker can't really put her finger on, she decided to tape part of the first side and all of the flip side. There was something vaguely interesting in young Presley's voice. She wanted her boss to hear it.

Sam Phillips listened to the record with mild interest. It could, he reasoned, be something like what he was looking for—a white who could sing something like a Negro. Phillips brought the boy into the studio for a few sessions but really couldn't make up his mind. The voice had a lot wrong with it. There was a lot missing. After several false starts, Sam Phillips had his doubts whether Elvis Presley would after all be the great white hope.

But Phillips was a kind-hearted man. He decided to give Elvis a chance to wing it with two local boys who were making a name for themselves, pianist-guitarist Scotty Moore and his neighbor Bill Black, a bass player. They helped make up a local group called the Starlight Wranglers. After doing a few pick-up songs, both Scotty and Bill were only marginally impressed with the new boy's talent. Perhaps the problem at that time was that Elvis Presley was not singing in the way he wanted to sing; he was singing in the way he thought *they* wanted him to sing.

One afternoon, when Presley, Scotty and Bill were together at the studio just drinking Cokes and making no particular headway, Elvis picked up his guitar and started to free style, wailing "That's Alright, Mama," by black songwriter Arthur Crudup. Scotty and Bill started picking up the beat, jam-session style. Suddenly Sam Phillips rushed out of the recording booth as if he were being chased by an enraged bull. Presley recalls that those early numbers sounded like he was beating an empty bucket, but Sam Phillips screamed at them: Whatever they were doing, do more of it! He had found the lost chord. This was the sound he was looking for.

Sam Phillips pressed the record of "That's Alright, Mama" and started to hustle it on the local disc-jockey shows. Many of the local experts had their doubts about the record—it was 1954, and the South was a long way from being integrated. Elvis sounded dangerously black.

Despite the misgivings, the record went on to sell seven thousand copies, a very respectable figure for Memphis in those days. It did so with the help of a popular disc jockey named Dewey Phillips—no relation to Sam—who had a program called *Red Hot and Blue* on station WHBQ. Sam Phillips pressured Dewey to play "That's Alright, Mama," and Dewey obliged.

Dewey Phillips, now dead, remembered one night when "I played the record fifteen times. Suddenly telephone calls and telegrams started to pour into the station. Everybody wanted to know who the new boy was. I wanted to get hold of Elvis for an interview.

Now, at that time a lot of folks thought Elvis was a colored boy. I got hold of Vernon, Elvis's daddy, who said he was at a movie, down at Suzore's Number Two Theater. I told Vernon to get his boy to the station. Before long, Elvis came running in."

Dewey told Elvis that he was going to interview him. Elvis replied that he didn't know anything about being interviewed. Among the questions that Dewey tried to emphasize was where Elvis had gone to school. "I wanted to get that out because a lot of people had thought he was colored," Dewey said. Humes was lily white. Finally Dewey thanked him and said good-bye. Disappointed, Elvis asked whether or not he was going to be interviewed. Dewey replied that the mike had been open all the time. He had been interviewed. Dewey recalled: "He broke out in a cold sweat."

Red West remembers the tune and the interview well. "I just sort of said to myself, shee-it, that ole Elvis Presley has really made it. Fancy, a guy I went to school with singing on the radio."

Red, of course, was in his final year at school. It was the beginning of fall, 1954, and he and his warriors were deep into serious football. The team was all set to play their arch rivals, Bartlett, across town. Red was boarding the school bus with his team, led by Coach Boyce, the man who had so strenuously objected to the length of Elvis's hair. "I was just about to get into the bus, and I noticed Elvis walking the opposite way. He was about to get into a battered old Lincoln coupe. It was green and about ten years old. His mummy and daddy had bought it for him. It was hard for them to pay for it, but it gives you some idea how much they loved him to scrape together that kind of money. Not many boys his age, nineteen I think he was, had a car of their own. No sir."

Protocol for football hero Red was reversed this time. Once it was the shy Elvis who would address

Red first. Now it was Red who waved and shouted a greeting: "Hi, Elvis." Red remembers he was decked out in a black-and-white drape cowboy jacket with black pants. "They were real sharp threads. Anyway, he waved back to me. I was impressed. Like in Memphis in those days, if you were on the radio, it was like being a movie star. Elvis was a celebrity. He was a pretty big deal." As the bus pulled out, Elvis fell in behind and followed the team over to Bartlett.

Red didn't have time to shoot the breeze with him. He was hustled into a dressing room and then to the field, where he played center. Red reports with no small measure of pride that Humes battered Bartlett.

"I noticed that Elvis was sort of hanging around quietly on the sidelines, just watching from under a tree, really quiet like. I was taking a shower, and one of the guys told me that Elvis was hanging around outside. I dried off and I went out to say hullo." Red remembers that Elvis's appearance had improved dramatically. He had filled out, and his face was no longer assaulted with acne. His hair was properly styled; although it still looked pretty outrageous, he seemed to have lost that greasy delinquent look, and there were real indications that he had the makings of genuine good looks.

Elvis seemed really pleased to see Red. "Hi, Red, how goes it? Nice game, man." Red was pleased with himself and pleased that Elvis was warm and friendly.

"Hey, thanks man. Hey, you're pretty big time. I hear your recording all over the place. It's pretty good. You're a star."

Despite his minor celebrity, Elvis smiled shyly. He was still a little in awe of Red West. It was almost as if Red was the guy that Elvis wanted to be. "Right then," says Red, "Elvis was the guy I wanted to be." They walked across the field toward the car. When they reached the battered green Lincoln, Presley said, "Hey, hop in, man, let's ride around a little."

"Sure thing, appreciate it," Red answered. "Well, what have you been doing with yourself?"

Presley still seemed a little unsure of himself. There was no mention of the hassles that Red had pulled him out of. Then suddenly Presley said, "Hey, why don't you come along one night? Maybe at the weekends. If you ain't doing anything, come along anytime you like."

Red West's social calendar wasn't exactly bulging. "Hell, yes, man, I'd sure like that. Sounds like a whole lot of fun." Right then, maybe Elvis didn't know it and maybe Red didn't know it, but from that moment until July, 1976, when a lifelong friendship started to fall apart, Red was Elvis's companion, friend, protector, the man who watched over him in the same way his twin brother might have, had he lived.

"I had a lot of laughs, a lot of good times with Elvis," says Red. "I also had a lot of rough times with him. Elvis over the years has changed since those days, unfortunately. . . . But I grew to love the sonofabitch, and despite everything—maybe I still do."

**7**

In the past twenty years, the adoration of Elvis Presley has far surpassed that of any entertainer in the twentieth century. According to a Gallup Poll, his first name, Elvis, has won more recognition than any full name in the entire world. The adoration has far surpassed that of Valentino, Frank Sinatra and the Beatles. In pure earning power, Elvis Presley has surpassed those three great talents combined. No fewer than 350 million of his records have been sold, a staggering achievement. The *Guinness Book of World Records* reports that he has had more Gold Discs (127) than any singer in recording history.

If there is any secret to his phenomenal success, it is that he is the only entertainer who at any given moment can appeal to both ten-year-old children and their grandparents. There is no longer a special age group that is besotted by Elvis Presley—he cuts across all age groups, all economic groups, all ethnic and national groups. The name "Elvis" is as well known in Tokyo as it is in West Berlin or Johannesburg.

Apart from the talent that got Elvis to this position in the first place, a lot of his appeal has to do with the image he projects. In a world of shifting sex mores, Presley today is every mother's dream of a son, every teenage girl's dream of a big brother, every young lady's dream of the perfect gentle, brooding lover. Presley is aware of his image, and he nurtures it by isolating himself from the press, and by avoiding interviews and public appearances other than his performances.

Within his tight circle of friends and among other entertainers, he is equally careful about his image. When a young lady claimed Presley was the father of her child, he did not, as so many other entertainers would have, ignore the suit or pay her a few thousand dollars to go away. He fought the suit until any shred of suspicion was wiped from the minds of his fans.

Presley is a man of immense sensitivity and intelligence. When meeting someone outside his immediate circle, he is a past master at the Dale Carnegie approach to winning friends and influencing people. Aware that people expect an entertainer of his stature to be something phenomenally different, he comes on with as much humility as time and circumstance allow. It is disarming.

Of course, like any other human, Presley has his highs and lows, his sunny moods and his dark days. Red West and Sonny West, like many of the Memphis Mafia, can at any given moment rhapsodize about Presley's overwhelming generosity—and in the next breath get downright bitter about what they believe is an obsessive compulsion to be an overgrown, selfish child. Presley never just likes someone; he loves them and will give to the point of suffocation. He never just dislikes someone; he has a rare ability to hate with an awe-inspiring passion. *Moderation* was never a word in the dictionary of Elvis Aron Presley.

Dave Hebler was a latecomer to the fold. Red and Sonny often say that few people could have lived to a hundred and worked at as many jobs as Dave Hebler has. Name a job and Dave Hebler in his checkered past has done it. "I know my mother,

Willy, who still lives in Massachusetts, always had that fear I would end up on the street with a cup in my hand," says Dave. When he first met Presley, in 1972, a lot of the singer's boyishness had worn off. The old brigade in the Memphis Mafia had been watching the irreversible changes in Presley's personality. But Dave had no such basis for comparison.

Presley's charm had the same impact on Dave as it did on fans and insiders alike. Even in his first two meetings with Presley on the karate mats, first at Ed Parker's karate studio in Santa Monica and next at his own karate studio in Glendora, when Presley seemed afflicted by some illness, the charm hit him like a cyclone. "Let's face it," says Dave, "I thought he was the greatest thing I had ever met. This guy didn't have to give me the time of day. But somehow he had that charm, or maybe it was a knack, of making me feel important at a time when it was important for me personally to be made to feel important.

"Perhaps, now, I see it clearer, but there is no getting away from it. I had never met—before or since—never read of, nor heard of, any man who could so totally disarm you with charm, generosity and what appeared to be spontaneous love, as could Elvis Presley. Today they use the word charisma. Well, Presley had it to spare in truckloads. He can walk into a room without saying a word and fill it with sunshine. I later learned that he could walk into that same room and fill it with black violence that got to be very hard on the nerves. He can manipulate your emotions like no human being I have ever seen. Suddenly you feel you're living your own life in a series of highs and lows dependent on his highs and lows."

Unbeknownst to Dave Hebler, Elvis Presley, after his first two encounters with Dave on the karate mats, had given him his stamp of approval. Dave was ideal for a Presley insider. He was quiet, respectful, closemouthed, and he deferred to Presley in a way that Elvis admired. Dave was also in trouble, and he was pretty much flat broke. In later times Dave realized, as did Red and Sonny, that this was an important requirement for getting close to Presley.

Approximately two weeks after Dave's first meeting with Presley, in the fall of 1972, Dave was attending a karate meeting headed by Ed Parker. "We were talking about organizing some tournaments," recalls Dave. "Parker was a helluva organizer. We made plans to make a bit of money for the art. Parker knew a lot of people, and if anyone can make something work, it's Parker. He is one smart dude, not to mention his skill—a rough mother. Anyway, as the meeting broke up, Ed mentioned casually that he was going over to Elvis's place. Would I like to tag along? Hell, yes, I would love to."

Dave didn't know it then, but nobody just tags along to see Presley. He does things with a lot more planning than many people think. Never is he spontaneous when it comes to meeting people. He thinks about it, discusses it with whomever he is close to and then acts. This is not because Presley was a born planner—far from it—but because, outside of entertaining, he has very little to occupy his time. Between the heady moments of driving an audience insane, there are very long periods of boredom. If Presley has a challenge to meet, everything is fine. But by 1972, a lot of the challenge had gone out of his life. One of the reasons he would change cars like some men change their socks is that there was absolutely nothing outside his work and immediate environment to interest him. Cars, mansions, women, gadgets, friends—they were all toys to break up the monotony of being a king in exile. So, in the past seven or eight years, when boredom has taken its toll on Presley, he has put a lot of effort into minor things. If ever there is the slightest change of plan that affects him or his entourage, he will have a full-scale meeting to discuss the problem, no matter how minute, in the same way a bank chairman will discuss a fiscal crisis.

Dave Hebler had been the subject of one of those meetings. His talents, personality, financial position and his ability in karate had all been discussed with the view of bringing him in as a potential insider.

"Elvis had taken an immediate liking to Dave," Sonny remembers. "So that night he actually told Ed Parker to bring him up to the house. The visit was quite planned." Presley at that time was living in another mansion in Beverly Hills, at 144 Monovale Road. It was a beautiful spread in the true movie-star tradition.

Dave picks up the story. "Elvis is just there sitting around quietly with the guys. Charlie Hodge, his rhythm guitarist, is there. So were Sonny and Sonny's wife, Judy. Sonny and Judy were living in the house with Elvis. It was a quiet evening, just shooting the breeze. As usual, I didn't say too much. Elvis gestured to me and took me outside into the drive. There were cars all over the place. Mercedes, Rolls, Cadillacs. It looked like an outdoor showroom for luxury cars. In the middle of all of this is this beautiful, gleaming black Stutz Blackhawk. Phew, what a car!" Elvis was extremely proud of this car. He smiled and led Dave over to it. He patted the car with a paternal hand and said, "It cost me forty thousand, Dave. Believe me, man, it is a lotta car."

The night was clear and crisp, and after a few more words, Presley said, "Hey, wanna go for a ride? Let's hop in and go for a cruise." Ed Parker had come outside to join them. Presley got into the driver's seat. Parker got in next to him and Dave sat behind them. Sonny and Charlie Hodge got into a Mercedes behind them. Presley gunned the car. It purred out of the drive like a contented panther. Sonny and Charlie fell in behind, and they went for a cruise, just for the pleasure of it. "It was about midnight," Dave says, "and we went nowhere in particular, and even though there were not that many cars around, just the sight of it caused quite a stir. In Hollywood in those days there weren't many Stutz to be seen.

"Then, of course, Elvis was highly recognizable. There were cars whipping U-turns all over the place. Other cars came speeding by with people gawking out of the windows. The traffic at midnight was going crazy. It was then I realized how this guy couldn't just go for a simple pleasure drive without it turning into a riot. He was the kind of guy who liked nothing better than to just get in a car and cruise around like any other dude. But this was denied to him, and although I was impressed by all the action, I couldn't help but feel sorry for him, forty-thousand-dollar car and all. It was no use. He had to turn around and go back home. We drove back and sat around some more in the house."

After a little more chitchat, Ed Parker quietly drew Dave aside. "Dave, we have a little something here to discuss, a small problem. I wonder if you could excuse us a while." Dave took the obvious cue and slipped into an adjoining room, turned on a big color TV, closed the door and sat quietly while the group inside discussed their business.

"I was sitting in the den," says Dave, "when the door opens and Elvis slipped inside." He smiled at Dave and said, "Dave, I was wondering if you could help out with something." "Sure, anything," Dave answered. Presley continued, "We have this here problem." Dave was apprehensive; it was the second time he had heard the word problem.

"Frankly," says Dave, "I thought they were having some trouble with some guys, so they got Parker and me up to the house to handle something like maybe a war or something against some guys who had been giving Elvis a hard time. I was ready for anything."

Presley motioned Dave toward the door. "Now this here problem . . ." Presley began as he opened the front door. Dave waited with apprehension. Was he going to face a man with a knife or what?

"Now," said Presley, pointing toward the driveway, "there is this goddamned car cluttering up the driveway, and I wonder if you could take it away from here for me—forever." Dave's mind did a flip. He wasn't quite sure what he was hearing. Did Presley want him to dump this car, this gleaming Mercedes-Benz? What on earth was he talking about? Presley motioned for Charlie Hodge, took a set of car keys from him, and put them in Dave's palm. "Go ahead," he said, "take it away, man. It's yours."

Dave paled. "What are you talking about? I mean, what's going on? Did I miss something?"

"It's yours, man," Presley repeated. "I'm giving you the damn car. It's yours."

"What? You're shittin' me. Is this some kind of a joke? I mean . . ."

When Presley finally convinced him that he was giving Dave a ten-thousand-dollar Mercedes 280 SL, Dave felt like he had been hit with an ax at the base of the skull.

"I remember, I sort of half fell into his arms and hugged him and gasped, 'You mean . . . Elvis, man, what can I say, you mother. I mean, Jesus man, thanks. What can I say? Thank you, thanks a million . . . Jesus." Dave remembers he got quite emotional, and a tear or two may have found its way into his eyes.

How often does somebody visit someone else and walk away with a ten-thousand-dollar car? It was all a little too much for Dave. Elvis acted like he had given away a paper clip. He smiled and said quietly, "Hey, man, enjoy it." Then he wandered inside and slipped upstairs to go to bed.

Back inside the house, Dave learned that the car had been originally bought for Charlie Hodge, but Presley had decided to make the gesture to Dave right there and then on the spot, so he told Charlie Hodge to "fix up the paperwork and get yourself a new one" —which meant buy a car right then, at three in the morning. That amazed Dave, but it was no big thing for the other boys there that night.

Charlie Hodge made a phone call to a Mr. Gold, the salesman from Hollywood Mercedes, at a few minutes after three in the morning. "They got him at home," says Dave. "There and then, Charlie fixed up with Mr. Gold to get a new Mercedes 450 SL on the spot." Dave turned to Sonny and, still in a daze, said, "Sonny, you know what Elvis just did, man? He just gave me a Mercedes." Sonny looked up. He couldn't be blamed if he seemed a little offhand. He had seen that scene a dozen times.

"Oh, yeah, I know, great" was his only response. Then he added, "Charlie is just getting a new one up here now, as a matter of fact." Dave looked quizzical. What is this? he thought. Are all these guys nuts? Two cars, two Mercedes-Benz luxury cars, all bought before breakfast. This is some trip.

Before dawn, Charlie Hodge had his new Mercedes. "Elvis did a lot of business with Mr. Gold," says Sonny. "Sure, he was going to get out of bed and fix up all the paperwork, if he could rely on that kind of business. Car salesmen should always have those problems."

The boys had ordered some Chinese food and were having an early-morning feast while the king slumbered upstairs. "I remember I was so excited I wanted to eat my Chinese food in the car." Dave had never bought a new car. He'd done his driving in a succession of broken-down secondhand jobs. Suddenly he is purring home along Sunset Boulevard in a gleaming Mercedes.

"It meant something else to me," Dave recalls. "I had split with my wife, and there was the trauma of splitting with the kids. I had felt pretty down for a long while.

"I had left my job and was working my butt off

to pay debts and stuff like that. Suddenly this. As I drove home on a cloud, I thought, maybe this is the light at the end of the tunnel. Maybe this is the beginning of something new. Maybe now will come a few breaks, a new era. And, of course, that's exactly what it was, a new era."

Dave became a regular visitor to the house in Monovale Road, although he would see Presley only occasionally. Elvis would drop down into the den, exchange greetings, be super polite and disappear. He never mentioned the exotic gift to Dave again. It was a gift, and there was to be no more talk about it. Every time Dave saw Presley, it would be just a warm "Hi, Dave, how goes it man? Good to see you." Dave saw a lot more of Sonny and Red. "I mean, Elvis isn't the kind of guy you can go down to the corner bar and have a beer with. So really, I got quite close to Sonny and Red, and Elvis would always have a big hullo whenever he saw me. I didn't want to seem like a hanger-on. I didn't always want to be under his feet." So for the next few months, he had an easy-come-easy-go relationship with Presley.

Then, in the spring of 1973, Dave was to help Presley in a way that was important to the superstar. It happened at the California State Karate Championships in San Francisco. Karate students from all over the U.S. and from other countries had gathered. At the time it was, in fact, the biggest karate tournament in the world.

"I went up there from Los Angeles with Ed Parker," Dave recalls, "and a crowd of my students. We were all very excited. It was the biggest time of the year for anybody interested in karate. Elvis was coming up to watch the tournaments. A man by the name of Ralph Castro was promoting the event.

"As we arrived in town on the Friday night, we noticed there were advertisements in the newspaper that Elvis Presley would be at the tournament in person. And at the entrance of the arena was a big marquee which said, Elvis Presley In Person. We thought nothing of it at the time, but it was to cause a whole heap of trouble. We went over to the Hyatt House, where Elvis was staying. We met up with Joe Esposito and Jerry Schilling."

Schilling is a good-looking man, a former star athlete for Memphis Catholic Schools. He keeps himself in impeccable shape and is a devotee of health foods. He was a Memphis boy and a loyal member of the Memphis Mafia. But Schilling and Presley had their differences. Schilling, along with Sonny, Red and Dave, was a lot more outspoken in his philosophy than a lot of the other members of the entourage. In politics, he seemed to follow a liberal line, and he would often offer convincing arguments in the long bull sessions the boys had with Presley.

Schilling was the first to admit that Presley had been generous to him with material gifts. But when angered, Presley would often refer to Schilling as "that bastard." Also, Schilling was a Catholic. Presley had been a generous contributor to various Catholic charities but, according to the West boys, he regarded Catholicism as a dangerous branch of Christianity. Despite all this, Presley kept him around. Their relationship weathered many storms before Schilling would quit the entourage.

Later that night, Dave remembers, somebody mentioned to Presley the fact that the news ads stated that he would be at the tournament in person.

"Suddenly, all hell broke loose," Dave recalls. "The word had got to Col. Tom Parker, and he was hopping mad about it.

"I didn't know what the fuss was all about, and then somebody ran it down to me. Apparently, the deal was that Elvis had to appear in Lake Tahoe within the next three weeks. There was a clause in the contract that said he could not appear publicly within a radius of six hundred miles within thirty days of his show in Tahoe. Now Col. Tom Parker is one of the hardest-nosed businessmen in the world. He drives an incredibly hard bargain. But once he gives his word, you can take that to the bank. He expects everybody to live up to their bargain, and he makes damn sure he lives up to his. If he wanted to, he could have told Elvis to go ahead and just sit in the front row and get up and wave at the crowd. That would have satisfied them. Probably, it would have been okay. But the old man didn't want anyone coming back to him and saying that Elvis appearing at a karate show constituted a public appearance. He wasn't going to even give a hint of breaking his word. He is fanatical about giving a handshake on a deal or giving his word. It's law, and that's why he carries so much weight in a world filled with double-dealers.

"Anyway, the order came down: 'Pull down the marquee.' And the word also came down that Elvis wasn't going to appear at the tournament. Elvis was very disappointed. And to me it was just another case where he couldn't enjoy the simple things of life. Now, nobody knows who took it upon themselves to put in the extra promotional bit about Elvis being there. I think it was just overenthusiasm on someone's part.

"But from where I stood, the consensus was that it was Ed Parker who got the blame for it, whether it was his fault or not. Anyway, for a while Ed Parker was on the outs with Elvis." There was still a problem: Who was going to get up there before ten thousand karate experts and tell them they had been conned into thinking Elvis Presley was going to make an official appearance there?

"Well," says Dave, "I took that little chore on myself. I got up on a ladder and tore down the marquee myself. Then came the hard part. I had to get in front of those ten thousand rough dudes and tell them that Elvis would not be there. It looked like as if we were pulling a con, and, frankly, although everybody was innocent, that looked like what had happened. Anyway, I got up and made the announcement. It's a very lonely feeling standing out there in front of ten thousand guys, every one of them handy with their fists and their feet, and telling them that the whole promotional gig was a big mistake. As I'm making the announcement, the guys behind me who were the organizers are saying, 'Go on, Dave, we're watching your back. If anyone makes a move on you, we'll get them' (and all the time laughing).

"That made me feel great. It was all right for those guys, but I was the one making the announcement. I really was worried that a riot would break out. There was a lot of booing, and I just finally told the crowd, 'Shut the hell up; we came here to watch good karate. Now if anyone wants their money back, just go to the window.' Well, they quieted down like lambs, and to my immense relief only four people asked for their money back. Thank God there wasn't a rush for the window, or I would have really wrecked things."

When Ed Parker was on the outs with Presley over the affair, Dave didn't know it, but he was also. "It was kind of like guilt by association. Probably Ed didn't know it either, because since then he has helped out Elvis a lot with security work, but he was getting the freeze."

Both Sonny and Red talked to Elvis about Dave, telling him how he handled what otherwise could have been bad publicity for Presley himself. Elvis acted like he knew all along. "You underestimate my powers," he told them. "I knew what sort of a man Dave Hebler was from the first day I met him. I can see these things long before other people can. I knew Hebler would handle it. Why do you think I gave him that car way back then?"

It was a typical comment from a man who sincerely believes he has supernatural powers, a special communication with the past, the future and with God. And, even though it sounds bizarre, Red West is not altogether convinced that Elvis doesn't possess certain powers. "A lot of it is pretty crazy stuff," says Red, "but I can't help believe there is something special about Elvis. Frankly, I believe a lot of the same stuff he does and so does Sonny. I have seen some strange things happen with that man, and I just can't think they are all coincidence."

After that Dave was a welcome visitor once again in the Presley household. He came mainly to see Sonny and Red, but would often stop by and shoot the breeze with Presley. At that stage there was no suggestion that Dave would work for Presley.

In July, 1974, Dave and Red West were working out on the front lawn of the house at 144 Monovale Road with some karate moves. Red was learning from Dave. Suddenly out of nowhere, Dave heard this bloodcurdling rebel yell from an open window. "I looked up and saw Elvis giving me a big wave. I yelled back to him and gave him a big wave," Dave recalls. "A few minutes later as Red and I are still working out, Elvis appears in the doorway of the house. He had a big smile on his face, which was pretty usual when he greeted me in those days." What was unusual was what Elvis was holding in his hands. It was a very lethal-looking Thompson sub-machine gun.

"Elvis pointed it at me," recalls Dave, "and yelled, 'Rat-tat-tat-tat-tat . . . sure as hell beats karate, huh, Dave?' "

Dave smiled weakly and said, "It sure does, Elvis."

"Here was this guy with a fucking great big machine gun," says Dave, still to this day showing some amazement. "I mean, tell me, where does a guy get a goddamned machine gun? It was wild."

Red answers, "I believe the gun came out of Chicago and had never been used. That's all I honestly know. He often used to tote it around with the damn M 16. But when you have chartered jets and stuff like that, you don't have to go through all that security stuff. Besides, most of the time Elvis was traveling in planes he owned, so he wasn't going to hijack them. So he didn't have to go through those electronic gates that would detect guns.

"Now because, coming from the South, all of us have been pretty close to guns, you grow up with them. But Elvis is absolutely kinky about them. He would buy an armory if he had the chance. He is kinky about guns and I mean kinky, man. How it hasn't got him into trouble, I'll never know."

**8**

Linda Thompson is more elegant than most models, prettier than most movie stars. She has, perhaps, more clothes than Jackie Onassis and certainly just as many jewels. She is not made any uglier by the fact that she has the cutest Southern accent this side of *Gone with the Wind*. Since his separation from Priscilla in 1972, and depending on Presley's moods, she has, on and off, been Presley's live-in girl friend.

In·February, 1974, Presley had just finished another standing-room-only performance at the Las Vegas Hilton. Presley, Sonny and Linda had repaired to the thirtieth-floor Imperial Suite, which had become the Presley home while he was in Las Vegas.

At a particular moment on this given night, the very elegant Linda Thompson was sitting in the well-appointed and luxurious bathroom of the Imperial Suite. Whatever might have been going through her mind at the time, her reverie was rudely interrupted. Suddenly she was shocked by a resounding blast. At the same time, a tiny rip appeared in the toilet paper on her right side. Almost simultaneously, the wall mirror on the closet door splintered into shards of glass. Linda arranged her clothing and dashed into the main room. Her pretty face was ashen. "What was *that*?" she yelled. The honey in her lilting Southern accent was decidedly absent. "What in God's name was *that*?"

Presley and Sonny had now been joined by Red West. Sonny and Red were shaken. The only person who appeared to be calm was Elvis. He was sprawled on a sofa, his head propped up by some pillows. In his right hand was the familiar outline of his favorite revolver, a .22 caliber Savage. The barrel was still smoking. "Hey, now, hon, just don't get excited."

Presley had just been doing a little target practice. Sonny remembers the incident—one of many when Presley surrendered to the urge of blindly popping off one of his arsenal of many guns. "Elvis is never without a gun," Sonny recalls. "Mostly he carries two or even three on him. Even when he is on stage, he carries a tiny four-shot Derringer in the top of his boot. He always rationalizes that he needs guns for protection against nuts. Well, I got to admit, there are plenty of nut cases around, but he has literally dozens of guns. Over the years he has bought hundreds, I mean hundreds. He doesn't need that many guns to protect himself.

"Now, I carry a gun, and I have a great deal of respect for what a gun can do. I take as much care when I'm carrying that gun as when I drive down the Hollywood Freeway, but Elvis is so damned careless with them, it's scary. I wouldn't be the slightest bit surprised if one day I pick up a newspaper and see that Elvis has accidentally shot someone."

"I think he was trying to hit a light holder on the opposite wall," Sonny says of that night. "Well, he's a lousy shot and he missed. The damn bullet went straight through the wall and missed Linda by inches. If she had been standing up next to the toilet paper holder, it would have gone right through her leg. If it had changed course or bounced off something, it could have killed her, man." That particular night, Presley pretended that everybody was making a fuss about nothing, but Sonny feels that inwardly Presley must have been shaken.

Presley's shooting urges can come anytime, anywhere. His passion for guns, coupled with the painful boredom of virtual imprisonment, makes him like a mischievous little child with a toy, but the toys are real guns, carrying real bullets. One night in this same period Presley and Red West were sitting in the dining room of the Imperial Suite. Red recalls: "Over the table there is this great-looking chandelier with about fifteen or twenty lights in it. It's very fancy.

"Anyway, Elvis is sitting back with his feet up on the table, and it looked like something out of a Robert Mitchum movie. He pulls out this gun—it just might have been a .22 Savage, if I remember rightly. Anyway, he just starts casually blasting away at these light bulbs. I don't know how many times he reloaded the damned thing, but he kept on reloading until he blew out every one of the light bulbs. There was plaster falling down from the ceiling like crazy, and there were holes in the ceiling everywhere." The management of the Hilton Hotel kept their complaints to themselves, but they did present him with a stiff bill.

It is difficult to say what makes a man obsessive about guns. Presley has not the slightest respect for them, although he does know the respect they can produce.

Red explains. "Now, I wasn't there when this happened, nor was Sonny, so we can only go on what 'E' told us. But it appears it was in the early days when I was away in the marines. Elvis was in a bar, or maybe it was a coffee shop or a restaurant on Lamar Avenue, back in Memphis.

"The way he tells it there was a sailor in there giving him a hard time about his clothes and long hair. Elvis takes this for a while, although he is burning inside. Anyway, after a bit he reaches into his pocket and takes out not a real gun—I think it was only a starting pistol. He walks up to this sailor, jams the starting pistol right under his chin and says—now this is according to Elvis—'Listen, motherfucker, I want you to stand to attention and call me sir.'

"The sailor is shittin' himself and he stands to attention. Then Elvis says to him, 'Now, I'm walking outside for some fresh air for a few seconds and when I come back I still want to see you standing to attention.' Elvis says he walked outside and got into his car. He says he drove around the block, and when he passed that place again he could see the sailor still standing stiff to attention. Elvis said that stuck in his mind, and he thought the gun was a helluva equalizer when it came to bullies."

On an average day, Presley will get up at four or even five in the afternoon. Soon after he gets up, depending on his moods, he orders a giant breakfast. Often, as he eats, he has one of his many guns at his side. While eating breakfast he always turns on the television set. For the sake of the television set and their nerves, the boys always pray there is nothing on that he doesn't like.

"For instance," says Red, "Elvis doesn't like too many other singers—at least living ones. He did admire Bobby Darin very much, but he has passed away. But generally Elvis will always have something critical to say about another singer. He doesn't like competition.

"Worst of all, he really hates Robert Goulet for some reason. I don't even remember whether he had ever met him or not or whether he had seen him perform live. Anyway, one afternoon in 1974, he is eating breakfast and on comes Robert Goulet on the big-screen television set. Very slowly, Elvis finishes what he has in his mouth, puts down his knife and fork, picks up this big mother of a .22 and—boom—blasts old Robert clean off the screen and the television set to pieces.

"He then puts down the .22, picks up his knife

and fork and says, 'That will be enough of that shit,' and then he goes on eating.

"Talking about it now, around normal people, I realize how weird that kind of stuff was. But at the time, I must admit, we all indulged him. Whenever he did something like that, we all laughed like crazy and made a big joke of it. I suppose when we did that it just encouraged him. But if that bullet had bounced off that television set and hit somebody, it wouldn't have been so funny.

"In fact, one night the bullet from a Presley gun did glance off a television set and it did hit somebody. It was in a two-bedroom suite at the Holiday Inn—or it might have been the Ramada Inn, I don't know, we hit so many places—but I remember it was just off the freeway in Asheville, North Carolina, and we were getting ready for the show."

In the room was Presley's father, Vernon Presley, and Dr. George Nichopoulos, a Memphis doctor of Greek extraction who would often travel with the entourage to look after Presley.

Dr. Nick, as he is called, is a short, good-looking man with a shock of white hair and a penchant for good rings, bracelets and watches—a preference that Presley has acknowledged with many expensive gifts. Dr. Nick has got Presley through some very bad times in his life, both physically and emotionally. He does his best, without always succeeding, to discourage Presley from an insane diet that would kill a hog, and exudes a distinctly paternal interest in the superstar. Dr. Nick's son, Dean, is often a member of the Presley entourage, and he is as close to family as it is possible to be without being a blood relative.

"I can't remember exactly what brought it on," says Sonny, "but just before the show, Elvis just whipped out a revolver that was tucked in his belt and blew out a damn television set in the main room. Now this time the bullet—I guess it was a .22—whizzed around in that TV set inside, bounced off and came out again.

It whistled past Vernon's head and hit Dr. Nick right under the heart.

"Thank God that by the time the thing reached Dr. Nick it was completely spent, and it just bounced off his suit and plopped on the floor."

Dave Hebler was on the balcony of the suite when he heard the gun go off, and he came racing in. By that time Sonny had very quickly dragged the dead television set from the room and replaced it with a live one from the bedroom. Sonny remembers that there were security guards for the show waiting outside. They were banging on the door wanting to know what was going on.

Another member of the Presley bodyguard team, a man named Dick Grob, a former U.S. Air Force fighter pilot and ex-Palm Springs policeman who had joined Presley on the permanent staff of the Memphis Mafia, had a little heart-to-heart talk with the other security guards and smoothed it over. "He just told them some kind of a story, but they went away satisfied," says Sonny. "It's not every day you hear a gun go off when you're supposed to be there protecting the ass of a superstar. Later on Elvis gave the chief of security a gold watch."

Predictably, the public and the ever-present press had no idea about the flamboyant show of gunplay. This was the closest the otherwise healthy Dr. Nick ever came to a heart attack. "Honestly," Red adds, "I can't tell you how many television sets went to their death at the hands of Elvis and his shooting. He would shoot out television sets in hotel rooms and in any one of the houses he has. He shot out a great big one at Graceland, in Memphis, the one he had in his bedroom. He shot 'em out in his place in Palm Springs."

Nobody would say a word to him about it, although there was one time he was asked to explain his actions. The reprimand came from his cute little daughter Lisa Marie, then seven. After seeing one of these shattered sets, she said, "Daddy, why did you shoot the TV?"

He smiled sort of sheepishly and said, "Aw, honey, there was something on it that Daddy didn't like."

Presley would regularly go on shopping sprees in sporting goods stores for guns. He bought them as he bought his cars—by the load. In 1970, on one particular Beverly Hills spree, for which Sonny still has the shopping list, Presley had a real ball giving Kerrs Sporting Goods the best business they had ever had. In just one month he bought thirty-two hand guns, one shotgun and a rifle. The arsenal included such goodies as a gold-inlaid .357 Colt python revolver, which cost $1,950, and a .44 Ruger Blackhawk revolver, also gold plated, costing $1,850. The rest ranged in price from over $1,000 down to $66 for a Derringer. The total cost of that shopping spree was $19,792.

"That four-shot Derringer that he carries in his boot on stage, well, one night it was irritating the side of his ankle," says Red West. "Elvis just stops between numbers and hoists it out in full view of everybody. There were cops all around. If they didn't see it or the audience didn't see it then they were blind. He put it on the stage right next to Charlie Hodge. Charlie just swept it up and put it in his pocket.

"One night on tour when he was wearing that damn big Magnum of his, we had flown in one of his private planes to Dallas, I think. Anyway, Elvis had slept all the way and was in his pajamas. He will often sleep on the plane in his pajamas and go straight to a hotel and back to bed again. But he was wearing this Magnum in the top of his pajamas. He had a coat over his pajamas, but the pajama top just wasn't strong enough to hold this great big Magnum. It just kept falling out. Elvis was out of it on sleeping pills and he didn't seem to know what was happening. We get off the plane at the airport and as he is walking down the steps from the plane the Magnum falls out in front of cops that are everywhere and a big crowd waiting for him. It was night and raining a little and here am I with this flashlight looking for a damned Magnum. I finally found it and Elvis just grabbed it from me like he had dropped a dime. Not a care in the world. I'll never know how none of this came out in the press because it was going on all the time. There are supposed to be some pretty sharp newspapermen around, but they never picked up on any of this, and it wasn't hard to find out because he seemed so damned open about it."

Elvis's guns, at least the ones he carries, are always loaded—but not fully; the first chamber is always empty. Sonny relates: "It is a habit he got from me. I had a friend who dropped his gun. It landed on the hammer. Anyway, it fired and hit him right through the heart, killing him instantly. Now after that happened I always made sure that when I was going armed on a security job with Elvis that I always left the first chamber empty for two reasons. First, I don't want the same thing to happen to me, and second, if I am wrestling with some nut case during a performance and my gun falls out, it might go off and hit someone in the audience, which would be a tragedy."

Presley might do it for those reasons, too, but according to Sonny he has a third reason. "Elvis knows what a real bad temper he has," says Sonny. "When he flashes, anything can happen. If he pulls the trigger in a rage, it will come up blank and give him just enough time to realize what on earth he is doing.

"I remember one time at the Memphian Theater in Memphis. That's the movie house that Elvis often takes over for himself and the boys to watch his favorite films. There was a crowd that night. Anyway, he went to the men's room. He seemed to be there a bit too long. Anyway, one of the guys—he wasn't a regular member of the crowd, just a friend—anyway, he started to bang on the door and sort of yell in a loud but joking way. I can't remember who it was, but I guess he was someone who wasn't close enough to Elvis to start getting too familiar. Anyway, Elvis yells back, 'Okay, man, okay.'

"But this guy just kept banging on the door, which was a damn fool way to act as he was to learn pretty soon.

"Apparently Elvis flashed. 'Goddamnit!' he yelled as he charged out the door. Then he screamed, 'Who do you think you are, you motherfucker?' With that he whipped out his gun, pointed it right at the guy and pulled the trigger. Jesus, thank God, he didn't have a bullet in that chamber; otherwise, he would have blown the man's head clean off his shoulders."

When the mood grabbed Elvis in any one of his many mansions, the place would sound like a shooting gallery. He has been known to pick up a gun or a rifle and just start blasting away for the sheer hell of it. Even when he was not in a state of excitement from his self-prescribed medication, he would spend hours on all sorts of target practice. An especially favorite pastime was to fill his pool up with balloons or light bulbs and blast away until the pool was a graveyard of burst rubber or broken glass. That in itself probably could be put down to boredom and, perhaps, was only marginally dangerous. "But," says Red, "what was really wild was when he would flash his guns on a public street."

Red and Sonny West and Dave Hebler have been with Presley on literally dozens of occasions when the star has been enraged simply by another car passing him. Many times he has every reason to get angry. Carloads of wise guys noticing Presley in a car would often burn past him yelling insults and making obscene gestures at him. But other times there have been drivers who, not noticing Presley at all, have simply passed him on the highway. When this happens there stirs in Presley the boyish ambition to be a cop. He will chase after the driver and yell at him to pull over, show one of his many police badges that he collects like some little boys collect marbles, and give the errant driver a lecture.

"He believes he is a law unto himself," says Dave Hebler. "You have to put it into perspective, however. In the circle of entertainment, he had every right to be that law. He is pampered, he is an industry, making a lot of money for a lot of people. That can be, to some degree, understood. But he loses sight of reality. Because when he gets out in the real world —your world, my world—he can't differentiate between the two. He still believes he is in charge. He is like isolated royalty, like the emperor of Japan or the queen of England. Despite his humble beginnings, he hasn't had contact with the outside world for many years. It's a genuine case of being a Howard Hughes. Elvis wouldn't know how much a slice of pizza cost in downtown L.A. He wouldn't know how much the average guy pays for a shirt. He is removed from all that.

"Now, when somebody passes him in a car going seventy miles per hour, he says, 'Who does he think he is, doing that? He can't speed'—even though Elvis speeds like a madman all the time. It's as if someone was trying to usurp his special privileges. I promise you, the man is a very interesting study. He has absolutely no self-control, hence the gun-firing stuff. Like a little boy who picks up a rock and throws it through a window for no real reason apart from the fact it was there, Elvis will pick up a gun and blast away with it.

"I can't honestly believe he always plays with guns because he is sinister. . . . Overall, I believe he is like an uncontrollable mischievous boy."

Dave remembers a perfect example. He was driving Presley along Elvis Presley Boulevard outside his Graceland mansion in Memphis. It was the summer of 1974, on a pleasant, warm evening just before sundown. Dave was just pulling into the entrance of Graceland. He slowed down as he came to the gate, because the entrance was jammed with the normal clutch of fans who keep a twenty-four-hour vigil.

"Just then," says Dave, "I noticed a car parked against the wall of Graceland. On top of it is a beer can. Now, as soon as I saw that beer can I instinctively thought, Oh-oh, target practice for Elvis, then figured, No way, he wouldn't do that in front of these people outside the damn gate. The hell he didn't. He whipped out a gun, leaned out and—*blam*—tried to knock the can off the roof. He missed by a country mile. He cursed. I nearly died. What if someone tells a reporter about the incident? Well, it didn't seem to worry anybody except me. Man, that crazy gun stuff drove me up the wall.

"I'm nervous around anyone who doesn't handle a gun with the same care as you would handle a rattler. I lost my eye as a kid because some crazy bastard got careless with an air rifle. After that beer-can incident, Elvis just laughed, and he put the gun back in his belt and we drove on through. In Elvis's houses, wherever he is staying, you just might flop down on a sofa and suddenly you're sitting on a stray gun. Sonny did that once, and this gun was jammed upwards between two cushions. He sat right on the point of the barrel, right up his ass. Man, that's sheer insane carelessness. There are kids sometimes roaming around those places of his."

It must be said that Presley's guns are quite legal, and they are all licensed. He goes to great pains to befriend law-enforcement agencies throughout the country. It isn't that he wants them on his side to cover anything up; it's just that—according to the West boys and Dave Hebler—he is impressed with the macho behind being a cop. He is obsessed with the authority that a police uniform or police badge gives. He will go to extraordinary lengths to get those badges of authority. He has long been issued a legitimate sheriff's badge from Shelby County, Memphis. In fact, all of his bodyguards, including Red, Sonny and Dave, possess legitimate Shelby County sheriff's badges. Even his doctor, George Nichopoulos, had one.

Presley arranges for these badges through his contacts in the sheriff's department. These are not honorary badges; they are legitimate badges that allow the holder to carry a gun. Holders of these badges are bonded and insured like a regular sheriff's deputy. "I guess he has troopers', sheriffs' and police badges from half the states in the Union," says Sonny. "If a local police organization offers him an honorary badge, he loses interest. If he can't get the real thing, he doesn't want it at all, and he ignores anyone who offers him anything less than the real thing."

Presley is a close friend of former Sheriff Bill Morris of Shelby County, a hard-working cop who can't be blamed if he is flattered by being sought out as a friend by Presley. Presley bought Morris a glistening new Mercedes but, in fairness to the sheriff, it was a spontaneous gift with no strings.

Sonny relates: "The sheriff was knocked out by the gift. He is a very good man. Very honest, very tough, but like everyone, he is human, too, and he is impressed by Elvis, like we all were."

Sonny recalls that in the beginning of 1971, Sheriff Morris arranged for Presley and Sonny to go to the National Sheriffs' Conference Building in Washington. "Elvis was very impressed by this," says Sonny, "him rubbing shoulders with the top cops in the country. He got off on that. Anyway, we get to Washington and we were very well looked after by the Feds, who were a great bunch of guys. They really gave us the red-carpet treatment. They took us into the Federal Building and showed us the files and exhibits of all the biggest crimes in history. It was like going through a museum, and both 'E' and I were very interested in it. Kidnapping, murder, assassinations—there were all sorts of exhibits and files. It was fascinating.

"Now before we went into the Federal Building, the

Feds who were showing us around assumed we were carrying arms. As is the rule, they very nicely asked us to unload.

"I took off my shoulder holster and locked it in the trunk of the car. I just guessed Elvis wasn't carrying, because he didn't make a move. I should have known better. Anyway, we're going through these exhibits and things and Elvis wants to go to the men's room. The Fed men came into the men's room with us. As is customary, Elvis always goes into a booth. He will never stand up alongside you in the men's room when you're taking a leak; he will always go into the booth. So when he comes out of the booth, there is me and the two Fed guys waiting for him. Elvis leans over to fix his shoe or something and as he does a .25 automatic tumbles out and clatters on the tile floor. God, my heart stopped. Here were these FBI guys, nice enough to take us around and take time off. They politely tell us to take off our guns because there are rules in the Federal Building about concealed weapons, rules which I fully understand and fully respect.

"Well, Elvis looks down at this gun on the floor, picks it up calmly and puts it in his belt. He just smiles boyishly at the Feds, and the Feds sort of smile back. He just charmed them off a tree and they didn't say a word. The old Elvis, when he turned on the charm, he could con anyone."

# 9

Presley is a mass of paradoxes, contradictions, complexities. His generosity vies with his selfishness; his sunny moments battle with his black moments; his demand for excitement clashes with his easy acquiescence to boredom. Of course, those contradictions exist in most human beings, but most human beings have the guiding force called maturity, that germ of moderation that sets off alarm bells when we have gone too far one way or the other. Dave Hebler says, "Without trying to be an amateur psychiatrist, the best way to explain it is that everything Elvis does, everything that interests him, everything that he takes up, he grabs, strangles and beats it to death. If he suddenly takes a liking for a certain food, he will eat it four times a day, every day for a month, until it makes him physically throw up."

There are reasons for this seeming lack of maturity. One is that since before the age of twenty-one, he has been constantly wrapped in his celebrity status, packaged and sold to adoring millions. There was no need to develop maturity. Perhaps immaturity is just what makes a man like Presley so irresistible to millions. He is one of the few Peter Pans who has managed not only to survive but to thrive. But the basic reason goes back to childhood. For the first seventeen years of his life, up until he left Humes High School, there had been little strong definition to shape his destiny. Paradoxically, despite the ordinarily clear-cut impact of an upbringing like his dirt-poor Southern background, the influences that molded him into manhood were a lot more confusing and blurred than one might think.

For poor kids life goals tend to be simply drawn. In many ways, straight-up-and-down, rough, tough guys like Red West had it easier. They seemed to have fewer choices, if only by virtue of the fact that they allowed themselves fewer ambitions. Youngsters like Red West never allowed themselves dreams in those semifeudal days of the South. If they did, they kept those dreams to themselves. Talking about dreams in Memphis was like wearing pigtails: somehow it just wasn't manly.

Red recalls: "I didn't have much confusion in my mind. I always wanted to be a musician or maybe a football player, but I never expected anything to come of those dreams. I recognized, I guess, that I was a bit of a hick, someone who was a bit suspicious of anything that didn't come from my immediate vicinity of Tennessee. I played football, had my share of fights. I came from a broken home, the same way as my daddy did. To me, a good steady job, enough money for a few beers, raising a family with a couple of kids was the very best I could hope for. You know, just get on with life."

In the past, lots of Southern boys thought the best and steadiest job was fighting in Korea or Vietnam. Red went into the marines, not knowing what he would do after that. Of course, despite his carrot-topped temper and his flying fists, Red was a sensitive kid, as his song-writing career was later to prove. But if there were any stirrings of that sensitivity in his early life, when he first met up with Presley, he knew better than to let it show too much.

With Elvis Presley, it was different. First, his only child status and his doting, self-sacrificing mother set

Presley apart from the other kids on the block. There was plenty of love in the South, but in those hard times it was parceled out. Presley seemed to his peers to have a whopping big parcel. One of the few aspects of Presley's life that has been puffed out accurately by a carefully controlled publicity machine is the portrait drawn of his mother, Gladys Presley. A beautiful, jet-black-haired girl when she was young, she grew to be a plump, benevolent lady whose interests rarely strayed from Elvis, Vernon Presley and the church, in that order. Neighbors from Tupelo, Mississippi, and Lauderdale Courts and Lamar Avenue in Memphis are all adamant in their description of her.

By all accounts she was indeed the saint that legends are made of. She was to die a young woman, only forty-two. Despite recurring liver problems and constant fatigue, Gladys Presley insisted on slaving at odd jobs to convince Elvis that they were not as poor as he thought they were. Her work in the sewing mills, as a waitress, and as a nurses' aide supplemented the meager salary from Vernon Presley's painfully boring job as a paint-can packer. Nothing was too strenuous, too hard, too wearing. And the worst thing anyone could remember her saying about the grueling life was, "My poor feet are killing me."

Young Elvis Presley was not insensitive to his mother's sacrifice. He did everything in his power to make life just a little sunnier for her. In November, 1950, when he was fifteen, he insisted on getting a job as an usher at Loew's State Theater for the princely sum of $12.50 a week. He pounded the carpeted floors from five until ten every night and gave every nickel to his mother. When he started to fall asleep in class, his mother insisted that he stop work, no matter how financially strapped they were. The following year, when money was still low, Presley insisted on going back to work at Loew's, only to meet with disaster. The theater manager, Arthur Groom, goes on record as having fired the world's most expensive talent. The girl who sold candy and popcorn appeared smitten with the brooding young Presley and favored him with some free samples. When another usher informed on him, Presley responded with a roundhouse swing that ended his career as an usher.

He next took a job with the Marl Metal Company. When his teacher again reported that young Presley was taking forty winks in class, his mother was genuinely horrified and vowed he would never have to work again while going to school. "That's no kind of work for a little boy," she said. "You quit. We're not that poor."

Presley quit, and when finances again got rough, Gladys went back to work at St. Joseph's Hospital in Memphis. Her health was appalling, but she never complained. Some friends remember Gladys Presley's doting on young Presley: "I can't remember right offhand when she didn't walk Elvis to school right up until he was maybe twelve or thirteen. She wasn't trying to turn him into a mama's boy, she just loved him something powerful."

Despite Presley's good fortune in having Gladys as a mother, poverty was ingrained in the Presley family in an especially tragic dimension. It was the birth of Elvis just before noon on January 8, 1935, that put into focus the real meaning of Southern white poverty. Gladys Presley in pregnancy was big, very big. Some people in Tupelo, Mississippi, thought she was going to have twins. The doctor at the time scoffed at the suggestion.

Now, as often happened with poor Southerners, white and black alike, giving birth was not a hospitalizin' affair. Going to the hospital to have a child was the choice of the rich, not the poor, who gave birth to the child in the same bed where it was conceived. When Elvis Aron Presley peeked into the world in the tiny frame house in Tupelo, Mississippi, Mrs. Presley was still writhing in pain. The doctor tried to soothe her. As little Elvis was getting cleaned up, she experienced still more spasms. It was the same pain because there was another baby inside. The doctor then worked on removing the second child from Mrs. Presley. Sadly, little Jesse Garon Presley, the identical twin of Elvis Aron, came into the world lifeless.

Red West remembers times when Presley in a mood of despondency would say, "Shit, man, my little brother died and my mama almost died because we couldn't afford to go to no damn hospital." To this day, Elvis Presley rarely travels without his personal physician. Red recalls that one of the most everlasting impressions ever made on Presley were the sacrifices made for him by his mother.

There was a beautiful brave stoicism in Gladys Presley that Red West can never forget. She seemed quite prepared to recognize the good life would never come in her time, but she did everything in her power to see that her son would have a chance at something better. While Presley in later years was to show mindless insensitivity toward others, he was keenly aware of every second of sacrifice by his mother. He relived every moment of silence with which she greeted hardship. When her son was struggling through Humes High School, how could she have known that the house where he was born would one day fit into the kitchen of any one of his many mansions? It was the stuff that American dreams are made of, and stuff that Elvis Presley made come true—perhaps too late. Because if Presley wanted riches for himself, he wanted them much more for his mother, a woman who deserved cars, diamonds and furs much more than the women on whom Presley has lavished exotic gifts.

Maybe that is the key to his overwhelming generosity. He has to give to somebody because the one person who deserved it all is no longer here to receive it.

Vernon Presley also had dreams. They would rarely show. But when Vernon looked at the grim life surrounding him, with little hope of anything better, he would seek temporary relief in a beer too many. He was never a heavy drinker; just a beer over the limit when the hopelessness became too relentless. And then young Presley saw the tragedy of a man who wanted something more from life than just a gold watch from the United Paint Company. To this day, with odd exceptions, Elvis Presley rarely indulges in boozing.

Then, too, young Elvis had his own complexities to come to terms with. He was in a tough town, in a tough neighborhood, in a tough school, but he was not especially tough himself. He was surrounded by crew-cut jocks, but he was not one himself. Perhaps if Elvis Presley had been born in New York, Boston or even Chicago, he might have fit in a lot better. In big cities there is more tolerance of a kid who wants to be different. But not in Memphis in the 1950s. "It was," says Red West, "as if he said to himself, Damnit, man, if I can't be like you guys, then I'm gonna be someone else." And he was.

When Red was driving around with Elvis in the battered old green coupe that day after Red's football game against Bartlett, Red looked at the fancy clothes, the wild hairdo and thought to himself, Man, this is going to be some gig, being on the road with Elvis. "Elvis didn't say so," he recalls, "but asking me to come along was his way of saying thanks for me pulling him out of those jams when other kids picked on him. He wanted someone his own age he could trust, and I don't think he knew anybody his own age like that. Let's face it, up until then we hadn't been really close buddies, but I guess I was the closest friend he had around. He was sort of lonely. It was his way of saying thanks.

"Elvis will never straight out acknowledge a debt to someone. Not in words. But he never forgets. When he first met Dave, and Dave helped him out of a few embarrassing moments on the mats, he didn't say thanks, but he remembered that Dave came through for him. He never forgets. So, you'll be with him and all of a sudden he will say thanks in a deed, like some fantastic gift.

"He likes to watch your reaction when he gives you something, but he doesn't harp on it. He never says, 'Remember when I gave you that thing?' He is very good like that. He will give you a sensational gift and forget about it. In return he expects total devotion and total loyalty. Sometimes, because of his moods, it's very hard to give all the time.

"After one of his wild temper fits, he will never say, 'Hey, man, I was wrong, I'm sorry.' But then one day you will be walking through an automobile show-room and he'll say something like 'Hey, man, that looks great, that car, don't it?'

"And somebody will say back to him, 'Sure does, Elvis.' The next minute, he'll tell you, 'Look, you fix up the paperwork, it's yours, you deserve it.' That's it. There is no argument, just 'It's yours, man.' When he does things like that, I have seen pretty tough guys just choke up with emotion. I have seen him do it, dozens of times."

By the end of 1954, Elvis Presley had been down so long it finally started to look like up. With the extra money he earned as a truck driver and the occasional gigs he got playing one-night stands, he had been able to contribute to the family finances to the point where his mother and father could move into a new apart-ment on Lamar. It was no mansion, but anything was better than Lauderdale Courts. A few bucks were roll-ing in. The disc he recorded, "That's Alright, Mama," sold a respectable seven thousand copies. Presley had become a minor celebrity with the support of Sam Phil-lips at the Sun Recording Company, Dewey Phillips, the disk jockey, and another popular disc jockey named Bob Neal. Presley was in big demand at the high school auditoriums and for one-night stands. Bob Neal had inordinate faith in Presley's potential, and he took over managing him. In a shark-eat-shark business, Bob Neal was, above all, very honest, had a lot of local contacts, and a genuine affection for the young, long-haired singer. And who wouldn't?

Young Presley was a manager's dream. Punctual, polite and without the slightest trace of big-headedness. He would get up and do his act, stay out of saloons, and never mix with the "bad" crowd that infested country music in those days. And there was a bad crowd. Although the rock groups of today are credited with being the high priests of the drug generation, the country and western crowd were gulping amphetamines like peanuts as far back as the mid-1950s, long before the Mick Jagger crowd ever got out of grade school.

After a gig, the most sinful thing young Presley and Red would do was to go to an all-night diner, eat a hamburger and suck on a double malted.

"He dated from time to time, like anybody," recalls Red, "but he wasn't girl crazy. He was more likely to have one steady girlfriend. He had one little local dark-haired beauty in the early days and, if I remember rightly, she jilted him. She didn't know what he was going to be or she might have thought otherwise. Lots of people thought he might have got married to her, but it didn't turn out that way. He was just a real good kid who liked very simple things.

"Apart from his wild drape coats, most of his money went to the one woman in his life that mattered more than anything—his mother. He wasn't a big show-off spender, nothing like that."

Despite the demands of local popularity, young Presley still loved to sing gospel songs. Occasionally he sang with local church groups, and at parties he would often be seen with a Coke in his hand, harmonizing with gospel groups. One very talented group at the time was a gospel-singing team known as the Blackwoods. They would often sing backup to Presley, and if anyone had recorded those sessions, they would be worth a fortune today. Even when singing a highly inspirational gospel number, Red noticed, young Presley had a highly unspiritual way of delivering his songs. It was something in the way his left leg would shake and in the way he swung his hips.

Red recalls: "Elvis told me later that he used to shake and swing himself around rather than stay still. He said he did this because if he stayed still the audience would see him shaking and quivering with fright. Of course, later on it wasn't nerves that made him shake."

Presley himself has said of the habit, "I remember sometimes in church, you would listen to the choir and all of them would have great voices. But it was often the preacher, who might not have had as good a voice, who was jumping around and getting them all worked up, who was the center of it all. It was like a bit of a show. And good."

By the end of 1954, despite the generous nibblings at success, young Elvis was making only "extra" money. He still had his job as a truck driver. Weeknights, when he sang in Memphis in local restaurant complexes like the Eagle's Nest, money at best was never more than fifteen dollars a night. Good money for the times, but no king's ransom. In the beginning, performing for adult audiences in semidarkened nightclub rooms, Presley was received politely, but without overwhelming enthusiasm.

"He did a damn good show," says Red, "but the older audiences in the South were pretty conservative, and they hankered more for traditional country and western stuff or straight ballads. Elvis would get up there on stage fired with more enthusiasm than ten men, but it didn't really drive the older audiences crazy. But when he got on the circuit playing high school audiences and opening drugstores and stuff like that, it was a different thing."

His un-self-conscious enthusiasm washed over the

younger crowds, and they got swept away. Elvis was *theirs*. He wasn't a hand-me-down from another generation; he was really theirs. "When I first saw him turn those kids on," says Red, "I didn't know what he had, but he had it to spare."

Red's duties in those days pretty well defined themselves. He would take turns with Presley at the wheel. He made sure that all the equipment was properly packed and generally just made sure things went smoothly. About that time driving facilities improved when Presley bought a pink Crown Victoria. Red recalls: "Of all the dozens and dozens of cars Elvis has bought, in my opinion it was that old Crown Victoria that Elvis seemed to love most. I'm sure if someone asked him today he would probably agree with me. Come to think of it, I loved that car, too."

When Red took up with Presley on the road, there was no suggestion that he be a bodyguard of sorts. He was there for company and friendship. Although Presley never asked him to be anything else, it worked out differently.

"I was on the road with him doing one-nighters on and off for about a month in 1955," says Red, "when I realized that Elvis was a really hot package. The girls just went crazy for him when he was up there on stage. He was still pretty shy, but gradually the waves of applause and craziness around him started to loosen him up a bit. He got a lot more confidence. Suddenly, to these young chicks Elvis was Marlon Brando and James Dean all rolled into one. I got an idea what the future was going to be like. When I saw these chicks leaping up on stage trying to kiss him, I knew we were in for some old-fashioned battles.

"Now, down South in those days if a gal was with a guy and she got up and tried to kiss the man on the stage, that was like asking him outside for a fight. I could see the faces of some of those boy friends sitting there while their girl friends went crazy about Elvis, and, man, they were as black as thunder.

"When Elvis saw the chicks reacting to all that wiggling and jumping around, he really laid it on. The girls went wilder, and the boy friends sat there and got angrier."

This was the South in 1955, when virgins were not necessarily an endangered species, as they are today. The wildest thing a girl from a good family ever did in those days before she was married was kiss with her mouth open.

For many of these girls, young Presley was virtually undressing in front of them and giving them what they wanted but were too frightened to let themselves do. The Presley cult was still a long way off from hitting the media, but on the high school circuit and at local auditoriums, girls scraped dust off the stage where Presley had stood to keep as a memento.

Instinct told Red not to forget how to throw a punch, because Presley was going to be the object of some pretty violent envy. His instincts were correct. "To be fair," Red says, "Elvis didn't mean this to happen; he didn't want me as a protector. He was making a gesture, a kind gesture for me to come along for the ride. But before very long, I found my job was looking after his ass. I did it willingly."

The first week that Presley had the new Crown Victoria, there was the trouble that Red had expected. "It was raining like hell," recalls Red, "and we all had to get to Grenada, Mississippi, about ninety miles from Memphis. We were running late, and suddenly we got stuck in the mud. Anyway, I get into the driver's seat and start gearing from first to reverse to get us out of the mud. Old 'E' is pushing the car from behind, nearly dying as he hears me ripping the gears all over the place. He was convinced I was wrecking the car. He was almost having a heart attack. Anyway, we got out, but not before he got a little spot of mud on his pants. His pants, if I remember, were those sort of light pink pants, pegged pants, and the mud really showed up on them. The mudspot figured in something that was to happen that night."

Presley did the show wet and with the mudspot on his pants. The girls in the auditorium did their usual riot routine. "Those Mississippi boys are looking at old 'E' like they're going to tear his head from his shoulders," says Red. "These girls were hugging and kissing him and Elvis is playing up to it a bit, which just made the atmosphere worse. The boys are getting madder and madder."

After the show Presley suggested to Red that they go see a couple of girls he had met on an earlier trip. They lived together in a house. "We went to their house," says Red. "We sat around, talked, drank a few Cokes, but nothing went on. No funny stuff. Anyway, we get up and leave and we go over to this combination gas station and diner to have a hamburger.

"Well, halfway through the hamburger, two big dudes walk in and I just know there is going to be trouble. They start mouthing off at Elvis. Then one of them says, pointing to the mudspot on Elvis's pants, 'He's so scared over there he is shittin' himself.' Oh, Lord, I know something is going to happen. Then one of them starts up on Elvis's hair and his fancy clothes."

Presley got a bit tense, and he said to Red, "C'mon, Red, let's get out of here."

Red didn't agree. He walked over to the two of them and said, "What seems to be the problem with you guys? What seems to be bugging you?"

The bigger of the two said, "You're messing with our gals, see? And that's gonna cause you a lot of trouble unless you get out of town."

Red was still pretty cool with his answer: "Man, we didn't know those gals were attached."

The big guy replied, "Well, they are our gals and you and your long-haired sweetheart better get the hell outta here before you get into something you can't handle. Look at him over there, so scared he's shittin' his pants."

Red glanced across at Presley. He had that same look on his face that Red remembered from back in Humes High School. Whether that look triggered a reaction in Red or whether he was just steaming mad, nobody knows. But if big Red needed an excuse to hit the big dude, it was given to him seconds later.

The loudmouth reached in his pocket for a knife, saying, "I've got something here for you."

That was a mistake. Red hooked him under the chin. The big mouth went down in a flurry of knocked-over tables and blood. Red leaped on top of him. As he did, the other bully jumped him from behind. Red turned around and hit him with two punches that sent him flying clean across the diner.

Red stood up and hit the second guy one more time, sending him unconscious on his back, his head slamming right between the feet of Elvis Presley, who was still sitting down.

The first guy by now had scuttled back behind the counter, where he held up his hands, yelling, "Okay, man, okay. We don't want no more trouble."

That showed some wisdom. Red dusted himself off, paid the check and turned to Presley. Elvis stood up, stepped across the unconscious form, and they both walked to the Crown Victoria parked across the street. Red had just finished the battle of Grenada.

"Now, it all happened too fast for Elvis to do anything," Red remembers. "But maybe he was scared or maybe he was just smart enough to worry about getting his face messed up, but Elvis really wasn't a physical guy. I don't hold it against him, because in those days Elvis would never start anything and expect me to finish it. He would never wise off to anybody and he never took advantage of who he was. He would never move in on another guy's gal—although that came later. It was, I figured, he didn't deserve to get into any fights because he was a perfect gentleman."

Before going out on a gig, Red would always go across to the Presley home on Lamar Avenue to pick up Elvis. "I liked going to that house, if it was just to see Mrs. Presley. She was sick an awful lot, but whenever I walked in, she couldn't do enough for me. She'd get up, cut me some pie or make me a cup of coffee and always seemed genuinely interested in what I was doing. She would just beam with warmth and you could see the love almost tumble out of her whenever she talked of Elvis. Elvis was the same way to her. If ever we stayed overnight on a gig, he would always call his mother at home and talk to her for ages. She wouldn't go to sleep unless she got that call. Whenever we were away, he would always buy her something.

"A lot of the fans gave Elvis presents; lots of them were teddy bears. Man, he had roomfuls of teddy bears that he would always bring home to his mama. He worshipped that woman and so did I. She seemed to like me a lot, although I don't think she ever knew about the fights and stuff. That would have worried her sick. But somewhere in the back of her mind she knew I sort of ran interference for him, and whenever we left the Presley house she would always say to me, 'Now, Red, look after my boy, just look after my boy.' They were words I was never to forget."

As Presley grew in popularity, the fights were coming thick and fast for Red. There was always some guy who had it in his mind that his girlfriend was in love with Presley. He was the number one threat to Southern womanhood. Sometimes Red would see the fights coming and cool it before anything started. Other times, if his back was to the wall, he would wade in. In those early years, Red knocked so many guys on their back, he could have sold advertising space on the soles of their shoes. Red waves his head from side to side in recollection: "They were fun times, but they were wild times also. Man, one night at a club called the Rio Palmisle—it was a place I think somewhere outside Lubbock, Texas—there wasn't a fight, there was a war. In Texas they do things in a big way, let me tell you. That night, it was lucky we all didn't get killed.

"Elvis was up there doing his act on stage and the way I remember it, some guy from the audience shouts an insult. Well, some other guy, a drunk, tells the other guy to shut up. Well, *bang,* it's on. They have a thing with each other. And then all hell breaks loose. Suddenly the whole place starts taking sides. It was like one of those movie scenes that Elvis and I used to do. Just one incredible brawl with tables and bodies flying everywhere. There must have been more than a hundred people beating the hell out of each other.

"Elvis is on one of those low stages. And now that all the men are fighting, the girls are swarming up to the stage. They didn't give a damn what their menfolk were doing. The fight is coming up to the stage and Elvis is still singing away with these chicks around his neck. One guy puts his foot right through one of Elvis's guitars, and it's getting bad. Some of the guys are dragging the women off the stage. There are punches and bottles flying all over. The guy who puts his foot through Elvis's guitar, I hit and I yell to Elvis, 'Let's get the fuck out of here.'

"Elvis wasn't taking any notice of me. He's now starting to sign autographs, and I figure any moment someone is going to get to him. He was encircled by gals. I grab through the circle of women and grab hold of him."

Red half-dragged, half-carried Presley out, all the while punching a hole through the crowd to escape.

Red continues. "When we get out in the open, the fight has now spilled out there. Man, it was one full acre of guys fighting, guys getting their heads splattered with beer bottles. Blood everywhere. I got Elvis to the car and I took off like a bomb. As we sped away, Elvis was laughing like a madman. He had never turned a crowd on like that before, and he loved it. He was laughing, and then I started to laugh, too. There was a civil war back there."

Like Butch Cassidy and the Sundance Kid, they rode out of town leaving chaos behind them. It was one of many such experiences that welded Red and young Presley close together.

Apart from his genuine love for Presley, Red always jumped to defend him for another reason. "Even to this day, man, I have never forgotten the face of Mrs. Presley sitting there and saying to me 'Red, you look after my boy.' It's always been in my mind, no matter where I was with him. And that's what I did to the best of my ability."

One night over a few beers at Hollywood's Hyatt House, Red hunched his shoulders and adjusted the shoulder holster carrying his .38, which is constantly with him. "You know," he said, "I guess I made that my main job, keeping that promise to Mrs. Presley. I can see her face like it was yesterday telling me to look after her boy. No matter what has gone on between me and 'E,' if I ever thought anybody was going to harm him physically, I just might blow the dude away."

# 10

By the end of 1955 there were no million-dollar deals yet on the horizon, but for Elvis Presley, singer, and Red West, sidekick, the year had been damn good fun. Elvis's father had signed a contract with disc jockey Bob Neal (Presley was only twenty, underage for such an undertaking), and Presley was on the road with pianist-guitarist Scotty Moore, bass player Bill Black, and drummer D. J. Fontana. They were called the Blue Moon Boys.

Of Bob Neal, Red relates: "He was a real good ole boy, a straight shooter. He seemed to be more in for the fun than the money. He was a pretty funny dude who might have made it as a stand-up comic if he had worked at it. Sometimes Bob would go out and warm up the crowd before Elvis and the boys came on."

Young Presley was on the circuit with some pretty heavy names at the time. Hank Snow, Webb Pierce and Eddy Arnold were the top-liners of the day. Elvis and another young man by the name of Johnny Cash were coming up fast. Presley put out a second disc called "Good Rockin' Tonight," and while it didn't set the country on fire, the writers at *Billboard,* the music bible of the day, knew how to spell Presley's name without having to ask.

The big boys in New York hadn't really heard of him, but Nashville knew who he was, and that was good enough, for the time being. It was just about this time that Elvis Presley made one of the big moves of his young life. He quit his job as a truck driver and from now on he was Elvis Presley, singer. The sophisticates in New York and the sharpies in L.A. still called country and western "hillbilly music," with a bit of a sneer. But in the South and Southwest, country and western was big bucks.

"Elvis, in a quiet way, was pretty confident that he was eventually going to make it," says Red. "He didn't have any idea how big he was going to make it. All the same, leaving a steady job as a truck driver was a pretty big step. Elvis had plenty of encouragement, but in those days there were hundreds of kids roaming around with guitars looking for the big time.

"He never said so, but I'm sure he had a lot of second thoughts about taking the big plunge of leaving his job forever. He always worried about having money for his mama and father." Red remembers, however, that the young Presley was pretty much "in the circle." He was liked by guys such as Hank Snow, Webb Pierce, Eddy Arnold and Johnny Cash, although, as in any profession, they were very aware of the competition he could present in the future. "Above all, we were having fun, and he was a good guy to be with."

Typical of the kind of thing they would do was a trip they took to Nashville in 1955. "We used to do things on the spur of the moment. Like this time we went to Nashville. We landed there flat broke. At that time there was a very big group known as Mother Maybelle and the Carter Sisters. June Carter, then married to Carl Smith, but now happily married to Johnny Cash, was a very sweet Southern gal. She always had a big hello for us. She once did a gig somewhere with Elvis, and she said something like, 'If ever you're in Nashville, look us up.'

"Well, we took her at her word. When we got to

Nashville, somehow we had lost her address. Anyway, we found out where she lived and hitchhiked out to the place. Well, June wasn't home. It sounds terrible today, but in those days things were different. We forced a window and broke into the house. We didn't give a damn. It was a beautiful place. Anyway, we made ourselves at home.

"First thing that happens is that we get hungry, so I wander into the kitchen to fix us something to eat. The kitchen was fantastic. All around the place were these beautiful copper pans and skillets. Me, being a dumb ass, thought they were regular pots and pans. What I didn't know was they were specially purchased antiques worth a goddamn fortune. Anyway, I cook up some bacon and some eggs in these pans. I can't understand why they suddenly melt. I ruined them completely. We didn't take any notice, we just ate up our food. Well, we got our bellyfulls, and like a couple of bears we then decided to get some sleep.

"We were dog tired and dirty. Anyway, we go up the staircase of this beautiful house and look for a bed. Well, fully dressed and dirty, we just plop into this big double bed in the master bedroom and go to sleep. We slept like babies all night. Now, June Carter and her sisters were on a gig outside of town. And her husband, Carl Smith, had been somewhere else. Now about nine the next morning I hear a voice and some movement. June's husband Carl had come home. First he sees the forced window, then he sees the ruined pots and pans and the dirty kitchen. It was like Goldilocks and the three bears. Who has been breaking into my house? Who has been eating my food? Who has been ruining my kitchen? And now who has been sleeping in my bed? I'm amazed he didn't arm himself with a shotgun.

"Anyway, he walks in when I'm still asleep. Elvis wakes up and says, 'Oh, hi Carl.' Now he sees Elvis, but he only sees a big lump under the blankets next to Elvis and it was me. You couldn't blame a guy if he thought Elvis was in bed with his wife, although June wasn't that kind of gal. But I have a suspicious mind, and I'm thinking, Jesus, maybe he thinks I'm June and maybe he is going to blow my ass off.

"Very meekly, I just peeked over the sheets and said in a very polite voice, 'Hi, Carl.' You would have thought he would have chewed us out for breaking in, screwing around in the kitchen and then sleeping in his bed. But he gave us a big hello and laughed. He showed us all around the big house, and that night June and her sisters came home.

"We had a big get-together, ate a great big Southern dinner and stayed up that night singing and harmonizing with them all. I mean, that's the kind of real decent folks they were. They welcomed us like long-lost brothers.

"You know, I would give anything to go back to those simple, crazy days. Elvis was such a great guy and we got along so well. It was old-fashioned good clean fun." From that night on, Red recalls, young Presley seemed to have a crush on June's younger sister, Anita.

"You must remember, Elvis is still pretty much of a shy guy. He still ain't no swinger, and whenever Anita Carter is around, he is like a kid with six pair of feet. It was kind of cute, looking back on it."

Elvis went to elaborate lengths to get close to the beautiful Anita. Red recalls that a few months later, Presley, together with Scotty Moore, Bill Black and D.J. Fontana, were at the Gator Bowl in Florida doing a support for the Carter Sisters. The show went over beautifully, and the crowd was eating out of Elvis's hand. At the end of his act, the Carter Sisters had gathered offstage ready to follow.

"Now," says Red, "Elvis sees Anita in the wings. Anyway, he comes to the finale and he starts to look very sick. He comes offstage, totters around and collapses right into Anita's arms. They lay him out and he's unconscious. Anita has his head in her lap and she is soothing his forehead. Anyway, we whisk him away to a hospital, and me and Scotty and Bill and D.J. are worried as hell.

"The doctors tell us to go back to the motel and await their word. They would give us a report as soon as they could. We thought that maybe he was dying from some mystery disease."

Worried, the boys from Memphis just sat around morosely in their motel room waiting for the worst. At one in the morning there was a knock on Red's door. The boys all looked up apprehensively as Red hurried across the room to open it.

"Damn, man, if it ain't that old sonofabitch Elvis standing there healthier than a herd of cattle, and he is grinning from ear to ear. Not a doggone thing wrong with him. We all pump him full of questions, and he tells us he is now okay. But when the other boys return to their rooms, Elvis makes a confession to me. The whole collapsing routine was just a big act so he could get his head on Anita Carter's lap . . . just so he could get close to this gal he had this crush on." The story of fresh young love didn't end there.

About six months later, back in Memphis, young Presley and the Carter Sisters were again on the same show. The same thing happened. Only this time it was Anita who fainted and it was Anita who was faking it. "There was nothing wrong with her, either," Red says with a laugh. "She just wanted some attention from Elvis. They were both too damn shy to make a move. They never did get together, but it was kind of nice, thinking back. In the show-business scene today, people jump into bed with each other before they know each other's name. We were very old-fashioned, and I guess Elvis was the most old-fashioned of all of us. But you know what? It wasn't bad. It sure didn't stop us from having a whole heap of fun. Later on, we all got a bit too fast and a bit too big for our boots."

Bob Neal was doing a good job for Presley and the Blue Moon Boys. His early morning disc-jockey show on station WMPS was a valuable promotion machine.

The show had a range of about two hundred miles, and in the beginning Bob Neal had as big a following as a comic as the Blue Moon Boys did for their music.

Often, when shows outside the show's radius would want the Blue Moon Boys, Bob would act as agent and promoter but would not always go along. The financial arrangement was that Bob took ten percent off the top, and ten percent of the take was set aside for advertising and promotion. In those early days the Blue Moon Boys played in gyms, auditoriums, church halls and schoolhouses in towns and hamlets so small that they have since actually disappeared from the map.

With the help of Bob Neal's talent as a comic, station WMPS, and some very complimentary notices in *Billboard* magazine, the Blue Moon Boys were starting to get a wide and solid appeal. After ten percent was taken for Bob and ten percent was taken for promotion, Elvis got fifty percent of the remainder. The rest was split among Scotty, Bill and D.J. The back-up musicians were not just "pick-up" side men. They had a distinctive sound of their own that in the early days was as much a part of the "Presley sound" as young Presley was himself.

The back-up was a much bigger sound than any group of comparable size. But as Presley got more and more confidence, it became obvious that he was the star attraction. As the appeal widened, there were more and more offers to play outside Bob Neal's two-hundred-mile radius, and often Neal would book them from Memphis into Louisiana, Florida, Arkansas and Texas. They would take off on these long trips, the faithful Red as "wheelman," and conquer another town.

There were times that young Presley would make as much as two hundred dollars a week, a giant sum for those hard days. He would buy his clothes, fill up the gas tank, buy a few hamburgers and Cokes and put the rest into the Presley household. Red West was along for the ride; he did not draw a single cent. Recalls

Red: "It didn't matter a hoot in hell to me. I was along for the ride, learning a lot about the business and music and having a helluva good time." Ironically, Red the driver knew more about the mechanics of music than Elvis Presley. He reads music like a master and since those days has written some best-selling numbers. The burly, auburn-haired Red doesn't look like the average songwriter: football player, bodyguard, yes; but not a songwriter.

"Elvis doesn't read a lick of music (and, strangely enough, despite all his jumping around, he's not much of a dancer either)," says Red. "But he had an uncanny sense of timing when he was singing and a great range. And he would surprise the hell out of me whenever he got on a piano. He's a real natural, just like Sinatra. He knows when a sound is right and he knows when it's wrong better than most conductors. He just has that ear."

The more exposure Presley got, the more Gladys Presley worried that her boy would forget about his upbringing and his church. The more widespread his acclaim, the more intense her plea to Red West, "Bob, look after my boy."

Toward the end of the year, things really started to rev up. While there was still no great Presley impact in New York and Los Angeles, he was fast becoming an idol in the South.

Red remembers a date in Florida. "We were playing in Orlando, I think, near there anyway. 'E' has really got the audience going nuts and he is playing them like a violin. If he noticed that a particular gesture got squeals and yells, then he would repeat it again and more so each time he did it.

"Toward the end of the act, it looked like one of those evangelist groups. He knew just when and how to bring them on. Just like one of those hot-gospeling preachers. I remember he was wearing a bright green drape jacket and black pegged pants. He leans over off the stage to kiss a girl's hand, I think. Anyway, she grabbed him and tore the sleeve clean off his jacket. That was the signal, particularly when Elvis played up to this.

"The next thing we know there are gals on stage and they have gone berserk. It looked like they were trying to eat him all up. They were tearing and clawing like animals. Then one of the legs of his pants went. Then his shirt was torn to shreds. It was just scary for me to see what human beings could be driven to. I had always known about the swooning and screaming, but this was incredible. We managed to get him off stage, in shreds.

"Of course, it was great publicity and the papers picked it up all over the South. When Mrs. Presley heard about it and Elvis called her with his regular telephone call the next day, she was worried sick. Elvis would always minimize the reactions of the crowd and tell his mama that the press was exaggerating. The thing was, the press stories were very accurate. There was madness out there that night."

Mrs. Presley became so obsessed with the safety of her boy that she would constantly dream about him at night. "There was always something very eerie about the things she would say," Red remembers, "like she was psychic or something like it. Whenever we had a particularly wild scene on stage or if a riot broke out, whenever Elvis called her she would somehow have some premonition that someone got out of hand even before reading the newspapers. Now both sides of the family, both Gladys and Vernon, were great dreamers. And both sides of the family had a history of walking in their sleep. Elvis inherited this, and when he wasn't shacked up with a gal, often one of his cousins, Gene Smith or Billy, would sleep with him in case he started sleepwalking.

"When we were staying in high-rise hotels or motels, we always locked the doors and windows just in case when he was on one of his sleepwalking trips he would go out a window. I tell you this because it always struck me as if there was something really strange about the Presleys.

"I mean, I believe all this sleepwalking and dreaming were somehow related to some kind of special powers, something like psychic powers or something I don't really understand or could put my finger on. A lot of that psychic stuff is a lot of bunk, but to some degree I believe in it. Elvis proved it to me again and again.

"Now, I remember vividly a case in Texarkana, on the border of Texas and Arkansas. We were on a gig there and I think we were driving in a rented Cadillac. Now this must have been about 1955. Anyway, somehow the engine overheated, and in just no time at all the thing went up in flames.

"It could have been a dangerous situation. Anyway, we could jump out and see the car just burn itself to pieces. The next day, Elvis made a telephone call to his mother. And what happened was scary. She had absolutely no way of knowing what had happened. It wasn't in any newspaper or anything. Nobody knew about it. Apparently at about two in the morning she just sat bolt upright in bed, snapped clean out of her sleep.

"She nudged Vernon awake and said, 'I see our boy, he is in a blazing car.' When Elvis called that morning, she said, 'Oh, thank God, you're all right. I dreamed you were trapped in a blazing car.' Elvis said he was all right and nothing had happened. Of course, he would never do anything to worry his mama.

"Now I was there at the other end of the telephone when that conversation went on, so I know that it was true. After the telephone conversation, Elvis and I looked at each other as if someone had just walked across our graves. It was eerie."

Bob Neal, with careful, colorful and very honest promoting, had by this time guided Elvis Presley's career to the point where he would pop in and out of the *Billboard* popularity poll regularly. The teenagers in the South were screaming for him. It was a vital market, but in those days they still weren't the extremely rich consumer market that they are today. Bob Neal was seeking a wider appeal. He had singled out young Presley from the Blue Moon Boys with the tag the Hillbilly Cat, which was chosen to attract a wider audience; hence the addition of the bop word of the day, *cat*.

It was important to convince the big-money boys in New York and L.A. that Presley was not just a hayseed hillbilly singer. He had something more, something new to offer, apart from his brooding good looks and three Southern boys backing him up. What he needed, reasoned Neal, was some national exposure. A big, nationwide television show would be ideal.

Bob organized an audition on the *Arthur Godfrey Show*. It was an exciting chance, and the Hillbilly Cat and the Blue Moon Boys took off for New York amid an air of optimism. This was going to be it: at last, the big time. From now on, no more driving one hundred miles to a gymnasium. They were going to sit back and wait for the big offers to roll in. They were going to do the picking and choosing of their gigs.

They flew into the cold grayness of New York knowing that as Southerners, they would probably hate the city, but willing to love it. They took one look at New York when they were on the ground and decided they would rather be in a swamp. The *Godfrey Show* audition team heard them go through their best and biggest routine and then decided that a swamp might be the best place for the Hillbilly Cat and the Blue Moon Boys. They may have been the cat's pajamas in the South, but in big bad New York they were just a bunch of hillbilly horses' posteriors. The audition team may have made the biggest mistake of their New York lives. The Hillbilly Cat and the Blue Moon Boys marched back South, beaten into submission by those damn Yankees. The big time, the really big time, was not for Elvis—just yet.

If ever the boys were suspicious of Yankees, their suspicions had been confirmed. But, although it was a bitter disappointment, the boys were still the rage in the South. If that's where their fame and fortune were going to be, then so be it.

Just about that time, a man named Oscar Davis happened to arrive in Memphis. Davis was a colorful figure in the South. He was helping his boss promote the Southern sensation of the day, Eddy Arnold. Oscar Davis's boss was even more colorful than Oscar himself. His name was Thomas Andrew Parker. Parker was a colonel, of sorts. One of those "Southern" colonels. He had been given the rank by Governor Clement of Tennessee in 1953. In 1968 Stanley Booth, a talented writer, described Tom Parker in *Esquire* magazine as "a latter-day Barnum out of W. C. Fields by William Burroughs." The description not only accurately fit the bill, it was one that Parker relished and he did everything to encourage its spread. Parker came from the old school of promoting: "Don't care what they say about you just as long as they spell the name right."

"I'm a great believer in fate," says Red West. "It was just as if Tom Parker and Elvis Presley were born and destined to meet. Tom Parker was and is amazing. With Elvis and him it was like a joint and socket who had been looking for each other. Things were about to take off."

## 11

Elvis Presley today is often fat and always older, but with a single bat of his long, dark eyelashes he can command the adoration of any one of several million women of any age. Women seem to forget they are in the twentieth century when Presley comes on stage, and revert to ancient idol worshippers' way of throwing caution and convention to the wind.

Whatever it is he has, it triggers a reaction that brings the Neanderthal out in women; perhaps it is similar to the way Farrah Fawcett-Majors affects men. But back in the days when Elvis was twenty and just about to board a roller coaster that took him on one of the most unbelievable rides in show-business history, he certainly was no stud in the modern sense of the word.

There were indeed adoring teenagers by the legion, but his natural shyness, and perhaps a belief that it "was all just showbiz," told him that it wasn't Elvis Presley they were adoring; it was just the image. He would poke fun at that image, amused at the caricature he presented on stage. Even today, in his calmer moments, he still doesn't take his image too seriously. When he comes on stage wearing some outrageous outfit, he is apt to tell the audience, "Here I am in this Superman outfit." It's an honesty that appeals.

And, early on, he held himself pretty much in check

as far as taking advantage of all the females who threw themselves at him. He was, according to Red, "more obsessed with making it as a performer for the sake of his mother than running around screwing everything that walked. He believed in his singing; he believed in living a clean life. He cared for his art. He wasn't no sissy when it came to girls, but he wasn't a runaround guy that crawled in and out of everybody's bed, at least in those days. More than anything, success meant saying thanks to his mother to show her that all the hard work and sacrifice weren't in vain."

Elvis's devotion to his mother, and her devotion to him constitute perhaps one of the truly great love stories of our time. And, had she lived, the excesses that Presley allowed himself would undoubtedly have been kept to a minimum. It is certainly not beyond imagining that a more disciplined personality might have evolved.

"Up until he went into the army," Red remembers, "he pretty much was only involved with two real girl friends, both Southern, both charming, and both very pretty. One was Dixie Locke and the other girl was a lady named Anita Wood. He never took advantage of who he was. But just around about 1955 to 1956 there was a gradual change.

"He still had some pretty strict rules when dealing with women. He would never tolerate any of the guys around him cussing in front of ladies, and he would really get turned off if any of his friends went with a married lady or even a divorced lady. Things changed, of course.

"He was every mother's dream. He would 'yes ma'am' and 'no ma'am' women half to death. He would always stand up when a woman came into a room. It was very natural at first.

"But then," says Red, "as Elvis got older it became part of his patter. He really developed that professional country-boy act with women. In the later years it was no longer natural, it became his line."

But where Red noticed a gradual change was "toward the end of 1955, and Elvis suddenly found that he was one helluv an attractive guy off stage as well as on. And he started to realize that women liked going to bed just as much as men did. One day in Memphis we were just cruising around in the pink Crown Victoria and we just came across two gals. I guess we knew them vaguely. They were more pick-ups than anything else."

Red and Presley pulled up alongside the girls and offered to take them for a spin. Homecoming queens they were not, and Red figured that he and his boss would get more than "just a spin" out of them. In another and earlier time, Presley would very likely have told Red, "I just don't think Mama would expect that of me."

"I was still living with my mother," Red goes on, "in the Hurt Housing Project. Mama—Lois West, was her name—was separated from Dad, and we lived together in the housing-project apartment. She worked during the day. Well, that day my mama was at work."

So he, Presley and the girls ended up in Red West's apartment. There were a few awkward preliminaries and then came the pairing-off time. Red took one of the girls into his room, and Presley disappeared with his girl into the bedroom of Mrs. Lois West.

Now, Red's mother had a painful back condition. The bed was very old, sagging and soft, but Red and his mother couldn't afford to buy a new one. Instead, Red had made the bed more comfortable for his mother's back by putting a large slab of hardwood under the mattress to give it extra firmness. Red and his girl were rolling around on his bed, doing what comes naturally, when "suddenly," says Red, "I hear this yell, this scream, this breaking sound, and a whole lot of giggling coming from my mother's room." Red hurriedly pulled on his pants and dashed out.

"Damn, I thought, maybe Elvis was getting into the

swing of things and she changed her mind and Elvis was trying to force the issue—although he was never that kind of guy. I didn't know what to think. Anyway, I rush in."

Apparently Elvis had been prosecuting the act of love with such inspired vigor that he had broken the slab of wood under the mattress. The beautiful moment of ecstasy had been punctuated by the sound of cracking timber. Red chuckles, remembering. "It must have been a helluva shock. Imagine the girl. There she is getting it on and suddenly the whole world collapses under her. I went into the room and there they are half-assed dressed and giggling like school kids in this broken bed.

"It was pretty funny, but at the time I thought, heck, man, old Elvis is starting to lose his shyness. Elvis then started to relax a lot more when there were gals around. Like everything. When Elvis does something, he goes all the way. Once he discovered how easy he could get girls, we were routing them through his bedrooms two and sometimes three a day. That boy sure had a constitution in those early days."

It was this newly found appetite of young Presley's that indirectly led to a bristling confrontation between Red and the show-business guru of all time, Col. Tom Parker. It was also Red's first meeting with the man whom he grew to like and respect over the years as "one helluv an old man."

It was 1956 and Colonel Parker had been managing Elvis for about a month.

"I think we were in some place like South Carolina," says Red West, "and Elvis had a showing the next night in Virginia. When we played those places back to back, there wasn't much time for fooling around. It was a case of do the show, grab a bite to eat, hit the sack and get moving the next day in the car to the next place. The pace could become very tiring.

"This particular night, Elvis and his newfound ways with gals picked up this very pretty chick. He took her back to the motel room and shacked up with her.

Fine. Now the next morning I get up and start beating on his door. I was banging and yelling, 'Come on, man, we got to hit the road. We got to get to Virginia.' We were already late. Well, whatever that gal was doing, Elvis sure liked her act because he wouldn't get out of the sack with her. When he finally emerged, he looked like he had been mixed up with an eggbeater. She really gave him a going over. Well, we're really late now. It's winter time and it's sleeting and raining, colder than hell. We jump in the car, I drive like a madman through snow and everything to Virginia to this auditorium. I don't know how we weren't killed in that drive—it was madness.

"Anyway, after a hair-raising drive, we arrive there. I guess we're fifteen minutes late, or something like that. Now it's still snowing like hell, but out in front of this auditorium I see this crazy guy in a T-shirt. I get out of the car and I notice he is puffing on this cigar and he has got an expression on his face like he is going to kill me. Now, get it, kill *me,* not Elvis. Then I notice that, despite the fact he is wearing a T-shirt in this damn snow, he is so worked up he is sweating. Oh, Lord, without him introducing himself I knew I had met the Colonel.

"He just looks at me as if he was going to rip a yard from my ass. Right away he starts in, 'Where in the hell you been? Do you know what time it is? I got these people waiting and you're damn well late. You can't keep people waiting. Who do you think you are?' Man, I wanted to dig a hole and dive in. Elvis didn't say a word. He just slipped inside and got dressed.

"I was scared to go near the Colonel all night. It started a trend. When anything went wrong with Elvis, it was always my fault. He would get straight to me. Later on, I learned that him holding me responsible for the star was his way of showing me that he respected me for the responsibility. And man, I got to respect that ole boy.

"With him, it was hard-nosed business all the way. He worked day and night for Elvis. Together they were like two half-pieces that when they were put together they became a whole. He was a tough businessman, but he lived and breathed his job of promoting his boy, as he used to call him. He made Elvis the fortunes that he got from unbelievable contracts.

"But as tough as the ole boy was, I never knew him once to go back on his word. I have heard all the stories about Colonel Tom, but I know one thing: once he gave his word and his handshake, he would have rather lost an arm than go back on it."

Stories about the cigar-chomping Southern colonel, Tom Parker, are as countless as stories about Presley himself. But the Colonel apparently chooses to ignore them. He lives quietly with his wife in an immaculate house in Palm Springs—which, the West boys swear, is so clean you could eat a three-course meal off the driveway. Most days he starts work at six in the morning, bellowing deals into a telephone. He has a loyal assistant, Tom Diskin. He has no great turnover of staff. Those who work for him have been doing so, in one capacity or another, since he has been in business. The financial arrangement between him and Elvis is not known, although some say that Colonel Tom owns fifty percent of the property.

Perhaps the reason the Colonel has apparently not taken time to deny some of the more outrageous of the stories about him is that virtually all his time has been spent promoting Elvis Presley. Or it may be simply the instinct of the true promoter: Don't worry about what they say about you, so long as they are saying it (and spelling your name right).

Until Tom Parker was eighteen, he worked at all sorts of odd jobs for his uncle, who at that time ran the Great Parker Pony Circus, which, despite its grandiose name, was as tawdry as most road shows of the twenties. After that he struck out on his own, specializing in catering for the circuses, but doing all sorts of other jobs, even, occasionally, some palm-reading.

In 1934, the twenty-four-year-old Parker decided to move to the periphery of the circus business. He became a press agent and promoter of sorts, and found he could make a satisfying living.

In those days, some of the bigger and better-equipped fairs, road shows and carnivals would feature one of the better-known names in the country and western field. Young Parker saw an even better way to make a buck in promoting music men: Put a coupon advertisement in a newspaper, offering a discount to the purchaser who would take the coupon to a certain department store or supermarket. The store would act as the ticket seller for a particular show—and would also be attracting new potential customers to their own business. Sometimes, Parker would even be able to talk the store into paying for the original investment of placing the newspaper coupon ad. He was thus one of the first men in the country to promote a show by "tying in" a completely separate party. The idea today is a cornerstone of promotion. There wasn't much grass growing under Tom Parker's feet even in those days, and that was in the South at the height of the Depression.

Tom Parker's first experience at actually handling a single talent came by way of Gene Austin, who swamped the record market with his hit "My Blue Heaven." He promoted a series of concerts for Austin in auditoriums and proved to himself that he had forgotten more about old-fashioned promotion than most veteran promoters had ever learned. It gave him confidence and focused his ambition. Music was, as they would say in a later era, "where it's at" as far as Tom Parker was now concerned.

Word of Tom Parker's obsessive work habits and his eye for promotion began to spread. Eddy Arnold, later to become a legend in country music, decided to hire him as an advance agent for one of his tours. Tom

Parker saw this as a chance to break into the big time.

Before Arnold ever hit a town there was a plethora of feature articles and stunt pictures lying on the city desk of the local newspaper all ready to go into print. They had been written by a freelance writer by the name of Tom Parker. Handbills, wall posters, newspaper stories, radio interviews—they were all there, waiting for the Arnold entourage to come, see, and conquer. Tom Parker left no area of exploitation untouched. Arnold was so impressed that he finally took him on as his personal manager. It was a move he never regretted. "Tom, why don't you get yourself a hobby?" he once asked Parker.

Tom Parker looked at him, dragged heavily on a cigar, and answered, "Eddy, you're my hobby."

Through his own talent as much as Eddy Arnold's, Parker was able to bring the great country singer under the wing of RCA Victor. That contact was later to launch Elvis Presley on his skyrocketing career.

The Arnold-Parker partnership lasted from 1942 to 1951. Whatever the reason for the split, it is not forthcoming from either Arnold or Colonel Tom. Both men have only the most complimentary things to say about each other.

There has always been a place for the "big promoter" in show business, but in the country-music field of the early 1950s, the radio stations of the South and the Grand Ole Opry—mecca of country music—both had their own talent-agency machinery. Parker was able to book a number of acts, but it wasn't until he picked up with Hank Snow in 1954, that his next big break came.

Snow, a Canadian, had come to Nashville and the Opry by a long, circuitous route. Although a household name in his native Canada, he was still an unknown in the United States. Colonel Tom changed all that with his old-fashioned hard-sell promoting and the all-important tie-in with RCA Victor. While Hank Snow was selling more than one million records of his "I Don't

Hurt Anymore," Elvis Presley was listening to him on the radio back in Memphis, between stints driving his truck at the Crown Electric Company. Never in his wildest dreams did Presley think he would one day eclipse the master.

Right at the end of 1955, Sam Phillips of Sun Records in Memphis was doing a good job in pushing out Presley's releases in the immediate vicinity. But Sam, who also had Jerry Lee Lewis, Johnny Cash and Roy Orbison in his stable, thought that maybe Presley was now ready for the big plunge. He went to Randy Wood, head of Dot Records in Los Angeles, with an offer to sell Presley's contract for $7,500, a giant sum in those days. Randy Wood was a good businessman, as was Sam, but he thought that, while Presley might make a few hot discs, "he was only a flash in the pan." Besides, explained Wood, he had a new hot property, a crooner who would last forever. His name was Pat Boone.

But even as Randy Wood was saying no to Sam Phillips, Oscar Davis was singing Presley's praises to Colonel Tom. Although the Colonel respected Davis's judgment, he didn't make a move until Steve Sholes started to echo Davis's sentiment.

"Sholes was an old friend of the Colonel's," says Red West. "He had been an A and R man for RCA Victor, that is, an artist and repertoire man. He told the Colonel about this here kid who was tearing them up on the Louisiana Hayride."

The Louisiana Hayride operated on much the same basis as the Grand Ole Opry, except that it was performed and broadcast at Shreveport, Louisiana. Colonel Tom went to Shreveport and listened to Presley. The conversion was immediate. And so was his recognition of a vital factor about Presley: he was the only male performer selling what so many female performers sold—sex. Since then, of course, all the top rock stars have got in on the act, but in those days male singers

were romantic, sad, heroic, inspiring, heartbroken—
but they were never sexy.

Colonel Tom met Presley and liked him at first
glance. He liked the way he reacted to direction; he
liked his dedication. And there was an added ingredient,
which Colonel Tom was to exploit for all its worth:
while Presley on stage was a writhing mass of sensuality,
offstage he was humble and polite. That contrast would
prove to be dynamite. Here was a man, the girls would
reason, who was always struggling to control the demon
inside him. It was stuff that made millionaires of many
people connected with the young truck driver from
Memphis.

"The Colonel," says Red, "offered to help Bob Neal
push Elvis into areas where Bob didn't know. That ole
man knew this country like the back of his hand. He
had traveled the route with Gene Austin, Eddy Arnold
and Hank Snow. It was only a matter of time before
the Colonel took over managing Elvis full time. There
was no bad blood about the takeover. The Colonel
didn't steamroll over Bob. It was by mutual consent.
Both those men have the highest regard for each other.
Elvis had outgrown Memphis, as far as performing was
concerned."

Some accounts credit Colonel Tom with getting Presley his first big break by putting him on Louisiana Hayride, although he hadn't seen him until he first went to
Shreveport. When questioned about that particular part
of Presley's career, the Colonel is likely to give that
belly-shaking chuckle for which he is well known
among his associates, and say, "Boy, I got him off the
Louisiana Hayride."

When Presley told the Colonel how he and the Blue
Moon Boys had got the thumbs-down treatment from
the *Arthur Godfrey Show* audition team, the Colonel
looked him in the eye and, in a voice that instilled
instant confidence in the young man, said, "Boy, we'll
have New York for you for money you can't believe."
If anyone around Presley thought it was an idle boast,

they were very soon to change their minds. Not three months after Randy Wood refused the chance to buy Presley's contract for $7,500, the Colonel's close contacts with RCA Victor paid off. He sold Presley's recording contract for $35,000, an unprecedented amount in those days.

"Now, just around this time, and maybe it was before he actually got the RCA contract," says Red, "Elvis was still on road shows. He was in a bigger bracket, of course, and there were times when he appeared on the same show as Johnny Cash and Hank Snow. Now, on those shows they work the sequence in which they would go on. Depending on the mixture of the act, the star attraction would normally go on last. Whenever Elvis was on with Hank Snow, Hank always insisted on going on last. It wasn't an ego thing, it was just that he was the star attraction.

"One night—I think it was in Alabama—there was a big show, a really big one, when all the top country-music stars were there, and Elvis was to go before Hank.

"Well, Elvis just ripped that audience apart. Now Hank followed, and did a great show, but as far as the audience was concerned it was a letdown after Elvis. Hank went to the M.C. and, like the real gentleman he was, just said, 'From now on, you better put me on before the boy.' That was an acknowledgement from one of the all-time greats that Elvis was the star. That's how those country boys were. No jealousy, nothing. You wouldn't hear of something like that happening in show business today."

The first disc Elvis Presley cut with RCA Victor was a number that sounded as if he were singing in an empty room, a long tunnel, an echo chamber. It sounded strange to uninitiated ears. It was called "Heartbreak Hotel," and in record time it was a million seller. RCA then re-released four Presley numbers, all million sellers. He went on to record "I Want You, I Need You, I Love You." Again a million seller.

The record industry was reeling. Where had this kid come from? The teenage market went berserk, and so did their parents. In 1956 Elvis Presley, by that stroke of Parker mastery, was crowned king.

Sonny West, who traveled with Colonel Tom and got closer to him than any of the other Memphis Mafia, relates: "That's why all those stories about him and his early days sound like rubbish to me. He was a tough, hard-working guy who had genius and old-fashioned horse sense."

In later years there were times when Presley would happily have got rid of Col. Tom Parker. "But," as Sonny observes, "without Colonel Tom there would never be an Elvis Presley. They are both part of a whole."

When RCA Victor bought Presley's contract for the fabulous $35,000, they generously threw in a $5,000 bonus for the young singer. The first thing he did was go out and spend it all on a pink Cadillac for his mother. It was almost as if he'd had a premonition that she would not be with him much longer.

# 12

$P$erhaps it was the eighteen months of intensive "training" put in by Presley and Bob Neal, or perhaps it was the instant magic wrought by the all-knowing Col. Tom Parker. In any case, 1956 was the year, says Red West, "when everything took off. Everything he touched turned to gold, he couldn't do a thing wrong."

It was the year Colonel Tom was going to prove his boast that he would have New York begging for Elvis Presley. If ever a town and its critics, who took a special delight in lambasting Presley, were going to eat their words, it was going to be New York and all the fancy-pants scribes. Ed Sullivan, a beloved veteran of the early days of television show business, would not be exempt. Taking his cue from the New York *Times,* the *Journal-American* and the *Daily News,* he had said loud and clear that he would rather run a sixty-minute test pattern than put on Elvis Presley.

Even in those early days of TV, the rating wars were just as hysterical as they are today. One of the shows that was suffering was Tommy and Jimmy Dorsey's stage show, broadcast from the CBS theater in midtown Manhattan. It was produced by Jackie Gleason and served as a lead-in to Gleason's own show, *The Honeymooners.*

The Dorsey show played opposite the *Perry Como*

129

*Show,* whose ratings seemed impregnable. Colonel Tom bombarded Gleason and his talent scouts with an impressive list of figures from auditoriums all over the country, bulldozing a reluctant Gleason into finally "giving the kid a chance" on an important nationally televised talent show.

Gleason was not really among the converted. He had gone on record as saying that he didn't think Presley's performance was the kind that would last. "But," he added, "if I booked only the shows I liked, I'd have nothing but trumpet players on the show."

It was a snow-choked Saturday night in January, 1956, when Colonel Tom led his caravan of Presley, Scotty Moore, Bill Black, D. J. Fontana and Red West into the CBS theater. All the boys were apprehensive. This was a do-or-die effort. The Colonel had got them an unprecedented $1,200 a show for six performances. That was fine, but the national exposure was going to either give them birth or execute them on the spot, forever. The CBS studio itself didn't offer any reassurance; it was only half full.

The stage was set, the group at their instruments. Presley, dressed in an off-white sport jacket with giant draped shoulders that made him look like a contender for a Mr. America title, pounced onto center stage with the agility of a jaguar that had been caged too long. He grabbed the mike, raked it across his body, threw his legs arrogantly apart and hunched his shoulders. His full lips formed a sneer. He gave that uncanny impression he still gives today—threat mixed with poise, half street-fighter, half ballet dancer. The lights shining off his patent-leather hair created an aureole effect around him. . . . And then he unleashed the hurricane.

His opening number was "Heartbreak Hotel." Here was this half-saint, half-sinner crying out for sympathy. Yet mixed with his pleas was the threat that the animal inside him could hardly be controlled. The legs quivered, the waist and pelvis did a whole 360-degree swivel, whose completion was marked by D. J. Fontana's banging drums, with Presley then flinging out his groin in unison. The face would contort in agony, and then the left-sided sneer would tell his women that the pain was gone and he was available anytime, anywhere. And then that groin would do its circle and D. J. would hit that drum again and it happened again. In a decade that yawns at *Oh, Calcutta* and *Deep Throat,* it should be remembered that this was going out on national television into millions of American homes at a time when the hottest thing on film was Doris Day, and Hollywood sets were only just beginning to include double beds.

The nation's holy, the nation's pompous, the nation's frustrated were sure to react to this drape-suited, gunk-haired Southern hick actually doing on television what had been reserved for bedrooms—with the light out. React they did, and the ratings went through the roof. For the first time, the Tommy and Jimmy Dorsey show eclipsed the *Perry Como Show.*

While the talent scouts were suddenly courting Col. Tom Parker, the controversy flared like a flash fire across the nation. Suddenly young Presley, a kid who still got a kick out of singing gospel songs, was the new threat to American virtue. This shy hillbilly, whose dedication to his mother was legendary, was the most evil thing that had come on the scene since the Charleston. He was immediately dubbed "Elvis the Pelvis," a name which nettled Presley.

"That's about the most stupid thing I have heard from a so-called intelligent adult," he said. The kids loved that kind of talk. He really *was* theirs. But it didn't quiet the uproar. The Reverend Billy Graham was applauded when he commented that he didn't think Presley was the kind of boy he would like his children to see. Newspaper articles had experts figure out that the decibel level of Elvis Presley's rock 'n' roll could deafen children. Children in the U.S., Australia and England were expelled from their schools when they refused to lop off their Elvis Presley style ducktails. Rock 'n' roll dances were banned in several American cities.

After a series of riots in which police broke up some rock 'n' roll concerts, and the teenagers gave the cops the worst of the evening, the New York *Daily News* demanded a midnight curfew for all people under the age of twenty-one and suggested that rock 'n' roll dances should be held only under the supervision of selected adults.

Elvis Presley's fan mail suddenly shot to ten thousand letters a week. Girls wrote offering themselves to him, outright threatening suicide if he didn't meet them. Some parents threatened homicide if he didn't cool down his act. And this "evil" had all started in a little white frame church on Adams Street in Tupelo, Mississippi.

Red West recalls that, apart from Presley's obvious jubilation at hitting it big, he seemed genuinely disturbed that anyone would regard him as a threat to their daughters, sisters and girl friends. "Heck," said Elvis, "I just go the way I feel. There ain't nothing bad about it. I would never do it if I thought it was bad. There is nothing planned in this. It's just music and singing, that's all."

His mother would bristle at any suggestion that her son had even the slightest passing acquaintance with vulgarity. "My boy wouldn't do anything bad, no such thing. He is a good boy, a boy who has never forgotten his church upbringing and he hasn't changed one bit."

The curious thing was that Gladys was pretty close to the truth; nevertheless, it seemed impossible to convince half the adult population in the world that Presley was not the devil incarnate.

Despite all the screaming crowds and the rioting fans, it was, according to Red West, always hard to believe how successful Presley had become. "We never seemed to have time to absorb it all," says Red. "We were all busier than a one-legged man in an ass-kicking contest.

We were hitting town after town in very quick succession. About then Elvis really started plowing through the broads. Every town was a different broad. Sometimes one in the afternoon and then one in the night. He was really taking off. He just left streams of gals behind him. And to be honest, there was plenty left over for me and the boys, too, so it was a good fringe benefit."

But Red remembers that was about all the benefits there were, because he never had got paid a cent up until that time. "There were plenty of deals going down at the time and there was big money coming in. Now, earlier I was there for the ride, but thinking back, for the work I did there should have been some kind of payment because, man, I worked like a dog. All the odd jobs, all that damn driving, anything that nobody else wanted to do, I did. I know that Scotty, Bill and D. J. weren't happy about their money setup. I believe in the end they quit because they weren't getting paid what they thought was right.

"And here is one of the most curious and puzzling things about Elvis. I have seen him give away some of the most incredible gifts imaginable. In later years he was to give away clothes and cars and rings, and even airplanes and houses, but he likes to be in control. Gifts are one thing. Money is something else. The point is that I believe somehow he believes money gives a person independence. He doesn't want people to have independence from him. He likes to be a father figure, or a God figure.

"For many years, with real seriousness, he called us his disciples. He was willing to feed and clothe and give you a good time, but he liked to be in charge of what he gave you when he gave it to you. Somehow he thinks if you get enough money together you can pull up sticks and leave him because you don't need him any more, and, above all, he needs to be needed.

"It's funny me not getting paid, but Charlie Hodge, one of the best guitar men in the business, wasn't even getting scale salary for musicians for many years. Elvis also doesn't like you to show any independence. That's why there was always that friction he had towards Jerry Schilling. Of all the boys who were called the Memphis Mafia, Jerry had seemed most independent. He didn't accept everything Elvis said without question, and Elvis didn't like it.

"If you look through most of the boys around him, none of us ever had any real money when we started with him. Me, Sonny, Dave, Joe Esposito, Gene Smith, Jerry Schilling, Lamar Fike, Cliff Gleaves. None of us had bread. We just jumped at the chance to do his bidding and work for him. Good times, bad times, but not much money. It was almost as if it was a requirement to work for him that you had to be broke. You had to need him more than he needed you."

Red remembers that just after the Tommy and Jimmy Dorsey show, Jean and Julian Aberbach, the two German-born brothers who owned Hill and Range Music Publishing Company—and who were to later take over the Elvis Presley Publishing Company—invited Presley and Red to New York's Brown Derby restaurant, which has since gone out of business.

"Now, there were the two of us, 'E' and me, at the classy Brown Derby. We were fresh out of Memphis, and we both looked like real rednecks, real hicks. I forgot what I had on or what Elvis had on, but the two of us felt about as comfortable as a black at a Ku Klux Klan meeting. Anyway, I made the mistake of going to the bathroom. I went and washed my hands, and this attendant in there did something I had never seen. He passed me a towel and I thought, "Well, that's a nice gesture and maybe New York is not that bad a town after all.

"I thanked him and started to leave. The sonofabitch grabbed me and said, 'How about the tip?' I never heard of tipping in a toilet, but this was New York. Well, now I haven't had a dime in my pocket at this time since I can't remember when. I may have just left

ELVIS: WHAT HAPPENED?

the biggest TV sensation in the country. I may be having dinner with two bigshots, but I ain't had a dime in my pockets for months, man.

"I've never been so embarrassed. I just said something about having left my wallet behind. I sat down to dinner and I worried that he was going to come out in front of all those important people and start demanding money for the leak I had in there. I've never been too fond of New York since then. But it gave you an idea the situation I was in."

Although the money for Red was scarce, the dollars were rolling into Presley's account. The first big paychecks were earmarked for something more important. Elvis wanted to buy his mother a home, a real home.

"It's something she always wanted but never talked about," Presley was to say later. "It was as if she didn't want to let anyone know about her dreams. But I knew. I wanted to get my mama a home."

He bought an attractive green and white ranch house on Audubon Drive in the outskirts of Memphis, installed a swimming pool, and built a fence around the property to keep out the fans. He also filled the garage up with two Cadillacs and a Lincoln limousine. "I guess," says Red, "the swimming pool was there for show, because Elvis really ain't that keen on swimming. I don't know whether it's because he doesn't like his hair being messed up or he is straight out afraid of the water. But he ain't no big swimmer, no matter what you have seen in the movies."

Presley's next offer came from the *Steve Allen Show*. He appeared with Andy Griffith, Imogene Coca and Steve Allen himself in a skit. Later he sang "Hound Dog." Within twenty-four hours it was on its way to becoming a number-one best-seller in the million-dollar-record bracket.

The Ed Sullivan people watched incredulously as Steven Allen's ratings started to rocket. It was only a matter of time before the Colonel got a call from Sullivan.

Nobody who was privy to that conversation is talking, but it would be hard to disbelieve that the old Southern horse trader in Col. Tom Parker did not make the mighty Ed Sullivan toast a little during negotiations for a Presley performance. He is obviously businessman enough to have asked for top dollars, but Colonel Tom is also Southern enough to have reminded the Yankee Sullivan of what he had once said about his boy. Whatever kind of conversation transpired, Presley got $15,-000 for a performance, three times higher than Ed Sullivan had ever paid anyone.

It was indeed a victory for Memphis that night. Only one thing, perhaps, took the edge off it. Presley, and probably the Colonel himself, didn't know it, but the TV cameras were filming Presley only from the waist up. In the end, Sullivan, sensitive to the bomb bursts of criticism and controversy swirling around Presley, was not going to risk getting grilled by his buddies on the New York *Times* and the *Daily News*.

Red West was, of course, happy that Elvis was making it big, but not too pleased about his own situation. "It was an exciting life for me, I guess, and maybe I shouldn't have complained, but hell, there was no union for being a professional companion, and I could see myself being that for the rest of my life and not getting paid.

"Sometimes the hours on the road were really tough. I often used to drive the car on ahead with the band's instruments. Vernon [Elvis's father] had this little bitty trailer cart made, which hooked on the back of my car. It looked more like a rolling toilet than anything else, painted pink and with one wheel. The way Elvis's dad went on about that thing, you would have thought it was a goddamned yacht.

"Anyway, on one of the times when I had to drive from Winston-Salem to Jacksonville, Florida, I was dead on my feet. I was driving like crazy, staying awake on a packet of No-Doz. A couple of times I almost went off the road. Anyway, outside of Jacksonville, the damn one tire on this portable john trailing behind bursts. Well, I get all the clothes out and the instruments, ditch the stupid-looking trailer, and load them all into the car. I got to Jacksonville about fifteen minutes late. It was amazing that I made it at all.

"Well, when I get there, instead of getting a hero's welcome, Vern Presley is fit to be tied. He wanted to know what had happened to his previous damn rolling toilet of a trailer that probably cost all of fifty bucks. He really went on and on about it. I think Elvis probably laughed at the time."

But Vernon's reaction to the loss of the "portable john" nagged at Red. "It was just a case of, you know, man, how long could I go busting my chops like this and getting abused into the bargain? Me and Elvis were very close, and I just didn't have the guts to say Hey, don't you think I should get paid a bit for what I'm doing?

"Now, Elvis was still a decent, good-looking guy who was very easy to get along with. We used to have a lot of fun, and I never saw him pulling any shit with me. But, damn it, I was too embarrassed to ask him for anything. If I had, he would have given it to me.

"So after this argument with Vernon, which really wasn't an argument, because I was on the receiving end, I thought there had to be a better way. I was getting to the age of having to go into the service. If you enlisted, you could choose your own service, so I thought I would get the service stint over and done with. I told Elvis that I thought I would take off and join the marines. I don't think Elvis knew that I was joining the marines really to quit being on the road, and I don't think he thought I'd quit over the Vernon incident. I just didn't want to cause a whole hassle, so I told him I was taking off. You know, it was an emotional thing, and we both shook hands and put our arms around each other. He was a good boy."

Red was posted for eighteen months in the Mediterranean and later assigned to a marine base in Virginia. He kept in contact with Presley and, especially, with Gladys, who seemed to have a real maternal concern for Red. So, whenever Red was on leave in Memphis at the same time as Presley, the superstar opened his house and hospitality to Red.

Presley continued to insist that friends he could trust be with him all the time. The hype, the publicity, the money, the managers all had their place. But when it came to relaxing and being himself, Presley more and more fell back on "his boys," and all the sharp Yankee money in the world and all the tough managers in the world would not change that.

If Red's departure left a gap in friendship, it did nothing to stop the incredibly booming career of Presley. When Red and Presley got together on Red's leave, they would marvel at the phenomenon they were witnessing, almost as if they were watching someone else's career and not Presley's. It was still very difficult for a pair of boys from Humes High School, Memphis, to understand what was happening around them.

Col. Tom Parker was in his element. At last he had a property he could promote with every stunt he had learned in the bible of razzmatazz. Elephants paraded in a conga line for no real reason except that they had Elvis Presley's name emblazoned on their flanks. Midgets marched down the streets of Hollywood presenting themselves as the "Elvis Presley Midget Fan Club." And then the merchandising hit with a bomb blast. Elvis Presley T-shirts, Elvis Presley jeans, Elvis Presley lipstick, bubble gum, footballs, shirts, socks, sweaters, pajamas, ballpoint pens, diaries.

There was no end to it. And all the time in the background was Colonel Tom chuckling his belly-shaking chuckle and showing them all how the old Southern horse trader did things right. Elvis Presley fan clubs sprang up in enormous numbers across the world. At one point there were close to one million card-carrying members of various fan clubs who owed their allegiance and love to Presley.

Gladys Presley was left a little breathless by it all. She wanted success and money for her boy—but this? Gladys did her best to make him proud of her, just as he had made her proud of him. She started to go on a weight-loss course to make herself look more like a superstar's mama. When it failed, she occasionally took a diet pill. There are some Presley detractors who have been so injudicious as to suggest that Mrs. Presley "got into the pills and booze." The notion that this lady allowed herself any excess, other than hard work and overindulgence in her only boy, is quite outlandish.

The pressures of being a superstar's mother were indeed taking their toll on Mrs. Presley, and that was compounded by the years of neglect of her own well-being and health. There were times now that she complained of tiredness, something she had never acknowledged as possible before. And she would often have an unhealthy-looking color. Her obsessive worry over whether her son was getting enough rest and enough food did not help matters.

Presley had collapsed from exhaustion in Jacksonville, Florida, after a marathon night of driving and a hectic, sleepless schedule. Perhaps those first grueling years left an impression on him, for, in his later years, he was to regard sleep with the passion he had once reserved for his inordinately healthy sex life.

In 1957, a year after buying the Audubon Drive house, Presley decided it was time to move. One reason might have been that it was too small to answer the needs and style changes of his skyrocketing success. Presley had collected quite an entourage, including uncles and cousins, and the house seemed to be bursting at the seams. Another theory to explain his decision is that the people on Audubon Drive looked down on their new neighbors.

Gladys Presley may have settled in a dream house,

but the lady was made of fine stuff and she wasn't about to forget her neighbors and old friends in the housing project and on Alabama Avenue. Those people were welcome in her new home. There is some suspicion that residents on Audubon Drive had resented the people from the other side of the tracks; neighbors once formed a committee that offered to buy the Presley house.

In any case, whatever the reason, Presley bought a bigger and more expensive house for his mama. It was a thirteen-acre property in Whitehaven, an upper-class suburb on the outskirts of Memphis. He paid $100,000 for it—a lot of money, considering it was 1957 and Memphis.

The house, a converted church, had beautiful white columns at its entrance. Presley named it Graceland, furnished it in purple, white and gold, commissioned figurines of himself with guitar to adorn the gates and installed the mandatory pool. While it might not be the kind of home a stockbroker would buy, it was deluxe class by the tastes of country-and-western stars.

Meanwhile, Hal Wallis, the genial and genius movie producer, had been talking turkey to Colonel Tom. A picture deal was signed for Presley to star in three movies. Presley was ecstatic, a reaction that would not last as the years and the scripts wore on.

No Presley movie ever lost money. Richard Burton, Laurence Olivier, Marlon Brando, Frank Sinatra— none of them could go anywhere near the earning power of Presley when it came to the box office. And yet, in the years to come, Presley would grow bitter. Red remembers: "He would sometimes see himself in a movie and he would get disgusted. He would say, 'Who is that fast-talking hillbilly sonofabitch that nobody can understand? One day he is singing to a dog, then to a car, then to a cow. They are all the damned same movies with that Southerner just singing to something different.'"

The first movie, *Love Me Tender,* started shooting in April, 1957. It started a package trend that made a fortune for Presley, the Colonel, the producers and RCA Victor. The package was the essence of simplicity. Churn out low-budget movies with predictable blank spaces for Presley to sing to his dogs, his children, his cars or his cows. Then release an album of songs from the movie track. Good packaging, good business, but not the stuff that Oscar-winning movies are made of.

During the making of *Love Me Tender,* as Presley was to later tell Red, he developed an uncontrollable crush on his female lead, Debra Paget. Presley talked to Red about it at the time. "If you look at her in those earlier pictures," says Sonny, "you will see she had a decided likeness to Priscilla Presley, whom he was soon to meet. She had black hair. When Elvis first met Priscilla he got her to dye her hair black. I think it's significant that his mother had black hair, too. Elvis in real life has very light hair. In that movie you can see he is almost blond. Later on he dyed his hair black, too. Of course, now, when he hasn't had a dye job done on time, his sideburns are almost completely white, like his daddy's."

Both Red and Sonny West recall that despite the handsome young Presley's shy attraction for Debra Paget, his passion was not returned. "I guess the way it went," says Sonny, "was that Debra really thought Elvis was just a nice handsome kid. She wasn't the least bit interested in him." So true. At that time, she was dating the fabled Howard Hughes.

In 1957, Presley's third movie, *Jailhouse Rock,* marked the first of the gradual changes in his personality. They were changes that would bring him endless hours of suffering.

The movie starred Presley in the part of Vince, a young man who goes to prison after accidentally killing a drunk in a brawl. There he meets his cellmate, Hunk Houghton, who is a one-time western singer.

After a jailhouse concert shows Hunk how much talent his young cellmate has, he signs him to a long-term contract, which is promptly forgotten, until they both meet on the street as free men. By that time, Vince has made it big. But with fame and stardom has come the inevitable star complex. Honoring the contract, Vince takes Hunk on as a manservant and dog walker. Vince meets a record plugger, Peggy Van Alden, who falls in love with the brooding, tough-guy superstar from the wrong side of the tracks.

Together she and Hunk try to turn his head around from being a spoiled, selfish brat who wants everything done on his command. It ends happily, with Vince seeing the error of his ways.

In real life, says Red West, Elvis became Vince. "Now, I don't mean he was selfish and big-headed all the time. But he took to fits of anger that none of us had ever seen before. He wanted to be treated as something special. Of course, he was something special, but he had never demanded that special attention. He was always one of the boys. He would often share the driving on long gigs. We had shared everything, even our women."

It was at this time that a young, star-struck fan by the name of Lamar Fike came on the scene. "The way I remember it," says Sonny West, "he climbed over the wall at Elvis's house in Audubon Drive and he never left. He still is with Elvis today. Lamar is three hundred pounds in weight and Elvis used to make him the butt of all his jokes. I'm not saying Elvis didn't like him. He really does. But when he speaks to Lamar it will always be 'Get your fat ass out of here' or 'Get your fat ass in here and take care of this.' Lamar, I guess, deep down is a very sensitive guy. I know he was sensitive about his weight, but he never let it show. He was the clown of the outfit.

"He was also the amateur psychiatrist. He would analyze everyone and everything. I really got to love Lamar. He is one of those jolly, funny and sensitive kind of guys you can't help love. But with Elvis, Lamar was always the butt of jokes."

Presley went on acting exactly like the character in *Jailhouse Rock*. Recalls Sonny: "He got to smoking those stubby little cigars and if nobody didn't light it for him straightaway, he would sit there and he would seethe. Then finally he would blow up and yell 'Am I going to sit here all day with this dry motherfucker in my mouth with nobody lighting it for me? If I am, then you can all get your asses out of here.'

"It would be the same," Sonny goes on, "with a simple glass of water. The glass would be in front of him. He would stay quiet and then yell 'Am I going to die of thirst or is some sonofabitch going to pour some water for me?'" It was a dramatic change from the gentle Southern boy who was apprehensive about Sonny West because he swore too much.

Sonny relates: "At first, man, we would only see flashes of those rages. But later on it was terrible. He would go into rages when things didn't go his way. He would wreck a goddamn roof or fire his guns off like a madman." There were times when he would assemble his "disciples" or his "boys," or his "Memphis Mafia" —whatever one wants to call them—and he would say, "I'm in charge here and if anyone wants to say different, then I may get hurt but somebody is going to die."

When Presley started to take his "special medication," he was like an unexploded bomb, says Red. "You could talk to him quiet, sensibly, about something and maybe that night you would say something that didn't quite go along with his way of thinking or doing things, but he would talk calmly about it and sort of see your way of looking at something. Then he would go to bed and get out of it on his so-called medicine, and the next day, man, wow. He would stew on something all night and then it would work up inside of him and he would lose total reason and just explode. On those days you would try to keep out of his way."

Sonny recalls: "When Elvis got into those rages and

took it out on Red, it would bring the worst out in Red. I would see Red sitting there trying to control himself for something said to him that was very unfair. Then he would go outside and get in a fight just to let off the steam. He could always bring the worst out in Red."

By the beginning of 1958, as Presley's career set record after record, the scene was set for the tragedy that would mark his life and change it. He was about to lose the person he loved most in the world.

# 13

The handsome face of Elvis Aron Presley was puffed and bloated. His eyes were narrow slits, and they were crimson. He was sitting on the giant-size bed in the purple-walled bedroom that he and Gladys Presley had decorated with an adventurous enthusiasm. The white trim had somehow dulled, the old fittings had suddenly lost their luster. Sitting on a makeshift bed next to the master bed was Nick Adams, the brilliant young rebel actor who was to end his life in suicide. Nick was now at Presley's side when the young superstar needed him most. Presley was afraid to sleep alone. He wanted Nick there to sleep with him for company. A doctor had just given Presley a shot to sedate him, but the pain wouldn't let him sleep.

Red West walked into the bedroom with a lump the size of a golf ball in his throat. His eyes were red-rimmed, and he found it hard to speak without bursting into tears. He closed the door gently behind him, looked at Presley silently. He strode quickly toward him; Presley half staggered to his feet. Both men collapsed into each other's arms, their fingers digging into each other's back.

"Mama's gone, Red. My mama's gone, Red. What will I do? I've lost everything. There ain't nothing to live for. She was everything. Without her I got nothing. It's all over, man."

Red couldn't talk for a long moment. "I know, 'E,' she was a fine woman. And now I've lost my daddy.

He's gone, too." The two men held each other in an embrace that only other men can understand.

Never before had Red West and Elvis Presley been so close as in this moment of profound loss. On August 14, 1958, Gladys Presley died at the age of forty-two from a heart attack triggered by acute hepatitis. Eight hours later, Red West's father, Newton Thomas West, also died. "I just can't explain how close I felt to him that moment," says Red. "Man, he was hurting and I was hurting. I knew what he was going through. I knew how much he had loved that woman, because I loved her, too. And I loved my daddy too. That was one helluva day."

Outside Graceland in the flat, oppressive Memphis summer heat, five hundred people, a respectful gathering of loyal worshippers, stood silent vigil along what now has become Elvis Presley Boulevard. Elsewhere in Memphis, more than two thousand Presley fans had streamed into the city from as far away as New York and Boston. Some of the people, unable to find accommodations, stayed on the couches or in the spare rooms of complete strangers who happened to live in Memphis.

There was a magnitude to the mourning that could be compared only to that given a head of state or a national hero. There were telegrams of sympathy from heads of state. Hollywood superstars flooded Graceland with telephone calls and telegrams. Somehow the legendary bond between Presley and his mother was something known in the most obscure places to the most obscure people.

The year 1958 had already surrounded Presley in hysterical controversy. He had signed a gigantic contract with Hal Wallis of Paramount to star in *King Creole*. The movie, thought to be a cut above the rest of Presley's acting offerings, was based loosely on the Harold Robbins best-seller *A Stone for Danny Fisher*. Presley would be paid half a million dollars and would receive fifty percent of the profits. It was his biggest deal to date, although his movie deals would get a lot bigger.

Presley was in the midst of another, less profitable big deal. His earnings, in fact, were about to drop from about $125,000 a month to $78 a month. His employer: the U.S. Army. Public protest was overwhelming, if the volume of mail to the Pentagon and fan-club demonstrations were standards by which to judge. Teenagers picketed recruiting depots, and many of the fifteen thousand letters received by the U.S. Government accused them of plotting to place Presley in danger of being killed or injured. The Pentagon actually had a file marked "Operation Presley." It was madness of the most humorous proportions. Senators and Congressmen, anxious for space in their hometown newspapers, got on the bandwagon.

Although no one had suggested otherwise, the wise men of Washington wanted reassurance that Presley would be given no special treatment in the U.S. Armed Services. One reporter with an eye for an angle really put the fox among the chickens when he quoted an anonymous army source as assuring him that Presley would be spared the regulation army haircut and would be comfortably ensconced in the U.S. Special Services, which has the responsibility of entertaining the troops. The source pointed out that this was the route chosen for Vic Damone and Eddie Fisher. It was not necessarily the route chosen by Damone and Fisher. After all, they were giving away for nothing what they had been paid a lot of money for. It was a point that did not escape the eagle eye of Col. Tom Parker.

Presley, for his part, was the model of public relations. He managed to quiet the roars from Washington: "All I want to do is to be treated like an ordinary G.I.," he said. "I want to do my duty and I'm mighty proud to be given the opportunity to serve my country." So everything died down.

But the sawdust was still to hit the fan. When Presley

received his notice to report to the induction center in Memphis, almost $300,000 had already been spent in prelocation shooting for *King Creole*. If Presley was to go in the army as scheduled, the movie would have to be scrapped.

At the urging of Wallis and Colonel Tom, Presley wrote to the Pentagon in the most respectful terms asking for a three-month deferment. Deferments, particularly in 1958, were extremely common. They were given on grounds of everything from hardship to college education.

No big deal. That is, until the news leaked out, and the bleats again came loud and clear from Washington. State Representative Nick Johnson, of Harlan, Kentucky, got more publicity than ever in his life when he resigned from the local draft board with the protest, "I cannot conscientiously ask any mountain boy to serve the country unless afforded the same treatment as Presley." Well, everybody had their say, the deferment was granted, and Presley finished his film.

Seven months before Gladys Presley died, while Elvis was involved with the film's prelocation shooting, Red West had visited at Graceland. He was on leave from the marine base in Norfolk, Virginia.

"While I was there," says Red, "she got on the telephone and called Elvis. He was glad to say hello, and when he found I had about two weeks leave, he invited me to come to Hollywood and spend some time with him. Great, I had never been to a studio before. I was to leave the next day. After the telephone call Mrs. Presley and I sat and talked some more. Man, I knew there was something wrong with her. I couldn't put my finger on it, but it was just the way she talked. Man, that dear lady knew she was dying. She never said anything like that, but the way she was talking, it was as if it was all over. She knew she didn't have long. When I got up to say good-bye, she just sort of called me back, and she said what I had heard her say a hundred times: 'Bob, look after my boy.'

"When she said it this time it was different. There was a sort of, I don't know, a sort of finality to the sound of her voice, like as if that was the last time she would ever say it to me. It was."

It was with an eerie feeling of sadness that Red boarded a plane the next day. "When I arrived in Hollywood, Elvis had one of his go-fers pick me up at the airport, and he drove me straight to the studio. I met up with him and we had a happy reunion. Man, there I was a crew-cut hick sonofabitch in a marine uniform on a Paramount movie set.

"I was really wide-eyed. Elvis took me around and showed me how things worked and I was really impressed. They had two more days shooting in Hollywood, and then they were going on to New Orleans for location. Elvis asked me whether I would like to come along. Man, would I!"

The party was to leave by train. Presley wouldn't fly. Red recalls: "A year earlier he had the scare of his life. He was traveling over the Ozarks in a small plane going from one gig to the next, and the way he told it to me suddenly this damn plane just lost all its power. The pilot couldn't do a thing about it. The pilot even was convinced they were going to crash and all get killed. Elvis said he was getting ready to die. He was sure that it was the end.

"Luckily, they made a forced landing and nobody got hurt, but it scared Elvis half to death. When his mother found out about it, she made him promise never to fly. He wasn't too keen on flying then. Of course later he lost that fear and bought himself almost his own air force. At one time he had five planes and four pilots."

Red boarded the train with Presley, Colonel Tom, co-star Carolyn Jones, her husband, Aaron Spelling, then a struggling writer but soon to become Hollywood's biggest TV producer.

Also along was Alan Fortas, one of Presley's Memphis Mafia. Alan, a husky, jovial young man, was from

Memphis. His uncle was former Supreme Court Justice Abe Fortas. Gene Smith, Presley's cousin, was there, too.

"Man, for me," says Red, "this was a dream trip, with all those important people." He stayed with Presley for a week, and the actors and crew treated him like one of them. "I knew then that I wanted to be connected to this life," says Red. "I didn't know what as, maybe an extra or a stuntman or anything, but I wanted in on this." Between takes, Walter Matthau, who had joined the group in New Orleans, would lead the cast and crew in card games, and that led to the first payment that Presley ever made to Red for his services up to then.

"The Colonel, Elvis, Mr. Matthau and some others were playing blackjack. Mr. Matthau went broke and wanted to play on credit. He was and is a pretty rich man. Nobody seemed to mind, except the Colonel. He was just as tough with cards as he was with business. The old Colonel just said flat out, 'No, you want to play cards, you play with cash,' and that was it. Mr. Matthau may have been a big movie star, but when it came to playing cards with the Colonel it was cash or nothing. Elvis then won a hand for fifty dollars. He just handed it to me and said, 'Here, Red, buy a few beers.' Like a dumb ass, that night I picked up this gal, and when we went back to the hotel room I went to the bathroom. I didn't know much about those kind of ladies at the time. While I was in the bathroom, she went through my pockets and took the fifty bucks. When I came out there was no lady, no money. It taught me a lesson."

On March 24, 1958, at 6:30 in the morning, Elvis Aron Presley arrived at the Memphis draft board accompanied by his mother, father, and faithful friend Lamar Fike.

Lamar wanted to join the army with Presley. The army doctors took one look at the scales and told a disappointed Lamar that he wouldn't be army material until he shed some of the poundage. Newspapermen from all over the country, as well as Canada, England and Australia, were on hand to record the induction of America's biggest entertainment name. Dodging photographers, who desperately tried to get a shot of Presley in the altogether as he was going through his physical, he yes sirred and no sirred his way through what seemed a never-ending barrage of ridiculous questions from the intelligent members of the fourth estate: Would he buy suede combat boots? Would he sing while he was marching to boost morale? Would he ask fans to send him Southern fried chicken? There seemed no end to it. Meanwhile, Colonel Tom was handing out eight-by-ten glossy photographs of Presley in the upcoming movie *King Creole*. He never missed a beat, this Colonel.

Later that day the "King of Rock 'n' Roll" became Private Presley U.S. 53310761, and a nation of girls mourned as he was herded onto a bus with other recruits to boot camp at Fort Chaffee, Arkansas, with a flotilla of pressmen following. At Fort Chaffee, it was the same scene over again. When an army barber cannibalized the famous hairdo, Presley smiled, and Colonel Tom looked at the locks on the floor and commented, "I know a lot of people who would pay a lot of money for that hair."

If life in Fort Chaffee was tough for the superstar, he went out of his way to make it look like he was enjoying every minute of it. He wasn't, of course, as Red was to find out. He took a lot of razzing from his fellow recruits, but after a while, when it didn't get anything but a shy smile, they forgot who he was and let him be another one of the boys. After six weeks at Fort Chaffee, he was transferred to Fort Hood.

While he was behaving outwardly like just another G.I., he was also making sure army life would resemble life in Memphis as much as possible. He rented a four-bedroom bungalow in a town called Kileen and installed his mother, father, grandmother (Minnie Presley), Lamar Fike and any of the Memphis boys, or girls for that matter, who dropped by. The house was a center of jam sessions, gospel singing groups and record parties. Nothing wild, mind you, but a little bit better than living in the barracks. Already he was making plans to have his entire family come with him to Germany.

It was in July of that year that the Presley family noticed the serious change in Gladys Presley. She was having trouble moving around. Her face was a deathly color, and the normally energetic and jovial woman seemed to have lost her spark. It was decided that she and Vernon should return to Memphis by train and check with the family doctor. Nobody was overly worried. After all, she was a robust woman of forty-two. Rest and a little specialist treatment would make things right.

Four days after arriving in Memphis, doctors at Memphis Methodist Hospital told Vernon Presley that his wife was suffering from hepatitis. On August 11, Vernon Presley called his son in Fort Hood and told him his mother was on the serious list. Presley got emergency leave and, despite his terror of planes, boarded the first flight out to Memphis.

He arrived at the hospital and waded through a battery of fans and reporters who were keeping a hospital vigil. Something told Presley that his mother was more than just "serious." When he arrived at her bedside, she rallied for the first time since she had been hospitalized. The young Presley kept a thirty-six-hour vigil at her bedside. Midnight Wednesday night, August 13, he went home to get some sleep, and Vernon took over the bedside watch. Three hours later he called his son with the news. His mother had died of a heart attack.

Presley arrived at the hospital in a state of shock. He threw himself across his mother's bed and sobbed convulsively.

When he emerged from the hospital, he could only mumble answers to newsmen at the scene. Back at Graceland, he stood for long minutes looking up at the building, then wandered through the house aimlessly.

When Red West heard the news on the radio in camp at Norfolk, Virginia the next morning, he went to his commanding officer and asked for emergency leave. "I had taken up all my leave time, as I only had two weeks left in the service. I couldn't get a weekend leave pass because Memphis was too far away from Virginia. I didn't know what to do. I just couldn't sit there in camp and not pay my respects."

Fate worked a nasty twist. Three hours later he got a call from his brother to say that his father, Newton Thomas West, was critically ill. Again he went to his commanding officer for emergency leave. This time it was granted. He couldn't get a direct flight, only a plane that took him to Atlanta, Georgia. "From there I hoped I could hitch a service flight or just hitch a ride."

From Atlanta, he called home. It was too late. His father had already gone. When he arrived in Memphis later that night, the whole city was in mourning, not for him, of course, but that's the way it struck him.

Red, busy organizing his father's affairs, could not attend the funeral for Mrs. Presley. Vernon Presley had arranged for a chartered plane to bring the Blackwood Brothers, Mrs. Presley's favorite gospel group, from North Carolina to sing at her funeral service. Elvis Presley remained standing throughout, in a daze of grief.

After the funeral, Red broke from his own mourning to pay respects to Presley at Graceland. The next day, at the same funeral parlor where Mrs. Presley was laid out, Red had to say farewell to his father. Red will never forget what happened, not because of his own loss but because of something Presley did. "Man, he had gone through a trial the day before at the funeral home. He was out of it. But just before the service started, Elvis appeared at the doorway. He was with Alan Fortas and Gene Smith and Lamar Fike. They were all very respectfully dressed. Elvis almost had to be carried over to me. He was there to mourn the passing of my dad. Damn, man, that took something. He came over to me and sort of half fell into my arms. 'My mama was here yesterday just where your daddy is, Red,' Elvis told me. He couldn't say too much more. He was so badly broken up. We just sort of held on to each other and I thought, This is one helluva guy to go through what he did the day before and then face it all over again to pay his respects to my daddy. Southerners can be great like that. I was never closer to any man in my life than that day."

Red returned to Norfolk, Virginia, to serve his remaining two weeks in the marines. Presley went back to Fort Hood and basic training. He had to forget, although he knew that was impossible.

Red recalls: "Elvis erected a great big monument at the Memphis cemetery in Forest Lawn. It's a beautiful monument. Big but showy. There's a big marble statue of Jesus erected over where she is buried. When Elvis is in Memphis, he always goes there to pay his respects. He never forgets. There are always fresh flowers there. Everybody breaks up when he loses a mother or a father. With Elvis I think it was a lot deeper. It was a heck of a shock to lose her when she was so young. Elvis had planned so much for her. He was going to take her to Germany with him, they were going to tour Europe together. She was going to be the best-looked-after mother in the world. And then this."

In the years to come, Presley gradually grew into a different person than he'd been before his mother's death. People close to him couldn't help speculating that her loss had more than a little to do with it. "I just can't help feel," says Red West, "that if she had lived, Elvis wouldn't have gotten into some of the habits he did. There was always that thought in the back of his mind: 'What would Mama say if she knew I was doing this?' "

Back in Fort Hood, Presley held open house in his home in Kileen. Lamar Fike was there, and Alan Fortas. Sometimes his old girl friend Anita Wood would drop by, as would Nick Adams and Cliff Gleaves. Elvis's grandmother, Minnie Presley, a feisty old Southern lady, had now become the matriarch of the house, taking over the duties of cooking and organizing the cleaning.

A week after Red West got out of the marines, Presley invited him to come to Kileen. He was trying anything to forget, and often the house was awake until the early hours of the morning with impromptu singing and gospel sessions. No booze, no dope, no fast ladies. "Pretty clean fun," Red remembers. "Sometimes a whole team of us would sit around with a guitar and sing ourselves hoarse." Gladys Presley had always fortified her son with the belief that "things would get better." It would be true as far as his career was concerned, but not necessarily for Presley personally. Suddenly he was a ship without a rudder.

Presley had been in the Second Armored Division. Now the army announced that his unit would make up a replacement in Germany in the Third Armored Division—General Patton's old outfit. Private Presley was assigned to the Scouts in the division. If anyone had speculated that he might have gone into Special Services, they were surprised to hear of his posting, which even in peacetime Germany was the least cushy place in the army.

Later it emerged that it was the army, and not Colonel Tom, who wanted Presley in the Special Services. "They want my boy to sing," said the Colonel, "then they are going to have to pay for it like anyone else." Colonel Tom took a giant gamble. Anybody who knew show business as well as he did knew that there was every danger of Presley's being a flash in the pan, that when the kids grew out of their Presley phase, his boy might have nowhere to go. The gamble he took was to take Presley completely out of show business for the entire two years he was in the service.

The psychology was double-edged, risky, but brilliant if it worked. First, with the right timing, the public would grow progressively hungrier for his boy when he came out of the service, provided he stoked the publicity machinery at home. Second, Colonel Tom knew it was time to expand Presley's audience to a grown-up group. If the chips fell the right way, Presley could emerge from his army exile with the loyalty of his established fans plus the millions more of an older group. And what better way to attract an older crowd than have the boy in the army—and in the toughest division in the U.S. Army—and thereby convince them his boy was a responsible citizen who put flag and country before anything else?

Red relates: "I always had a suspicion that the old Colonel maneuvered so Elvis would be in that Third Armored Division just so as nobody could say that he was a soft delinquent-type guy."

In the middle of September, 1958, Presley got his marching orders. He was to go by train to Brooklyn Navy Yard and join U.S. troop ship *General Randall*. "We were all there to see him off," Red remembers, "his dad, Minnie Presley, Lamar, myself and Anita Wood. It had been decided that Vernon and Minnie would follow Elvis over to Germany when he settled in and Elvis would live off base. The farewells were going strong and Elvis gave Anita a good-bye kiss."

And then Presley did something quite unpredictable. He turned to Red and Lamar, and just about his last words were, "How y'all like to come across, too?"

Lamar and Red looked at each other, and before they could speak, Presley added, "Now, my daddy will fix up the tickets. When Daddy and Grandma Minnie come across, you fly across with them. We'll have ourselves a ball."

## 14

While the rest of the world recognizes that Elvis Aron Presley is something more than an ordinary human being, the one person who believes that most passionately is Presley himself. He is addicted to the study of the Bible, mystical religion, numerology, psychic phenomena, and the belief in life after death. He firmly believes he has the powers of psychic healing by the laying on of hands. He believes he will be reincarnated. He believes he has the strength of will to move clouds in the air, and he is also convinced that there are beings on other planets. He firmly believes he is a prophet who was destined to lead, designated by God for a special role in life.

If it sounds a little bizarre, Sonny West, Red West and Dave Hebler, who have sat with him for hours discussing religion and philosophy, are prepared to believe he does have great powers to control.

"He believes there was a master plan," says Red, "by God in singling him out for his fantastic success. Now, while it does sound a little wacky, I have often given it a lot of thought and have often felt that maybe there was something to it. I mean, how does it happen that a skinny little kid from a dirt-poor family in Tupelo, Mississippi, suddenly becomes the best-known name in the world? How is it that he commands all these fortunes and has all these millions of people who love him?

"I don't know. I'm not overly religious, but it does have a ring to it that maybe this all was destined. It was almost magic that Elvis and Colonel Tom got together. That seemed destined. I often felt that I'm in the aura of some very special human being. He genuinely believes that he is a prophet and we were his disciples. He demands fanatical loyalty, expects it. There have been times that I have felt that Elvis bordered on being a bit of a nut, but look at the loyalty we gave the man. We broke our backs for him. We've risked our lives for him.

"I have risked getting my fool-ass head blown off for him. He certainly had a power over us. He certainly had a control over me, I admit it. We didn't do it for the money, because we never got much. We didn't do it for the women, because we had all had that and we are all married. We didn't do it for the excitement, because we were all a bit old for that kind of thing.

"I mean he had me going where I was making telephone calls about getting Mike Stone hit. I am no killer, but I would have broken arms and legs for him. He really affected me. If I had a blowup with him or we argued, it would get so that I would get into a mood and go out and get in a fight and kick some guy's ass. It was crazy, but I did it. He could reduce us to tears, and he could get us praying for him when we thought he was hurting himself. That's the way it was."

All three men believe that in another time Presley could have been a great evangelist or even a politician. Dave Hebler relates: "I have seen him manipulate crowds like he was Hitler. It was weird, man."

Presley's fascination with death and the life hereafter, perhaps triggered by the death of his mother, borders on the frighteningly bizarre. His loss was so great that, to ease the pain, he believed she came back in another life. "He believes in reincarnation but not for everybody," Sonny says. "He believes that only strong people who show they have power on earth will be reincarnated. He would often say, 'If you are powerful enough on earth and are strong enough, you will come back. Weak people can't bring themselves back from the dead. Only strong people.' "

His fascination with human corpses is downright terrifying. Red recalls: "There was a very nice guy, a Memphis policeman who ended up an inspector. His name was Woodward. Well, he took a real fatherly interest in Elvis right from when he just left school. They were very close. Well, in 1961, the good old guy died. I'm sure Elvis was sad about the whole thing, but do you know what he did, man? He watched a mortician embalm his friend, this old man Woodward.

"Can you imagine that? Someone watching someone else slicing into the body of a friend. Elvis could tell us details about embalming that would impress a doctor. He knew all the right terms, and he would tell us how a body is bled and blood is taken out and replaced by the embalming fluid. It used to make me sick.

"There were other things that were weird too. When he was at funerals, he would act in the most strange way. I'm not talking about his mother's funeral, because he was genuinely shattered. But even way back in 1964, when Dewey Phillips, the disc jockey, died—the guy who got Elvis all the breaks—well, Elvis is at Dewey's funeral, and suddenly he got a fit of the giggles. Just laughed his head off. I've seen him at other times start cracking jokes."

Sonny West's experiences with Presley were even more bizarre. "He would love to go on these damn trips through graveyards," says Sonny. "He would just tell us to see if we could scare ourselves. He's pulled up on a dark road with Red and just walked down a lonely road to feel the experience of being scared. But worst of all was his trips to funeral homes. He used to return to the funeral home where his mother was laid out, on Union Avenue in Memphis. I don't mean he would just go there during the day and look around. I mean he would go there at three in the morning and wander around the slabs looking at all the embalmed bodies. It scared the shit out of me."

One night in 1972 Presley, as was his practice, took over the Memphian Theater to see a movie. Sonny relates: "Elvis loves horror movies. So this night we see a horror movie, and it must have got his mind working. Anyway, Linda Thompson was there this night. It's about three in the morning. We all hop in the car and suddenly Elvis says, 'Let's go down to Union Avenue.'

"Already, I've got it in my mind what he wants to do. We pull up outside the funeral home. We go around the back, and Elvis is leading the way as calm as if he was going to a movie. Anyway, three in the morning, the door is wide open and we just walk in, Elvis, Linda and me. I can't believe there is no security guard or something, but we don't see a person.

"Anyway, Elvis just wanders around calm as anything trying doors to some offices. Some are locked, others are opened. I've got my jacket open ready to go for my gun. I'm scared some security guy is going to come along, see us, think it's a robbery or that we're grave robbers or something and start blazing away. I'm as nervous as a cat, because we don't see anyone and it's dark and eerie.

"Then I get the shock of my life. We come into this big room with heads sticking from under sheets. They were bodies, and they were sort of tilted upward, feet first. This was the damn embalming room. I'm horrified. But this was apparently what Elvis was looking for. He is happy he has found the room. Then he starts lecturing us on how people get embalmed. He is walking around and lifting up the sheets looking at the bodies, and he is telling us all the cosmetic things the morticians do when people are in accidents. He is showing us the various veins. The jugular veins and things like that. How a body is bled. Then he shows us where the bodies were cut, and because the cuts don't heal, there is only the stitches holding the body together. He led us into another room, and he is still lifting up the sheets pointing out various things that have been done to the bodies.

"Well, man, I'm flipping. First of all, I'm convinced that a security guard is going to come in and start blasting away at us, and the whole thing is making me sick. I mean, three o'clock in the morning on a tour of a mortuary. Damn madness. In the meantime, Linda Thompson is just as interested as can be. She is ooing and aaahing and saying 'Oh, my goodness, will you look at that' in that sweet little Southern accent of hers. It didn't seem to affect her.

"Well, we were there about forty-five minutes, and nobody so much as showed a face. It was amazing nobody was around. But it just shows you what a night out with Elvis might end up like. Red has also been with him on trips to embalming rooms, and I know he used to hate it, but that's what Elvis wanted and you just went along with it."

Dave Hebler says Elvis has the same fascination with birth. Dave was driving Presley, Linda Thompson and Dick Grob, another bodyguard and former Palm Springs policeman, to a movie in the spring of 1975. "We were going to the Memphian for a private showing. Linda mentions that her brother Sam Johnson and his wife Louise have just had a baby. She is talking about how thrilled she is and suddenly, at one in the morning, Elvis decides to go see the baby. We finally get in the back entrance and, once inside the hospital, we're causing a riot. Nurses are dropping patients everywhere and running to get his autograph.

"Anyway, it's against hospital rules for strangers to come and look at a baby at one in the morning, but Elvis cons the nurse and, sure enough, we get the baby. Then someone wakes up the mother, Louise, and she comes out. Then her husband Sam is brought to the hospital to join the party. Then Linda's parents show up. Then there are the doctors and nurses. We had a convention here.

"Anyway, down the hallway there is a bit of activity. Elvis sees some doctors and nurses wheeling this woman along on one of those mobile stretchers. She is yelling in pain. I notice she is in labor, and they are rushing to get her into the delivery room.

"The next thing I know, Elvis has stopped the emergency charge toward the delivery room and starts talking to the lady. Here she is in labor, but Elvis comes along and she starts flipping out despite the pain. Anyway, as he sees her in pain, he lays his hands on her stomach, and he starts saying serious in a sort of mystical way, 'Now, there, it won't hurt any more. It won't hurt any more. Everything is going to be fine. You're not going to hurt any more.'

"He's laying on the hands and taking the pain from her. Well, that might sound pretty ridiculous for a woman in labor, but the funny thing was she is saying 'You're right, the pain is gone, you're right.' Well, the doctors there are doing flips. They want to get this lady into delivery, and Elvis is doing his psychic healing. Then he asks the doctor, 'Can I come in the delivery room? I have never seen a baby born. I want to see life.'

"Well, the doctors finally said no, but they were thinking of letting him, especially when this lady kept on pleading with them to let Elvis Presley see her give birth. Some people, man."

Sonny West says that Presley is convinced he has the power to heal people. He will lay on his hands and say that their strength and the power of concentration will draw out the pain.

Red relates: "Since my days playing football, I've always had a bad back, and sometimes at the top of my neck it gives me hell. Well, after a while I learned not to complain about it when I was around

Elvis, because I knew what would happen. Whenever he knew I had the pain, he would ask me to sit down in front of him, and then he would lay on his hands, telling me over and over that the pain would go away, that he was drawing out the pain. Well, I would sit there and he would say, 'It's going away, Red, the pain is going away. It's going away, Red. You're going to be okay.'

"I would say, 'Yes, boss, I hear you.' Then I would tell him, 'Hell, man, you're right. The pain has gone. That's fantastic. It really has gone.'

"He would give me one of those little secretive smiles that told the world that he had these powers, and he would walk away pleased with himself. I would walk away and my back and neck were still hurting like hell. It was a case where I didn't want to tell him that he was kidding himself, because he really had the best of intentions, but he was convinced that he had fixed me up."

In Vail during a holiday that Presley was on, all the boys were out on the slopes at three o'clock in the morning, horsing around. "We were on those snowmobile things," says Sonny. "Well, Dean, son of Dr. Nick, was along with us. He often travels with the team and helps out in various ways. A real nice kid. Well, we were on these disc sleds, and somehow Dean's went skidding out of control and he hit a fence and hurt his leg. We thought it was broken, because he was in a lot of pain. We carried him back to the chalet and laid him down, and he was groaning in pain. Then old psychic healer Elvis comes along. He starts laying on the hands and grabbing the leg. Poor old Dean is nearly passing out with pain. But Elvis is convinced he is fixing the leg. Now, as it turned out, it wasn't broken, just a very bad bruise, but if it had been broken, Elvis's fooling around and grabbing it could have got it worse.

"When Elvis heard from a doctor that the leg wasn't broken, he gave one of those satisfied little know-all smiles, and he said, 'I know, it isn't broken. It's okay now.' He was taking credit for the fact that the leg wasn't broken."

Dave Hebler, who has a cynical sense of humor, sometimes found it difficult not to laugh at Presley. Like the others, he would indulge him no end, but he was always battling with his laugh button.

"Man, I remember one day at the Palm Springs house in Chino Canyon Road," says Dave. "It was hotter than hell, over a hundred degrees. Anyway, Elvis wants to suddenly hop in the car and go down to the shopping area to load up on some stuff. When he goes, everyone goes. We all jam into this car. There were four or five of the other guys along. God, it was hot. Elvis was talking about the power of metaphysics, although I'm not quite sure whether he knew the real definition of the word.

"Anyway, the sky is desert clear, not a cloud in the sky except for this tiny little cloud a long way away which was minding its own business.

"Suddenly Elvis yells out, 'Stop the car. I want to show you what I mean, Dave. Now see that cloud? I will show you what my powers really are. Now I want you all to watch. All of you, look at that cloud.'

"Well, we all look at the damn little cloud up there like a bunch of goats. Elvis is staring a hole through the damn thing. Well, the perspiration is dripping off us. Not a sound in the car, just a whole lot of dummies dying of heat stroke looking up at the cloud.

"I'm near dying and I am praying that the sonofabitch would blow away. At the same time, I'm really having a problem not to burst out laughing. Well, after about ten minutes, thank God, the damn thing dissipated a little. I mean, if you watch a single cloud, anyway after ten minutes, it will move or dissipate to some degree.

"I saved the day by noticing it first, and, because I didn't want to die of dehydration, I said, 'Gee, Elvis, you're right. Look, it's moving away.' That was just the right thing to say. Old Elvis gave me one of those sly little smiles that told me he had done it again. 'I know, I moved it,' he says. Then we drive off."

Red West, perhaps because he saw the miracle of Presley's rise to the top from the very beginning, is not quite as cynical as Dave. He remembers driving across the desert in a Dodge mobile-home trailer that Presley had bought.

"It was just after we made the movie *Wild in the Country*, and we had a group along with us. Elvis was making it with this girl he had met on the movie, and she was along, and Larry Geller was there, too. Larry was his permanent hairdresser. He was one of the best and most expensive in Hollywood. It was Larry who first interested Elvis in a lot of psychic phenomena books. He was into it.

"Anyway, we are driving back from Arizona. Now in those days many of us used to follow Elvis in popping those damn amphetamines just to keep us high. But, I swear, on this day I hadn't taken a thing. I was very straight. Now we are talking about some of this heavy psychic stuff, and Elvis is talking about how he believed he was destined to do something very big in his life apart from show business. I'm agreeing with him. Anyway, suddenly just to show me what he is talking about, he says, 'Hold on, Red, stop the trailer. Look up there, see what I mean?' Anyway, I look up and I'll be a sonofabitch. There is a giant cloud formation above us, and I don't know whether it was auto-suggestion or what, but this cloud formation is formed in the shape of two very definite likenesses of two heads. One was Elvis Presley and one was Joseph Stalin.

"Now, I don't want to sound like I'm a candidate for the funny farm, and I don't know whether it was my imagination, but I know what I saw very clearly. Elvis Presley and Joseph Stalin. Wow, that shook me.

"And I said to him, quite sincerely; 'Yeah, sure, boss, I see what you mean.' And I'm not going to say that I don't believe in a lot of that stuff. Some of it is pure crazy, but there are too many unexplained things to dismiss it completely."

Presley knew that Red felt Presley's control over him, and he would often write him kind of fatherly letters containing advice and psychic philosophies. He would sometimes dictate such a letter to Linda Thompson and have it delivered to Red by hand. Red remembers one in particular because, he says, "it shows you how he had to be the dominant figure. He wasn't content to let his show-business status speak for itself. He had to have control. You were his subjects, you did what he said. He even called us disciples."

"That comes in with the Mike Stone incident," adds Sonny, "I thought he was trying to get my mind to go kill Mike Stone and putting the gun in my hand. I thought he was trying to overpower my mind."

Sonny says that when Presley talked about his powers, he would say that the pain was being transferred to his fingers and that's why he had the ability to cure with hands. Presley, who was brought up in the First Assembly Church of God, knows the Bible extremely well. He would often sit with his legs crossed yoga fashion and read to his Memphis Mafia and their girl friends for hours.

At other times he would mix Bible teachings with philosophy. His favorite book is *Voice*, which Sonny says is one of the many books on highly complicated philosophy that Presley has with him all the time. "But Elvis often gets up in his acts during his performances and reads these things to the audience," says Sonny. "One night at the Riviera Hotel in Las Vegas, he got up there and stopped a whole performance." Don Rickles was in high gear doing his "insult act." Rickles decided to introduce Presley, who was in the wings. Sonny recalls that Presley could hardly wait to get on stage. And when he did, instead of saying the perfunctory "Hi" to the audience, he produced *Voice* and insisted that Rickles read passages from it. It was an extremely embarrassing scene. What could Rickles do? He didn't want to insult Elvis, so he read on and on until he looked at Elvis and said with a smile, "Hey, where are we going with this?" Presley looked at him, dead serious, and said, 'Keep reading, Don, it's very important." Sonny was embarrassed for Elvis: "Jesus, was I glad when the reading was over. The audience clapped politely, but they didn't know what the hell they were clapping for."

Sonny recalls how Presley would tell his boys how his powers went beyond healing humans. "He said," says Sonny, "that his powers could be transferred to bushes and trees. He would have this gimmick where he would put his hands and fingers over a little bush or a leaf. Then he would move his hands back and forth in a vibrating motion. Well, after a while, of course, there would be movement in the air, and the bush or leaf would move naturally.

"Now I would do it, knowing that the movement of his hand had actually moved the leaf. I would stick my hand out stiff, and if I moved it, I would move it slowly. And, of course, nothing happened and I would say, 'Gee, boss, I can't do it. How did you do it?'

"Well, old Elvis would smile that smile of his and he would say, 'I can do it and so can you, but you're going to have to learn how it's done.' We weren't ass kissing. It's just that he is so certain of these powers, you don't want to throw it up in his face. It's like spoiling someone's fun and we just went along. None of us would ever want to rain on his parade."

Dave Hebler relates: "Now, there are experts in the psychic phenomena field who are very hard to discount. A lot of their stuff stands up, and I am tempted to believe in it quite a bit. But with Elvis, while I believe a lot of his homegrown philosophies, it's quite obvious he has only a very surface knowledge of this stuff. The ludicrous part was him passing himself off as an expert, particularly in this healing business.

"I think he sincerely wanted to heal someone's pain. But at the same time he was trying to elevate himself above ordinary humans. He sort of had this superman complex."

There were times, says Sonny, when Presley, halfway through a Bible reading, would stop and interpret, and change the wording. "There is a passage somewhere in the Bible which mentions that a rich man, if he is only rich, cannot get into heaven. Well, Elvis turned that around and would tell us, 'The Bible says that a rich man's chance of getting into heaven is like a camel's ass trying to get through the eye of the needle.' Now that wasn't meant to be funny. We weren't supposed to laugh at that. Then he would say, 'Well, the Bible didn't mean it that way, because I'm rich and I'm going into heaven.' We would always nod our heads and agree with him."

What really would break up the Memphis boys was Presley's way of preaching. "There was a time," says Sonny, "in one of his homes—it might have been down in Palm Springs. Anyway, Elvis was all dressed up, and there was a period where he would carry a cane. Actually they were sword canes, and some of them had daggers in the bottom of them. Anyway, we're all gathered around, and Elvis with this damn cane jumps up on a coffee table and he starts giving us the Sermon on the Mount.

"But the way he gave it was a little different from the Bible. He stood up there and held his hands up for silence, and in a loud preacher's voice he yelled down to us as we sat around with our faces turned up to him, 'Whoa, all ye motherfuckers, of kind thoughts and good deeds . . .'

"He went on in this vein and it really was funny. There were a bunch of girls there sitting on the floor, and when they saw that we weren't laughing, because we knew better, they kept their faces straight like they were in church listening to a sermon. Anyway, he starts talking about Moses and he says, his voice still like a gospel preacher, 'Moses, that white-haired sonofabitch, comes running down from this big mountain. Now his damn hair had turned white because he had seen the Lord, and those things can happen when you see the Lord. Anyway, he came on down from the mountain, and how he got down was the burning bushes directed his ass on down.' "

Sonny recalls that the Bible teachings were really a scream, but nobody dared laugh. Presley was deadly serious. Sonny recalls: "He doesn't realize he is saying these things. His mind is always running very fast, and it jumps ahead of his talk, and sometimes he doesn't know what he is saying and he says the first thing that comes into his mind. He would say the funniest things in quoting the Bible. Now whenever he mentioned Jesus, he would just say aside, 'Now, Jesus, he was getting it on with Mary, the woman at the well, you know, Mary Magdalene. It ain't in the Bible but it's true. She got stoned, but Jesus took care of her and they traveled around a lot together.' "

Red West recalls: "He would say, 'Jesus said he was old and of age and he fell ass backwards in the dust.' Later on, after we got together, we would laugh our heads off because it was hysterical."

The boys say that he was fascinated by intelligent people. "Just so long as he wouldn't get into all that other bullshit," says Dave, "he had a very good and very inquisitive mind." When he'd hear somebody tell a story that interested him, he would absorb it, build on it, and make it into a whole monologue.

"Typical," says Red, "was an incident attached to the song 'Softly,' which is one of the songs he would sing on stage. Now, one night backstage, some guy who was feeding Elvis a line said, 'Do you know the story behind that song?' and Elvis pricked up his ears and said, 'No, I thought it was a love story.'

Anyway, this guy tells him it wasn't a love story. The lyrics, this guy says, were written by a dying man.

"Elvis gets to thinking about this. And, as is his way, he will often talk to the audience about the song he is going to sing. So he has made up this incredible story. We heard him tell it on stage so many times we started to get to where we believed it. He would get up there and tell them: 'Now this is a story about a man who is dying. He was in the hospital and his wife was there with him. She sat with him for three days and three nights. On the third day, she lay down beside him and went to sleep. Just then this man felt himself dying. He didn't want her to see him pass away, so he reached for a pad and a pencil and he wrote these words: "Softly." ' Then he would sing the song.

"Well, I guess the audience ate it up. Anyway, I spoke to a guy who knew the writer of the song and told him this story, and the guy looks at me and says, 'Oh, bullshit, it's a love story.' But Elvis to this day will tell that story on stage. His imagination is great."

Elvis firmly believes there is life on other planets. He believes there are flying saucers and that visitors from other planets often come down to earth. "When he started talking like that," Dave Hebler says, "he never got much of an argument from me. I mean, it's pretty arrogant of us here on earth, a tiny little planet in this giant universe, to think we are the only ones here. So I would listen pretty closely to his ideas, and they often went along with mine."

Sonny West remembers a time in 1966 when Presley believed there was a visit from outer space. "It is still a bit of a mystery to me. We were back in his mansion in Perugia Way, Bel Air. We were in the back of the place, and suddenly Elvis says to me, 'Do you see that?' I looked up and I could see this light coming through the trees. Elvis was getting very excited and said, 'It's a flying saucer.' I didn't take much notice. I thought it was the light of a plane or a reflection from a plane, and I just waited until I heard the sound of the motor. Well, I didn't hear any sound. The light kept coming, and it went through the trees and sort of over the top of the house.

"The light disappeared, and it seemed to have dropped in the front of the house and we were in the back. Elvis tells me to go back in the house and get Jerry Schilling. I rush in, grab Jerry and we go outside looking for the light. When we got outside, we couldn't find Elvis. We're hollering and yelling, and we run in front of the house and we still can't find him. Finally I hear him yell, 'I'm down here.' We run down about two or three houses, and he is in the driveway of one of these houses. He is looking off toward Westwood.

"I say to him, 'Jesus, that light thing scared the hell out of me. I thought they had got you.' When I said that, I was only half joking, because I believed I had seen some kind of flying saucer or a phenomenon of some kind which I can't explain.

"Anyway, he just kind of grinned and he said, 'They will come but they won't hurt us. If they make contact, we can't be afraid, because they are not going to hurt us.' He was convinced there was a flying saucer with people on board, and I don't know what I believe, but I do know I saw something I can't explain. And I agree with Dave—I can't believe this earth is the only planet with life on board."

Sonny and Red believe that a lot of Presley's mysticism started with his mother's and father's dreams. "Like his mother, who dreamed that his car was on fire and was right, Elvis told us about his dad, who also had these weird dreams and would walk in his sleep, like Elvis did," says Sonny.

"He told us of a time that his dad had this dream that the house was on fire. So his dad jumped up and ran toward where Elvis, who was three years old at the time, was sleeping. He grabbed little Elvis, and he thought he was throwing him out of a window to escape the flames. Of course, the house wasn't on fire. He threw Elvis out of his cot, and Elvis landed butt first against the wall."

Red remembers that once, the teenage Presley sleep-walked right into the street in his underwear. A girl he knew saw him and yelled out to him. It woke him up and when he saw himself there in front of the girl, he was so embarrassed he ran off and hid until she went away.

"When he first went to the Hilton International in Las Vegas, there were nights where I sat up awake all night, just sitting by the window, while Elvis was asleep. I just stayed there, because I was scared to hell he would walk in his sleep and jump out the window. It was a genuine fear.

"There's a lot of strange things to Elvis, a lot of strange things. That's why I don't believe he is any ordinary human."

# 15

On September 26, 1958, the U.S. Army's most famous recruit sailed from New York on board the U.S. Troop Ship *General Randall* bound for Bremerhaven, Germany. With the death of his mother hanging heavily in his heart, Private Presley kept pretty much to himself during the voyage, but there was one soldier who struck up an acquaintance with him—a short, sharp-looking guy from Alabama, Charlie Hodge. Presley felt secure in the company of a fellow Southerner, and besides, Private Hodge played a good guitar. For four days they talked and sang together. Today Charlie is still playing guitar as one of Presley's musicians. He has become so closely identified with the star that he even has his own fan club.

When the *Randall* arrived, the cold, gray docks of Bremerhaven had never looked so decorative. There at dockside, behind sturdy fences, were fifteen hundred shrieking fräuleins waiting for their hero. Harassed army officials whisked Presley and his fellow soldiers off to their camp at Freiburg.

Meanwhile, the Presley rearguard action was about to rendezvous with their leader. Vernon Presley, Minnie Presley, Red West and Lamar Fike were on their way.

"The first thing Vernon did," says Red, "was to

173

organize a place for the whole of us to stay together. It had been agreed that Elvis could live off base, which was no special privilege, really. I mean, it wasn't against army rules if you could afford it, and naturally Elvis could. Well, Vernon organized this place to stay in Bad Nauheim. It was a hotel. Now I have read stories saying that this hotel was a luxury hotel. Well, it wasn't. It was called the Gruenwald Hotel, and as soon as I saw it, I knew it really wasn't the place for us to stay. It was a sort of outpatients' hotel for heart-attack victims. There wasn't anyone there under sixty, and every one of them looked like they had one foot in the grave and the other one on a roller skate. Anyway, we get this three-bedroom apartment with a living room, kitchen and bathroom. Grandma, Vernon and Elvis would sleep in the bedrooms, and Lamar and I would bunk down in the living room, which was more than fine by us.

"Now, Grandma, who is still alive, thank the Lord, and must be now about eighty-two or eighty-three, is a real character. She had never been outside Tupelo, Mississippi or Memphis. She had never flown before, and here she is with a superstar grandson, her son and two men. She is real down-home country, and if you think I have a Southern accent, you should hear her.

"Well, as soon as we land she started getting dreadful reactions to the vaccination shots. The vaccination scab on her arm was the size of a half-dollar coin, the poor old girl's arm swelled up to twice its size. She couldn't get out of bed, and for about a week there I thought maybe we had done the wrong thing bringing her, because I thought she was going to die, and that would have finished Elvis off.

"Well, from death's door Grandma seemed to come out of it. She was tougher than ten horses. In about a week's time she was ruling that house like a real Southern lady. She did the cooking and cleaning, even though there were chambermaids (thank God for those chambermaids, but I'll explain that later).

When she got well, we were all one big family, and I was sort of raring to go to enjoy myself. But then whenever I went downstairs and saw all these people who looked like they were going to die, I sort of had second thoughts. This was not the place to have fun—although, looking back, we did have a ball. All of us, particularly Elvis, liked the Germans. They weren't Southerners, but they were kind of straight people who were very honest and looked you right in the face when they talked to you. One guy who particularly looked us in the face was the manager of the hotel, Herr Schmidt, who wasn't too happy about our invasion. He obviously thought that after we were there a while, there would probably be a few corpses on his hands. I'm surprised there weren't. Herr Schmidt was a strange guy, who used to be followed around by this ratty half-breed dog."

Trouble started straightaway for the Presley party. "There was this old gal below us," Red continues, "and as soon as Lamar walked around, she would thump on the ceiling and shout something in German. Lamar would respond by jumping up and down on the floor, yelling something about Hitler. If it didn't kill her off, it damn near killed Vernon off. He had visions of the publicity if ever we got thrown out of the hotel—which, of course, we eventually did."

Private Presley rose at about 5:00 A.M. every morning and headed for the base, where he was assigned to the Scouts. It was, naturally, an ordered life, but occasionally something would go wrong or else a superior officer would hassle him. "That's when Elvis got in a bad mood," Red recalls, "and he would say, 'Man, what the hell am I doing here? That old sonofabitch the Colonel, he could have got me out of this. He could have fixed it.' But most of the time he fitted in well.

"Quite obviously, the big attraction straightaway was the women, and the women were as frantic there as they were here but, generally speaking, the German fans seemed better mannered. I mean, you could joke around with them, talk to them without getting ripped apart. Of course, there were exceptions."

Red remembers their fun at the Gruenwald Hotel with affection. "We never stopped playing games. Each week we would have a different kind of fight. We always had water pistols, and Elvis, Lamar and I never stopped fighting with these water pistols. We would be in the hallways of this hotel, squirting hell out of each other, and suddenly we would see some old broad look at us with shock like she was about to drop dead from a heart attack. And only then we would stop.

"Then there were the shaving-cream fights and the pillow fights and all the time pushing and wrestling each other on the floor. When I think of it, me, Elvis and Lamar wrestling on that floor, I often wonder how long after we left did that old girl underneath us live. I'm sure we shortened her life."

The best time of day, particularly for Red, was early morning. "Now that's when the chambermaid would come in to make up the bed. I would give her a quick roll in the hay, and then she would go back to work."

When Red and Lamar weren't having water-pistol fights and shaving-cream fights and pillow fights, they would spend their time in the Beck's Beer Bar, around the corner from the hotel.

"I guess I was there more than Lamar, but I couldn't do much damage there, because I never had any money. Both Lamar and I were back on Elvis's payroll, which meant we didn't get paid. We got our three square meals a day and we had a roof over our head, so I guess we couldn't complain; we were there because we wanted to be there, and nobody forced us. But the most we got was a few marks here and there, and in Germany in those days a mark was worth about twenty-five cents. So I would go over to the bar and nurse two beers all night."

When Red wasn't doing that, he admits, he got into a little bit too much trouble in the Beck's Beer Bar. "Always seemed I was getting into fights. Some guy would say something, and one thing would lead to another and things started to get a bit physical. It was pretty stupid, I guess, but hell, I was only about twenty-three and didn't know much better. See, Elvis wouldn't go into a bar and drink, and he just didn't figure that a guy needed a few bucks here and there. We did plenty for him, and he guessed we were happy with just being there serving him, which was right, but a few bucks would have helped because there was no way we could do any work there to earn any money."

Red admits that he had himself to blame for the way Presley relied on him to do odd jobs. "For instance, at night sometimes, when I had nothing to do, I started polishing Elvis's army boots. I learned all that spit and polish stuff in the marines. And Elvis really started taking a pride in his dress while he was there in Germany. Well, I showed Lamar how to shine his shoes, and between us we would have those boots of his so shiny you could have shaved in them. He got used to it where he expected it, but we didn't mind doing it."

While Red was making an impression on some G.I. jaws at the Beck's Beer Bar, and Minnie Presley was making her impression on the kitchen, and Presley was making his impression on the U.S. Army, Col. Tom Parker was not actually dozing, himself. He had thwarted all attempts to have Presley put in the Special Services, and Elvis's fans were now resigned to hearing only silence for the next two years. So Colonel Tom had RCA Victor release the movie album from *Love Me Tender*. When that reached the saturation point, the album *Loving You* was released, followed by *King Creole*. All were million sellers. Then some of the old songs were re-released and brilliantly repackaged. Presley may have been up to his knees in snow in Germany, but he was still warming the hearts of his American fans.

News stories and pictures in U.S. newspapers and wire services about Private Presley were doing their work, too, and, predictably, an older generation was gradually seeing Presley in a different light. No more was he a swivel-hipped menace to womanhood, but a clean-cut Southern boy out doing his duty for his country and his flag. By the time he returned to the States, he was every parent's idea of what a good son should be. Up until then, no singer had ever managed to appeal across generations, but Colonel Tom wanted *everyone* to want "his boy," not just one age group. He wanted him to be around for decades, and that is exactly what happened.

Red recalls that RCA Victor was frantic. "They wanted to keep the ball rolling. They wanted him to cut a disc in Germany. When that idea was hit on the head, they even pleaded with him just to sing a song into an ordinary tape recorder. They would do the instrumentals and the dubbing back in New York. But the old Colonel, I guess he knew what he was doing and he knew the time wasn't right." Presley would never be snowed by pressure. No matter how he was harangued to cut more discs, he would politely shake his head and say, "Just take it up with the Colonel."

Fun and games at the Gruenwald were reaching raucous proportions. Herr Schmidt had a suspicion that one of his chambermaids was doing more to the beds in the Presley suite than just making them. Lamar Fike's marching around the suite was pushing the old lady underneath closer to her Maker, and Red and Presley had gone just a little too far with their water-pistol, shaving-cream and pillow fights.

"If I remember rightly," says Red, "the straw to break the camel's back came when Elvis and I are having a shaving-cream fight. I kept hitting him in the face with this stuff, and he ran into one of the rooms and locked the door. I guess I wasn't too satisfied with this so I put some paper under the door, lit it and decided to smoke him out. Well, you guessed it, it caused a little fire. Nothing serious, I don't think, but there was a lot of smoke coming out of the windows, and Elvis and I are dying laughing as we try to put this damn thing out. Suddenly Herr Schmidt, the manager, appeared on the scene. He was one very pissed off German hotel manager.

"I thought he was going to explode. Meanwhile, all the old biddies are running around downstairs thinking that they are going to be barbecued.

"No matter how bad our German was, we got the drift of Herr Schmidt's strangled shouts. He said one word in English very good and that word was *out*. Vernon was pissed off as well, but old Minnie Presley, funny old gal that she was, she thought it was very funny. She had never had so much fun."

A decision was made to move into a three-story, five-bedroom house nearby on Goethestrasse. Red remembers it was a comfortable, big, old place, which the landlady charged an arm and a leg for. "She saw us coming, man," says Red. "We paid close to about eight hundred bucks a month for the place. That was a gigantic amount of money for Germany in 1958 and 1959. It was at least three times what a German would have paid for it.

"The landlady was a gal we'll call Frau Gross (which is not her real name), a big, big, busty broad who could have played linebacker. We take over the place, move in and find something very strange. Even though we're paying the rent, Frau Gross decides she doesn't want to move out. One of the main reasons for this was that she very much liked the idea of men company—not Elvis, but his dad, Vernon. He didn't want to be alone with her. She would rattle away at him in this very fast German and Vernon would just nod his head. She never stopped talking to him, but not a word of English. He didn't understand a word she was saying, but she just kept talking and smiling. It was very funny. But what was funnier was to see her and Grandma Presley together. Now Grandma couldn't talk Yankee, let alone German. But Frau Gross would be in the kitchen and she would talk to Grandma in her German and Grandma would talk back to her in this real Mississippi country accent of hers and, man, they would talk for hours. It was a scream.

"But Grandma didn't like anybody trying to take over her kitchen. One time there was a dreadful confrontation, and Grandma decked this big Frau Gross with a broom handle. Oh, Lordie, what a house."

Presley and Red had a passion for fireworks and, on occasion, would engage in fireworks fights with local German youths. Once, Presley accidentally sent a Roman candle into the back of a young German man, who told Presley that he had put a hole not only in his leather jacket but almost through his back. When Presley offered to pay for a new jacket, there were no more problems.

"Elvis liked the Germans for that sort of thing, because if that had happened in the States, someone would have sued him for a hundred thousand dollars. He liked the Germans, the way they didn't make a fuss about things like that. They were good people."

Presley was cementing U.S.-German relations in other ways—with the women. "I remember one day," says Red, "I saw this pretty little thing out by our front gate. Now I just went out there and said hi and we couldn't communicate at all. But I just said the word *Elvis* and pointed up to his bedroom. We didn't say another word to each other. I smuggled her past Frau Gross, who didn't like other women, particularly young women, around her house, and I just put her in Elvis's bedroom and left her there without a word.

Elvis came home a little later and I just said, 'Hi, I've got a present for you upstairs.'

"He looked at me, shrugged his shoulders and didn't say another word. Well, he came down about a half-hour later, and he had a smile on his face that just about split his head in half. Little presents like that tend to break up the day."

Red remembers one particular girl whom Presley got hot and heavy with. "I can't remember how we met up with her," says Red, "but what I do remember was something that would never happen in the South—even today. This girl took him home with her to her mother. And that night he slept there—with her mother's blessing. I know it must have shocked the hell out of Elvis. Those things didn't ever happen to him. I guess she was a pretty liberal mother."

Presley felt very much at ease with the Germans. He and Red would go into the park with young Germans and roughhouse with them. "It was like sort of friendly fighting," says Red. "No punching in the face but wrestling each other and throwing each other on the ground and tackling each other. Nobody went too far and the German guys were having as much fun as we were.

"I remember one time we were battling with them and having a ball. We were getting swamped by them. Elvis pokes his head out from under a pile of legs, arms and bodies and yells to Lamar to come and help out. Well, there was some ice on the ground and Lamar is on top of a hill. Old Lamar yells out, 'I'm coming Elvis, I'm coming.' Well, he came all right. Lamar slips flat on his ass at the top of the hill and slides from the top of the hill, the whole three hundred pounds of him, right past us where we were wrestling, and he keeps on going like a great big giant human sled right to the bottom of the hill.

"Well, that broke all of us up. Elvis, me and the German guys went hysterical. I've never seen anything like Lamar. It was like he was jet propelled.

Old Lamar didn't think it was funny; he climbed back to the top of the hill with his ass out of his pants. Lamar was always doing something like that. Somehow he didn't mind being the clown. He was a great guy who was just so funny without even trying, and he had a heart of gold, too."

Other diversions consisted of football games set up by Presley and Red. Some of the G.I.s they played against were to become college football stars, and a few of them even made the rookie pro ranks. "The only thing about this field where we played," says Red, "the most dangerous thing about the game, was the fact there were a lot of shepherds in the area.

"Well, we would have to stop our game as about a hundred sheep would pass over the ground. Only problem was that half them damn sheep would take a crap in the middle of the field, and we found ourselves playing ankle deep in sheep shit."

Presley spent some of his free nights fairly quietly at home. Charlie Hodge, the Southern boy Presley had met on the boat to Germany, would drop over. So would another Southern boy, Rex Mansfield. Together with Lamar and Red and Vern, they would all get together for an old-fashioned Southern night singing and harmonizing around a fire, with Minnie Presley cooking up heaps of Southern food.

"It was like a big family and we enjoyed ourselves," Red remembers. "Rex Mansfield ended up by marrying a beautiful little American girl called Lizbeth who worked with another girl handling fan mail. It was a pretty tight group, even with Frau Gross hovering in the background."

The mail that Presley was getting was staggering, something like ten thousand letters a week, some of it just addressed simply to "Elvis, Germany." All of them were answered.

Red remembers that, despite the rare complaint that Colonel Tom could have gotten him out of the Third Armored Division, Private Presley was a good soldier. "He took the job seriously and asked for no special treatment, and the guys really liked him. There were a couple of alerts that sent Elvis right up to the East German border, where he could actually see the Commies on the other side. One time there was even talk that shooting might start up there, and Elvis was right along there, up to his ass in snow and as gung ho as the rest of them."

Because he was so well received and because he made an honest commitment, Presley would get particularly annoyed if he thought any superior officer was picking on him. "One particular incident I remember," says Red, "was to do with the BMW sports car that Elvis used to drive. The Germans called it an Elvis-wagon. Anyway, he was driving off base, and when he got to the gates, this big MP starts giving him hell because there was mud on his license plate. He just jumped all over Elvis for no real reason. I mean, he was just trying to show off that he could push Elvis around. Well, Elvis came home and he was in a bad mood. He was saying, 'That sonofabitch of an MP tried to embarrass me for no reason. I'd like to kick his ass.' "

Red had never liked to see anybody push Elvis around, whether it was in Humes High School or in the United States Army. Presley gave Red a description of the offending MP, and it clicked in Red's mind. "I knew who the big sonofabitch was. They called him 'Indian,' because I guess he had a bit of Indian blood in him. Anyway, I recognized him from the Beck's Beer Bar just across the street, where I hung out. I just said to Elvis, 'I'll just go check it out.' "

Red went across to the bar and within a minute had found the MP who gave Presley the business. When Red walked over to him, the "Indian" knew right away he was in a spot of trouble. Red's reputation in the bar had preceded him. "I want you to come with me," Red said.

The MP looked up from his beer. "I know what it's about," he said. "I made a mistake."

"Well, why don't you come with me and we'll talk about it," Red replied. Red took the "Indian" back across the street to the house, and presented him to Presley: "Is this the guy who was giving you all that shit?" Presley nodded. "Now," said Red, "why don't you two guys go into the living room and talk it out." Red closed the living room door and stood outside.

"The next thing I know," says Red, "this guy comes out with a rag in his hand, and he goes out to Elvis's sports car and he cleans the license plate himself. Elvis just walked out with that little grin on his face and it was all over." What did Presley say to the MP? Did he threaten him with Red's awesome reputation with his fists? "I don't know," says Red.

"I don't want to look like a bad ass. I just fell into the situation and handled it. To tell you the truth, what I really think happened was that Elvis gave the dude a hundred bucks to go out there and clean the license plate, and then Elvis would look good in front of me, as if he had handled it himself. . . .

"That was the only problem that I recall. Of course, there were girls always chasing him, but he was pretty cool about them. He chose his broads pretty carefully. I remember one time there was a little carnival nearby, and Elvis and I and Lamar went along. We were just playing around when suddenly a group of girls recognized him from a long way off. They charged. Elvis and I took one look at them and started to run for our lives. So we're running like hell and just then a bunch of G.I.s go past in an open car. Without saying a word, we just dived in the back of this moving car to escape. Unfortunately there was Lamar running like crazy to catch up. He couldn't make the car and was running so hard across the street he couldn't stop himself. Well, he crashed right into a wooden fence. You should have heard him cuss when he got back to the house. You could always rely on Lamar for comic relief."

While at the Gruenwald Hotel, Vernon Presley met an attractive blond army wife. Her name was Davada "Dee" Stanley. She was married to Sergeant Bill Stanley. Red remembers the first meeting very well. "She was a very pretty woman in her thirties. She had three children, Billy junior, David and Ricky. Billy was about five, and David and Ricky, I guess, were only about three or four years old. She introduced Vernon to her husband, Sergeant Bill. He was a pretty nice guy, pretty typical career-army type. Well, Vernon got so thick with the two of them, he would go out with them, like a triple date. They would go out drinking together and they were good friends. Well, when Sergeant Bill was on maneuvers, he didn't mind Vernon taking Dee out if she was lonely.

"Well, I guess one thing led to another and Vernon and Dee got involved. I remember one night Vernon, Dee, Sergeant Bill, Lamar and I went out on the town. We all got pretty swacked, but Vernon and Bill really got drunk. We all ended up at Sergeant Bill's apartment. Luckily Sergeant Bill Stanley just passed out in his chair, because things were getting rough. Vernon was mouthing off. David and Ricky were crying and I put them to bed.

"Anyway, Lamar and I, over the protests of Vernon, just dragged him out of there and bodily carried him to a taxi. He was cursing and yelling that he was going to have us on the first plane back to the States. But just as well we got out of there, because if Bill Stanley had woken up and heard all this going on, it might have got out of hand. He didn't know that Vernon and Dee were more than just seeing each other. Of course, from then on it was pretty obvious that Dee and her husband were going to split, because Vernon and Dee got pretty close. Later on they got married."

Vernon's relationship with Dee Stanley didn't please

young Presley. "It really got him pissed off that Vernon would marry again," says Red, "but he would always say calmly, 'Whatever Daddy wants is okay by me. Whatever makes him happy.' But the truth was, he never liked Dee Stanley. The thought that Vernon was replacing his mother really burned him up. It wasn't anything he talked about then, although he did later."

There were two habits that Presley picked up while he was in Germany. One of them was a fascination with karate, a passion that became an obsession. He would practice karate for hours on end with Rex Mansfield, who willingly acted as his karate dummy. In years to come, someone's enthusiasm for the sport often qualified him for a place on Presley's team.

The other habit wasn't quite as innocent.

As Red recalls: "There were times on maneuvers up close to the border when the G.I.s really had to be on their toes, and they wouldn't sleep sometimes for a long time. Elvis knew a sergeant, whom I'll call Sergeant Johnson (which is not his real name). Well, Sergeant Johnson wanted his men to be sharp, and he didn't want them falling asleep at their posts. So from time to time he would give out these Dexedrine pills to keep his men awake. Now, Elvis had never had anything to do with pills or booze up until that time. He still doesn't have much to do with booze, only occasionally."

Presley "really took to them pills," says Red. "He liked what they did for him. And he started taking them regularly. So did we all. On some of those movies we made we were higher than kites all the time." But Elvis didn't stop at Dexedrine.

# 16

It was 1975. In Las Vegas, before a packed house of 2,500 in the show room of the Hilton International Hotel, Elvis Presley had just finished his last scheduled number, but instead of disappearing backstage and sprinting to his dressing room, he remained standing in front of the mike. The majority of the press reports were totally wrong, he told the audience, and he wanted to tell it like it was, set the record straight. For instance, he said, "the other night I had the flu real bad. Someone started the report that I was strung out. If I ever find out who started that, I'll knock their G.D. head off. I've never been strung out in my life!" Nor, he went on, had he ever taken drugs.

This brings a smile to the faces of Red West, Sonny West and Dave Hebler, who were all working for him as bodyguards at that time. According to them, Presley, like many show-business personalities, had considerable experience with many types of drugs.

Recalls Red West: "He takes pills to go to sleep. He takes pills to get up. He takes pills to go to the john, and he takes pills to stop him from going to the john. There have been times where he was so hyper on uppers that he has had trouble breathing, and on one occasion he thought he was going to die. His system doesn't work any more like a normal human being's. The pills do all the work for him. He is a walking pharmaceutical shop. He has smoked marijuana, but he doesn't like to smoke it because it burns his throat. He takes uppers and downers and all sorts of very strong painkillers, Percodan and the stuff they give terminal cancer patients. He has often got prescriptions in the names of a lot of the boys, and from time to time he had a doctor (not one named in this book) who used to make up his prescriptions, but has since vanished. Yes, he knows a lot about drugs."

Sonny West shrugs and says, "There is a whole sickness thing that is going to happen to him. His system is just shot to hell."

Dave Hebler, a man who has dedicated the past eighteen years of his life to the study of karate, is more incredulous than Red or Sonny. "After getting to know the scene with Elvis, I was surprised. It is absolute insanity that a human being would want to commit slow suicide, which I feel he is doing with the drugs. I can't understand how anybody can deliberately set about to do himself in. Here is a guy, one of the most popular persons in the world. He can have anything he wants. He has the means. He could have been a fantastic physical specimen. It is hard for me to understand how he can deliberately set out to destroy himself. It seems he is bent on death.

"The thing about him is that Elvis doesn't care. He doesn't give a fuck. I can't find the words to say it strong enough. I mean he is a fascinating person, the most fascinating human I have ever met. He is a composite of contradictions. He is like a Ping-Pong ball going down the hallway. You never know from one minute to the next whether he is going to point a gun at somebody, or he is going to kiss them, or what. It sounds bizarre, but I am really struggling to find the words to emphasize that particular facet about the changeability in his personality."

Red West is convinced that the massive doses of

various pills have taken a toll not only on Presley's body, but also on his personality. The continual confections of great highs and lows have completely warped his senses.

It must be pointed out that the bodyguards, particularly Red West and Sonny West, were not innocent bystanders. From the very first time that Presley discovered what a mild Dexamyl or a mild Dexedrine could do to lift the spirits or kick off a day after only a few hours' sleep, they were right along with him. Both Red and Sonny openly admit that from 1960 all through the period they were on movie locations with Presley, they were flying most of the time on uppers.

"There was no other way we could keep up with him," says Sonny. "He would never get any sleep. Then comes six in the morning for an early call, and we would be beat. So he would give us these uppers and we would drink coffee all day. After a while, we graduated with him into stronger pills like desbutal and escotrol. We were there, right in with him.

"Don't get the idea we're angels. And if we were still wired when it was time to go to bed, he would give us tranquilizers, like Valium, although we have taken much stronger stuff than that toward the end. Stuff like Placidyl, which really knocks you for a loop. He would give us this stuff.

"Some of the time we would ask him for it, but other times we really just wanted to get some sleep, natural sleep. On some of those movies, while Elvis was wired and high as a kite, we would sometimes sneak away off the studio lot and go to a vacant studio and hide under props and stuff and sleep while he was before the cameras. It was the only way we could get any real sleep, because he would be going like a steam train all day and only get a few hours' sleep. In the early days that man had a tremendous constitution. He would never stop. There were other times when he was going to get high, he sort of demanded that you get up there with him. Sometimes he would stand in front of you and watch you take the stuff because there was some stuff he gave me, I don't know what it was, but I would break out in a sweat. So often he would give me a handful of pills and I would ditch them. He knew this, so he would stand in front of me with a glass of water. The past several years, I just plain refused them and this upset him. Eventually, he quit offering them to me." In the light of Presley's traditional image, the bodyguards' stories seem incredible, but all three back them up with offers to take a lie-detector test if anyone cares to challenge them.

Red West says that during the 1960s, Presley was mostly involved with uppers, amphetamines. "But toward about 1970, he started taking the downers. He had taken them before and that's when he had his first weight problem, but he started into them heavier in 1970 and got particularly heavier into them in 1972, after Priscilla left him for Mike Stone. It went on right up until we left him in 1976, when the situation had gotten ridiculous." Despite all Red saw, however, he could never say that Presley ever had any experience with heroin.

The fact that his pills were an important part of his life was demonstrable as far back as 1960, just after the completion of *G. I. Blues,* Presley's first movie after his return from the army. Presley had planned a weekend's rest and relaxation in Las Vegas for his Memphis Mafia. The group—Presley, Sonny West, Joe Esposito, his cousin Gene Smith, Lamar Fike and Charlie Hodge—took off from Los Angeles in a white Cadillac limousine and a Mark VI Lincoln. "Elvis," says Sonny, "had been to Vegas back in 1956, but me and a few others had never been there. We were all excited. Well, we take off in high spirits, and halfway there we stop at Barstow. Elvis asks Gene to give him his kit bag. It was Gene's responsibility to look after Elvis's kit bag. Elvis said that he wanted to brush his teeth or something. Well, we really knew what he wanted. He kept his uppers in his kit bag. It was then we discovered that Gene had left it back at the hotel in Los Angeles. Instead of shrugging it off, Elvis really got mad, so mad that he said for us to get back in the car. We were not going to Vegas now. We were going back to L.A. We were all down. So after being halfway there, he decides to drive back because he hadn't got his little kit bag with his pills in it. Elvis decides to do the driving, and he is cussing and yelling at us.

"We're down and we're tired and Gene starts to doze off. Every time he does, Elvis hits him on the chest with the back of his hand and yells at him, 'There will be no goddamn sleep, do you hear?' Old Gene jerks awake. 'No, boss.' Joe in the back is dozing off and chewing gum at the same time. 'Joe, goddamn it, I said no sleeping.'

"Joe replies, 'I wasn't sleeping, just looking out the window.'

"This is the way it went all the way back to Los Angeles. He was so pissed off at us; he was behaving like a damn child because he didn't get his way."

The party trooped back to the Beverly Wilshire Hotel. Charlie, Lamar and Sonny undressed and fell into bed. Just as they are dozing off, the telephone in their room rings. It's Joe Esposito: "Come on down. Let's go. He decided to go again." Sonny remembers that when they got to the car, Presley had retrieved the kit bag and was dispensing uppers for the long ride to Las Vegas.

Presley got high. Outside Los Angeles the sparkling new car's left front tire blew out and the hubcap came off. Presley was mortified. "We can't go to Las Vegas without a hubcap. Damn it, I want to sell this car." They finally found the hubcap and continued their journey.

They arrived in Las Vegas at about eleven in the morning, all wearing black mohair suits and sunglasses. "I think that's where we got the tab 'Memphis Mafia,' " Sonny remembers, "because we dressed like Mafia guys. Elvis in those days always demanded we wear suits and ties."

As soon as they arrived, Presley went to the crap tables. In a few hours he had lost ten thousand dollars. "After that," says Sonny, "he found out he could play with the house money, where he would not win or would not lose, just sort of like a shill. After he started playing with the house money, he had the most incredible run of dice you had ever seen. One guy who was betting on his throws won a fortune and wanted to give some money to Elvis, but he refused." That weekend, according to Sonny, with a little help from Presley's "friends"—the pills—they slept about two hours. In the early days, says Red West, the uppers were really just a way for Presley and his boys to squeeze a bit more fun out of life. "I know they are dangerous, particularly the way we took them, but it really didn't start out as anything sinister."

For instance they came in very handy when playing football. "Elvis organized a touch-football league called Elvis Presley Enterprises," says Red. "We also had a pick-up side when we lived in Los Angeles and played other teams from the television and movie studios. Lee Majors was a big player in those days; so was Michael Parks and Gary Lockwood and a whole lot of other stars. Elvis played, but of course we gave him plenty of protection.

"At these games we would swallow a couple of uppers, and we have played as much as four and five games in one afternoon, going into the night. People would see us and wonder how we could do it. Well, that's how. Occasionally, Elvis would give us stuff to take for our injuries, and our aches and pains and bruises and sprains. They were painkillers."

"After being five or six hours in the fairground in Memphis on those Dodgems," Sonny remembers, "we were bruised all over, so we gradually got into the painkillers. But still nothing like Elvis was taking toward the end.

"I have seen him with literally dozens of bottles of every different kind of pill. Now, he knows a lot about them. He knows what pill to mix with another pill. He knows the dosages and the exact result. Sometimes he has miscalculated and had bad effects, but most of the time he knows what he is doing, at least he thinks he does. He has got medical directories on the pills and he knows the color codes. Show him a pill or tell him its color on the capsule, and he can identify it in a second."

Red says that the movie-going public would notice the difference in Presley if they could compare his pre-army films with those he made after he got out. "From *G.I. Blues* on, you can notice the way he speaks. He had to make a real effort to slow his speech down. He would talk like a machine gun in those movies where he was wired with uppers. He was high the whole time—and we were most of the time, too."

Any kind of overindulgence in drugs can produce bizarre behavior. At times it has triggered Presley to go on the most lavish and generous of spending sprees. Someone with him would have only to hint at wanting something, and Presley would buy it for them on the spot. Of course, there were many times when he gave simply for the pleasure of giving, his generosity could never be in question.

There are other times, when he is "wired," to use Dave Hebler's expression, in which his moods and actions assume a black, frightening violence. There were two occasions when violent rage was turned on Red West, the man who has given most of his life to the protection of Presley.

In 1973, Presley was performing in Las Vegas at the Hilton. Suddenly, at the end of a song, he completely lost his voice. Red and Sonny cannot say what caused that to happen, but both theorize he had taken so many pills that his throat suddenly dried up. He came offstage in a panic, and Red and Sonny called in Dr. Elias Ghanem and Dr. Sidney Boyer. Dr. Boyer, using special equipment, cleared Presley's throat of a substantial amount of mucus and congestion. After less than ten minutes, Presley was able to go on with his show. Red recalls that Presley had a lot of faith in Sidney Boyer, well-placed faith, because the man was an expert in dealing with various throat problems.

"Around about that time," says Red, "he was going to Dr. Boyer every day, and Dr. Boyer was doing a great job in clearing his throat. It got to be an obsession about going to Dr. Boyer, although there was no doubt the guy knew what he was doing. One night, after he had kept us up all day, we finally hit the sack. I took a sleeping pill and was just dozing off. It must have been about nine in the morning. I knew it was ridiculous to expect to get any sleep. Suddenly, I got a telephone call. He wanted to see Dr. Boyer right away. I may have said something like, 'Hey, man, you don't go on until tonight. What is the reason for getting it done so early?' Anyway, he was bugged or something. I told him I had just taken a sleeping pill, and he said, 'Well, go back to bed.' I knew the tone in which he said that. He was sort of saying I was letting him down. I said, 'No, I'm up. It's my job. I'm going with you.'

"I hurriedly got dressed and went down the hallway and into his suite. Sonny was there and he could see I was pissed off. Well, Elvis goes into his room and grabs his M 16. He says, 'I'm going to blow your fucking head off.' "

Red, despite his rough and readiness, doesn't resort all that much to heavy swearing, but he was angry. "Shoot, you motherfucker," he said, "go ahead, shoot. . . . We only have one life to give you. Shoot."

Sonny West was trying to calm everyone down.

Red was madder than hell, and there was this man pointing an M 16 gun at him. "I thought something was really going down," Sonny recalls. "Red was angry and Elvis had the gun and he is bugged. Then the next moment, Elvis turns away and winks at me, like it was nothing at all. That's how quick that guy can change."

It was after that incident that Presley dictated a long, rambling letter to Red on philosophy and psychic strengths.

About six months later, a similar confrontation took place, once again between Presley and Red West. Presley had finished a show and was holding court in his suite at the hotel. There were five or six women in his suite. There was no romantic interest involved. Presley was simply showing them his karate tricks. One woman, a married lady, was entranced by the show of karate and asked Presley how he did it. In the ensuing demonstration, Presley broke the girl's ankle, completely by accident. Sonny and Red remember the girl limping from the bedroom trying not to cause a fuss. One of the main reasons, of course, was that her husband did not know she was in the suite, and she didn't want him to know, lest the incident be misinterpreted.

Whether Presley was aware he had broken the girl's ankle is not clear, but both Red and Sonny recall he made no effort to inquire about her well-being. She did have an operation which involved having a pin placed in her ankle, and at one point there was some question whether or not she would sue Presley. But before there was any talk of a suit, Red recalls, he had to run interference to keep the girl's husband away from Presley. She had eventually told her husband what had happened, and he wanted to straighten a few things out.

"The bad night started in the showroom of the Vegas Hilton. It was 1974. I'm backstage. Now Elvis has this thing of throwing scarfs out to the audience.

This night this girl had a scarf of her own, and she threw it to Elvis and he would throw it back to her. This went on and on. I guess she wanted him to come over and kiss her. Well, he was high. He threw the scarf back at her and told her not to throw it again. He started walking off stage, and she threw it again and it hit him right on the shoulder . . . no big thing. . . . I saw this and I mentioned it to the security guard, who stopped it. But Elvis was really mad.

"Down in the dressing room he called us all in—now there was a security guard there while all this was going on—and he said, 'How come somebody didn't stop that chick? . . .' I told Elvis if I had gone out there and taken a scarf away from a girl, it would have looked bad . . . I would have made a fool of myself. All he had to do was keep the damn thing and the whole thing would have stopped there. That's what I said to him but no more than just that. Well, when we got in the suite, he blew up. 'Goddamn, don't you ever talk back to me in front of a security guard. You work for me.' He went apeshit."

Presley called Red everything in the dictionary of swear words and insults. "You red-headed cocksucker, you motherfucker." No man had ever called Red West those names and stayed with both feet firmly planted on the ground for too long. Red was sitting on a stool at the bar of the suite and Sonny West was there, once again seeing an ugly situation develop. There was enough adrenaline pumping to light up a dozen city halls. Sonny had a bottle of water in his hand and said what he thought to be soothing words: "Oh, come on, Elvis."

Presley flared. "You stay out of this," he said, knocking the water from Sonny's hand. "You never talk back to me in front of those guards." Red tried to explain that he wasn't talking back, just trying to say the way it was.

"I was shocked," Red remembers. "The whole group

was in there while he was swearing at me. Nobody has ever called me those names."

When Red continued to try to explain, Presley reached for his long-barreled .22 Savage revolver, which was on his hip. Sonny recalls: "Red was starting to go white and I saw it in his eyes, he was just this far off coming off the stool and decking Elvis. Elvis was about to pull that gun out and Red says, 'Don't do it, Elvis. Don't pull that gun.' And Elvis stopped dead, because he knew Red was ready to go to war and kick ass. But he wanted to pull it. He couldn't have got it out fast enough, but something in him saw something in Red's eyes."

Red says that he just sat there and took it. "I knew if I had got off that stool that would have been the end of my job and security for my family. I thought, hell, let the crazy fool get it all out. Then I told him, 'The husband is out here looking for you. We've been trying to keep him away. You know, the husband of the gal whose ankle you broke in a karate demonstration?'

"And he yells back, 'Where is the motherfucker? Bring him up here.' His father, Vernon, was trying to cool him down, but Elvis was so high and so bugged nobody could talk to him. And all the time he is wearing this gun on his hip. It was a hairy situation. Jerry Schilling tried to talk to him and Elvis said, 'Get the fuck out of here.' Jerry didn't take too much of Elvis's shit either, and he just walked out of the room."

Later in a calmer moment, Presley did face the situation of the girl whose ankle he'd broken. She signed a release not to sue. Presley paid all hospital bills and picked up the tab for her and her husband and some friends to see the show and stay at the hotel.

Despite the obvious results that Presley's pill-taking binges have, he seems to learn very little from his excesses. In August, 1975, he canceled out on his Las

Vegas schedule after two appearances. Red relates: "Joe Esposito called and said that an ambulance had taken Elvis away. . . . He had taken so much of something that it had affected his breathing. I was at home in Memphis when Joe called me. They said it was exhaustion or pneumonia. I had seen those breathing problems before."

When Presley canceled out in Vegas, there was a problem. At one point he wanted to cancel right before a show, after the people were seated. It was typical that Colonel Tom told him, according to Sonny, "I can get you out of the shows tomorrow, and we are going to have to make good the money. But I'm not going out there now that the people are seated and tell them you're not appearing. If you want to do it, go get your daddy to go out there on stage and tell them." Sonny recalls that nobody was too keen to do that. Presley went on that night, and the Colonel told him to clear out of Vegas if he was sick and cancel his remaining shows.

Red West remembers what started the whole situation. Sonny was in Vegas waiting, and Red, Charlie Hodge and Presley were to arrive on a Jet Commander private plane. Presley had bought the plane only four or five days before the engagement.

"On the plane he took some of his pills," Red says. "He started to get very hyper. He was in the back of the plane." Suddenly Presley yelled, "I can't breathe! Drop the oxygen mask, drop the oxygen mask." Red recalls that his boss was gasping and that he and Charlie Hodge got very apprehensive. The oxygen mask didn't seem to do Presley any good. "His breathing was badly messed up," says Red. "About that time I noticed an air vent on the floor, and there was a lot of air coming out. Well, I told Elvis to lie down on the floor and put his face over the air vent where the air was whooshing through."

Then Red and Charlie heard words from Presley that shot them through with fear. "I'm not going to

198

make it," he gasped. "Land." An emergency landing was made in Dallas, and Presley and Red and Charlie went to a motel for five hours while the pilot changed planes. "He was okay soon after that," says Red. "The effects of the pill had worn off."

Sonny and Red say that they have seen Presley wiped out on the painkiller Demerol, complete with head nodding and slack jaw. They recall that on one such jag, it was suggested that someone take a photograph of him so that he could see what he looked like at those times.

All of them agree if it had not been for the eagle eye of Dr. George Nichopoulos, Presley may have had a lot more trouble with drugs. Both Red and Sonny say that Dr. Nick, like Joe Esposito, would often take capsules and drugs that Presley had had smuggled in and replace them with harmless vitamins. Dr. Sidney Boyer, who treated him for his throat problems, and Dr. Ghanem were not as close to Presley and probably knew nothing of his abuses.

Red, Sonny and Dave have all seen Presley in a complete stupor from his pill-taking. "There have been," says Sonny, "actual shows that he has done that he can't remember. The audience must know something is going on. Sometimes he gets up there and talks and talks to the audience instead of singing. He will give his philosophies on life and it's very boring. People go there to see the old Elvis magic.

"One night he did a damn karate exhibition for twenty-eight minutes straight in Las Vegas. People were walking out all over the place. I never saw a word in the press about it. He lives a charmed life. Sometimes, he will forget the sequence of songs, and he will forget the lyrics to songs. Other times there are songs scheduled to be sung, and he will just refuse to do them." On the other hand, says Dave Hebler, "when he is straight and he is slimmed down and he is just going on his own energy, there is no showman like him on earth. He is a born performer."

The whole Memphis Mafia knows about Presley's incessant and potentially dangerous habit of taking every conceivable kind of upper, downer and tranquilizer. And there are others who know, to some degree, about Presley's pill-popping habits—two undercover narcotics detectives.

While on tour in the various cities, Presley, with his passion for anything to do with police work or playing cops and robbers, often had very close contacts with the local cops. There were several detectives in the Denver Police Department whom Presley got particularly close to.

Colonel Tom always had close contacts with cops throughout the country. If the city concerned would allow cops to moonlight, he would often recruit them to help out in security work, paying exactly the same rates the city would. This practice always promoted good relations between Presley's entourage and the local police. The detectives that Presley got to know in Denver introduced him to some undercover narcotics policemen, who, by virtue of their job, will remain anonymous. Red relates: "Wherever you go you can pretty much assess what kind of a police department a city has got. These Denver cops—and Sonny and Dave can back me up—are about as sharp and as professional as you will find anywhere in the country. They are sharp, straight, and there is no nonsense, no corruption. Well, we had been in Vail, and Elvis somehow got this really heavy painkilling stuff. He had the prescription. Don't ask me how he got it, because it will mean we have to put someone on the spot. Anyway, in Denver he had this infection from an ingrown toenail. Now the police doctor comes along, who is introduced by these two narc cops. Now the cops don't know at this time anything about Elvis's habit. But then Elvis asks for a heavy painkiller, and the police doc won't give it to him. Then, the police doc shows this prescription that Elvis has to the undercover cops. Now the cops know that this is very very heavy stuff. When the cops see this, they start to wonder."

The narc cops kept a close eye on Presley. Suddenly they noticed his highs and lows—and they are experts at this. Presley was entertaining them lavishly, but the undercover police were getting uneasy—Presley seemed to be getting high. Dave Hebler recalls that both detectives mentioned their observations to him and Red. They were evasive, but it was obvious the cat was out of the bag. Nothing was said to Presley. He left Denver, but returned a few weeks later, in February 1976.

Dave Hebler picks up the story: "Now we go into Denver and we check into a hotel. It's at this point these two undercover cops have a talk with Elvis about what they thought was going down. Well, we hadn't been in that hotel more than two hours when all of a sudden we're leaving. Elvis tells us we have to go into Las Vegas and not to bother bringing our stuff.

"The reason he is leaving is that the police had talked to him about going into a sanitarium and drying out and that he was a complete embarrassment to them because they were narcotics officers and he's stoned out of his mind. He's stoned out of his mind and flaunting it right in front of them. You know, this is kicking them right in the chest."

Red West adds: "It must be stressed that these guys told Elvis that no one would know; it would be handled right. They would oversee this drying-out process personally. His answer was, 'You think I'm hooked. You think I can't handle it myself. I'm strong enough to take care of it. I'm strong enough to get off the stuff.' Now these cops had seen all these pills, and they knew he was taking all sorts of stuff that would screw him up. They couldn't live with themselves that Elvis was doing this to himself, because they liked him a lot. They felt the same way we felt about him. We just wanted to see him straight, that's all. The greatest present that anyone could give me was to tell me that Elvis Presley is straight, slim and handsome and just the same as when I knew him way back. A lot of what went on was as much our fault as it was his because we would indulge him like a child."

Dave Hebler relates: "God, that man can sometimes act like he is a two-year-old. Sometimes, you think you are looking after a child. You can't help love the guy, but it gets you so pissed off at him."

There was a time in 1975 when Red, risking Presley's wrath, decided to have a heart-to-heart talk with him about how he had changed. Red treated him as if he were his kid brother, although Presley is eighteen months older than he.

"This night he wasn't high. He had taken a tranquilizer, and I just sort of came out with it, because when you start to think of all the gifts he has bought us and all the good deeds he has done, it's hard to just sit there and take it without caring for the guy. I mean, man, I love the guy. There were times I felt like beating the shit out of him, but there is no getting past it: I love him even if he doesn't love me. This night I told him that all the shit he was swallowing had changed his personality. I told him I wished he could get back to like he was in the old days. Well, he surprised the hell out of me. He didn't flash with anger, he just said quietly, 'Yeah, I agree with you.' And he didn't have too much to say that night. So I thought I had done a really good deed. I left with tears in my eyes and all that jazz. I was a bit emotional and I thought, well, things may be different from now on. The good old fun days are going to come back.

"The next morning I get up, and he is on the couch in the suite at the Hilton and I ordered breakfast for him. I knew something was bugging him. I could see his face. He was building up to something. He said to nobody in particular, but I knew it was aimed at me, 'So, I'm not myself any more, huh? Goddamnit.

I don't want to hear all that shit. . . . I wish people would stay out of my personal life. I'm going to do what the fuck I want to do. I don't need anybody preaching to me.'

"At this time I moved out into the kitchen. I was mad. He had been stewing on that talk all night and suddenly he does a complete reversal thing. I was so mad I punched the refrigerator, and he follows me out and he has calmed down and he says, 'What do you think I give you guys all these gifts for? It's to make up for the hell I put you through, for the work you guys do. That's why I give you these gifts.'

"I replied, 'Yeah, but the talk we had last night didn't mean anything, right? It was just going in one ear and out the other.' And he said, 'I'm going to do what I want to do and that's the way it is.' At that stage, I gave up on him. I never talked to him about the drug stuff ever again."

In Las Vegas, in the inner circles, rumors about Presley flew thick and fast. Vegas is a small town and secrets are hard to keep. Some of the rumors were half true; a lot of them were outrageously inaccurate. But the boys did their best to keep the rumors to a minimum.

Sonny West remembers a time when there was a particularly bad rumor going around, but one that wasn't far from the truth. Still, he felt it was his job to take any steps necessary to have it quashed. "Jackie Wilson, the singer, was a good friend of ours. He was a very nice dude, and the people who worked for him were very close to us. Anyway, one of the guys who knew him called me up and told me there was something he wanted to talk to me about. Well, I went over to the Flamingo Hotel, where Jackie was playing, and this guy who knew Jackie introduces me to two guys. They were from New York, if you know what I mean.

"This was at the end of 1973, and Elvis used to get a lot of massages from a guy who worked for one of the hotels. I won't say which hotel because that would identify him. But this guy used to get a hundred-dollar tip from Elvis every time he massaged him. Also, Elvis would sign a chit and it was in triplicate. This guy not only got paid and tipped, but he had a scheme where he would present the bill twice, until I caught up with him. So, he was a con man right from the word go. I'll just call this guy 'Big Bill' (which is not his real name).

"Anyway, it seems that one of these guys from New York was getting a massage, and this Big Bill starts shooting his mouth off to him that he has massaged Elvis Presley and that he is a head [drug-taker]. My mind gets buzzing, and I think, if Big Bill told a perfect stranger this, how many people has he told? Well, the guy who knew Jackie Wilson says that he is telling me this because he knows how much Jackie Wilson loves Elvis and I thank him for his concern. Now one of the guys from New York is pretty heavy, if you know what I mean.

"He says to me, 'How do you want to handle this? If you have any problems, call me, and I will take care of it.' I mean, Big Bill was out in the desert outside Vegas if I had given the word to this guy. I could have very easily given the word. All I had to do was call up and say 'Do it.' Someone in that city would have done that guy in, and they may have found his body in the desert. . . . It would have been another unsolved case of finding a body in the desert. . . . But I didn't want any of that stuff—that was going too far. But we had to shut the guy up. Anyway, I got the telephone number of Big Bill and I called him.

"I said, 'Could I speak to Big Bill?' He answered the telephone and then I said, 'You don't know me. I'm just telling you. You have been shooting your mouth off about a certain celebrity that used to give you a one-hundred-dollar tip, and you have been talking about how he is a head . . . and I tell you now, stop it, man, or you are gone.' I then hung up.

"Elvis didn't tell me to do it. I was acting on my own. In fact, I never told him about it. I just handled it that way because there was no use getting him upset over something if it could be handled."

Red says it was often best to keep a lot of their talk away from Presley because he would often do things to test a person's loyalty. "I remember," says Red, "one time we were in a hotel in Colorado, and he called my room and told me to come see him, that there was something he wanted to talk to me about. Well, I got straight to his room and Elvis is lying out of it on the floor. I thought, Oh well, he just whacked himself out with something. So I undressed him and put him to bed. Just lifted him up and put him in bed and covered him up. But later I got to thinking. When he spoke to me on the telephone, he was completely straight, like he hadn't taken a thing, and I got to that room in less than a couple of minutes. Now no drug hits you that hard. So then I suspected that he wasn't asleep or out of it at all. He was wide awake and just faking it, just to see how I would handle him. He tested us a lot of times like that.

"He always wanted to know if we were really dedicated to him. . . . Of course in those days, there was very little any one of us wouldn't have done for him."

# 17

No matter how many women Elvis Presley has had in the past and no matter how many he may have in the future, it is clear there is only one woman to whom he will always have a strong romantic attraction. And that woman is petite, sophisticated Priscilla Beaulieu Presley. They both had genuine love for each other, and even though she left Presley for another man, no other man has had as lasting an influence in her growth as Elvis Presley. After all the glossy fan-magazine pictures and stories are digested, it must be remembered that Presley virtually raised Priscilla from the time she was a fifteen-year-old schoolgirl until they finally split in an explosion of anger, selfishness and misunderstanding.

The Presley "groupies" who chart both lives from day to day, often theorize that eventually, when Presley is sixty and Priscilla is fifty, after a lifetime of "doing their own thing" apart, they may reunite. It is not an altogether bizarre theory. There is an incredible bond of loyalty between them, as well as their beautiful daughter. Neither will permit a word to be said against the other.

Presley met Priscilla in Germany, in the closing months of his army service. Red recalls: "I had got back to Memphis before Elvis. I was sort of causing a bit too much trouble in the bars, and I was getting nowhere fast. I left soon after a brawl in the Beck's Beer Bar with some bully they called the 'Mexican Bull.' "

One of the customers who watched Red's demolition of the "Mexican Bull" that night was Joe Esposito, the sharp-witted recruit from Chicago who was later to pick up with Presley and become "one of the boys." "Diamond Joe" was impressed with Red's action and in later years was only too happy to let him head up the "Royal Bodyguard."

Presley returned to Fort Dix, New Jersey, on March 3, 1960. Col. Tom Parker had stoked the fires of publicity to hysterical proportions. Only World War III could have kept Presley off the front pages that day.

Within a week, he was back in Graceland and had swapped his army boots for his blue suede shoes. Red, who was in Los Angeles at the time writing songs, soon made his way back to the Presley mecca in White Haven. "He had a girl friend at the time," says Red, "and I won't mention her name because what Elvis said to us all just might embarrass her. But he said, 'It's about time I got a girl who was a bit more sharp.'

"We didn't know what he meant, but after a while he kept on talking about this girl Priscilla he met in Germany after I left. When he told me she wasn't yet fifteen, I nearly had a heart attack. He assured me that this girl was different, much different from the average Memphis girl, and I was prepared to disbelieve him. Anyway, she had been introduced to him by a guy in Special Services by the name of Curry Grant.

"Elvis started to talk more and more about this girl as the year wore on. And I believe he even wrote her a letter, which I can tell you is almost unheard of for Elvis. A lot of things were happening. We started our movie schedules, kicking off with *G.I. Blues,* and . . . we would always bring girls over to him. It's not that we were procuring, but he was still a little shy about making the first approach. That night they would be in bed. That charm, man, it just dripped off him. But he still always got back to talking about Priscilla.

"We were having a lot of fun those days in Memphis, when we weren't in Hollywood. Sonny had joined the gang, and we were at Wimpy Adam's amusement park riding the cars and the roller coasters, and we were skating like fools at the Rainbow Skating Rink."

Despite the many women Presley was seeing, he always harked back to the little girl in Germany. He made several long-distance telephone calls to her. And to the boys, Red, Sonny, Lamar Fike, Charlie Hodge, his cousin Gene Smith, Alan Fortas, and a new addition, the Yankee, Joe Esposito, it seemed their boss was finally in love. Presley arranged for Priscilla —daughter of an Air Force captain who was later to become a colonel—to visit him over Christmas, 1960. Presley wanted to see just whether he was indeed in love, or whether he was just smitten by a fresh and beautiful schoolgirl.

Sonny was at Graceland at the time. "Elvis went to the airport alone to greet her," he says, "and all the boys were in the living room at Graceland. We didn't know what to expect, but we were Southern boys, and a fifteen-year-old girl in Memphis was someone who giggled and talked about a boy's acne. Anyway, that afternoon, just before Christmas, he walks in with her. Man, she was everything he had said she was. She looked much older than fifteen, but not in a cheap way—she was very mature-looking.

"She had been a child in the service and had lived all over. She knew nothing about men, hadn't any experience with them from what I know, but she seemed every bit as mature as all of us guys put together. Elvis had made arrangements with Priscilla's dad that his daughter would stay in Vernon's house. Vern was living with Dee in another house across from the back of Elvis's house at Graceland. There was a pasture and then Vern's house. The whole time she was there, about two weeks, it was a very quiet event. Dinners at home, small parties with the boys, and I guess we went to the amusement park and the movies, but no wild times. Priscilla had a very easy way with her. She had a nice easy laugh. She was neither over-awed with Elvis and the boys nor uppity. She was just right. Man, she fit in perfectly. There was no doubt that Elvis had got himself a great chick."

After Priscilla returned to Germany, Presley polled the boys on their reaction to her. It was the early days of the Memphis Mafia, and it was a lot more demo-cratic than in years to come—members of the entourage didn't necessarily say what they thought Presley wanted to hear. However, to a man they agreed that Priscilla was the greatest thing since fried chicken. Presley was quite impressed at their reaction.

Sonny remembers that Presley made up his mind he couldn't go on living in the States if she was going to live in Germany with her parents. "He started making arrangements," says Sonny, "to have her come back to the States. He spent a lot of time talking to her father on the telephone. Now Captain Beaulieu was a pretty smart customer. He wasn't suddenly going to let his daughter wander off and take up with a sex symbol, just like that. Elvis really had to pour it on. Elvis told her father that he needed her, loved her and would respect her in every way that her father wanted her respected. He told him that he would marry her one day, and he undertook to put her through school. He would tell us that Priscilla was the one he wanted, because he thought he deserved something better than the girls he was running around with in Hollywood."

Presley finally won over Captain Beaulieu. It was decided that Priscilla would live with Vernon and Dee and that Presley would put her through school. The boys were out in force to meet her at the airport when she arrived, and Sonny remembers she looked even better the second time around. Red saw her soon after. "I was in the kitchen at Graceland, and I saw her there—wow—every bit as good as the build-up. The great thing about her was her easy manners. You always felt easy with her. She did look a lot older than fifteen, and she spoke a lot older, very sophisticated."

Priscilla was a Catholic, so Presley had her enrolled at the school of the Immaculate Conception, which stood on the corner of Park and Lamar Avenues. The boys used to call it "Virginity Row."

At the beginning of her school days, Presley would often drive her to school in one of his huge fleet of cars. For the South in those days, it was somewhat bizarre, but there was very little comment in the press. Once again the skilled hand of Col. Tom Parker was felt. Red and Sonny are still amazed that more was not made of the romance by the press. Even the fan magazines trod fairly lightly. Colonel Tom convinced everybody that Priscilla was living with Vernon and Dee, and that absolutely everything was above board.

As soon as Priscilla was old enough to drive, Presley bought her first a Corvair and then a lavender Chevy sports coupe. She lived in a mansion, she had the best schooling, everything money could buy—and the sex symbol of all sex symbols as her romancer. What more could she want? As the years went on and Priscilla's personality developed, she found there was much more in life than just riches. She was, she realized—right up until 1972—a virtual prisoner in a gilded cage.

Presley always kept Priscilla on a pedestal. "It was like everything he does," says Sonny. "He got what he wanted, put it away in storage, and went on to something else. Priscilla could have anything she wanted, but the thing she wanted most was Elvis. In the last couple of years she was with him, he was away from her eighty-five percent of the time. She wouldn't see him for seven weeks at a time. Then they would spend the weekend together and then he was off again. She could buy all the clothes and jewels she wanted and Elvis would not have said a word, but she didn't want that. She was not a heavy spender when you think of other girls who have been around him. She just wanted a normal life. But toward the end, Elvis's life consisted of staying in bed all day getting swacked out of his head. There were times when we wouldn't see him for a week. He would just stay up in that room taking downers, watching television, and watching the closed-circuit television which covered the entire house. She didn't want that kind of life. Toward the end she wanted to do something with her days, get out and enjoy life. She didn't want to stay in a hotel room all day or the bedroom of Graceland all day, asleep."

But in earlier days, Presley lived with genuine vibrancy, even if it was helped along by popping a Dexedrine here and there. He had a lovely, irresponsible lust for life that never seemed to be satisfied. He was romancing several ladies in Hollywood on his various movie assignments, and he would even play a little in Memphis. The Memphis Mafia hung out in the back room of a place called Chennaults. It was especially cordoned off for them and there was plenty of action.

Red remembers that Presley couldn't care less about his various girl friends' knowing about each other. "But he was always careful never to throw up anything in Priscilla's face," he says. "Any suggestion that he was playing around was fiercely denied by Elvis. Later on, when the gossip columnists started picking up stuff, a lot of which was true, he would just deny it outright and call it all publicity and lies. He was very convincing, because by the time the columnists got onto a story about a girl he was seeing, he would be back in Memphis, and he would turn it around that these columnists had him out with a girl while he was at Priscilla's side. When she was younger, I guess she swallowed it, not so much later on. But in those days when he was with her and not running around Hollywood, he was very attentive, very affectionate."

Those early times at Graceland are thought of as the best years in the life of the Memphis Mafia. Presley was making up to three million dollars a year, and he was going to make sure it was spent on fun for him and the boys. Red and Sonny remember those years before he married Priscilla as Presley's "cowboy period." It was the beginning of some very bizarre buying habits.

"Well," says Red with more than a hint of nostalgia in his voice, "it started off with Elvis buying Priscilla a horse. Now she didn't have anyone to ride with, so Elvis bought his cousin Patsy Presley a horse so she could ride with her. Then he bought himself one. And when he saw us looking on forlornly at them riding horses, he decided we all should have horses. He bought every one of us a horse."

Graceland had only thirteen acres, and when Red once accidentally ran Presley down on horseback and dislocated cartilage in his chest, Presley decided it was time to get a special place for the horses so they could ride them without running each other down.

He found a nice little place across the Mississippi border, not too far from Graceland. It was a beautiful estate of one hundred and fifty rolling acres, owned by a local rancher named Jack Adams. He paid in excess of a half a million dollars for it. It had a gleaming lake with tributaries running off it and picturesque bridges —the works.

"Now," says Red, "he decides we all should have chaps and cowboy hats. And we were going to be ranchers. We had to have cattle, so he bought some cattle that were developed by King Ranch. He didn't know how valuable they were, but they were really prime cattle. Now every ranch has to have a truck, so he bought a Dodge truck. Then all hell broke loose. He started buying trucks for everybody. All the boys, they all had these ranch trucks. Rancheros, Cameros, El Caminos, I think Sonny remembers the price—

ninety-seven thousand dollars' worth of trucks in one buying spree.

"When word spread about this, there were truck salesmen lined up outside the ranch. He called the ranch Rising Sun. Outside of the place there was every kind of salesman in the world. We would try to stop him from walking outside, literally try to force him from going out there, unless one of us was with him, because sure as hell he would buy something from them. All cash. He would sign for it and say, 'Give the bill to mah daddy.' I remember one salesman there had a great big three-stall truck you could haul horses in. Anyway, a guy comes down to survey the place, a very quiet kind of guy. He was just going about his business, and Elvis looks at this three-haul truck that he had no use for. He said to this surveyor, who he had never laid eyes on before, 'You like that truck?' The surveyor looks up sort of sleepy-eyed and says, 'What?' Elvis just gestures to the salesman to make out a slip, and he gives it to the guy and says, 'Take it, man, it's yours.' The surveyor nearly dropped dead on the spot. I think he sold it for cash the next day."

Sonny continues: "Alan Fortas tells me of a funny anecdote. They are standing in front of the ranch, and all these truck salesmen are there. Elvis goes out with Alan Fortas. He looks at all these trucks, and he says to Alan, 'Take your pick,' pointing to these ranch trucks. Alan replies, 'But "E," I already have one.' Elvis then looks across at a salesman, who he doesn't even know is the salesman: 'Well, give it to him,' and Alan says to him, patiently, 'But he's got one, too.'

"So Elvis looks at Alan as if he is nuts and says, 'Well, hell, man, find some sonofabitch to give it to.'

"It was going on like that all the time. Show him something and he would buy it for someone. Now it didn't stop there." The Memphis Mafia, ten strong, led by Red and Sonny, would be at the ranch all day, racing their horses, drag racing their ranch trucks and keeping their spirits high with the little white pills Presley would generously dispense. But the tragedy was they had to go home at night and leave behind this fabulous toyland.

Red relates: "Elvis, when he was at the ranch, would stay in this very nice, very comfortable brick cottage in the northwest corner. Now for some reason one of the salesmen standing outside grabbed him and somehow sold him a trailer, not an ordinary trailer, a beautiful three-bedroom trailer that was more a house than anything else. In those days, in the middle sixties, I guess it cost over fifteen thousand. Well, that started it. We all got trailers. In no time he had bought eight trailers, at a tremendous cost, and they were all lined up in a row. Then he had a guy come out and put concrete under them and connect gas lines to them to make them permanent. We all moved in.

"We stayed at the ranch for days at an end. Some of us moved our wives in. It really was sensational. We raced horses all day, played at target practice with all his guns. Elvis had a beautiful gold palomino horse, which he called Sun, and to see him all pilled up riding that horse was like watching Lee Marvin on the horse in *Cat Ballou*. It was a scream."

"Long before communes, man," says Sonny, "Elvis wanted us to have a commune, a place where we could have all the fun in the world and not be bothered by anyone. He wanted to have a sort of Garden of Eden, just an ideal community. He was very happy there and so were we."

Red remembers that after the horse-buying spree, the truck-buying spree, and the trailer-buying spree, Presley decided he needed a tractor. At first he got a small tractor, but that wasn't powerful enough. Then he got a full-size farm tractor.

"We would put a saddle on the tractor and ride it around like madmen. Often a rider would get bucked off the saddle, and we would all have to run after the tractor, which had suddenly become a driverless runaway machine. We were all pilled up and slightly crazy, but there was nothing bad going down. If ever we were Elvis's disciples, then it was during that time just before he married Priscilla. Priscilla seemed to love the action and she liked all the boys."

In July 1961, Red married his wife, Pat. "Elvis came to the wedding half an hour late, and even then, at the wedding, he came loaded up with two guns in his waistband," Red says. "But we all thought it was a bit of a joke. Anything he did, we laughed at."

The spending sprees never let up, with Presley always paying cash. "His old man, Vernon, would just gasp when he got those bills. Elvis would laugh and say, 'Hell, man, there is plenty more where that came from.'"

Unlike other entertainers, Presley made no fancy tax shelters for himself. He has always let the Internal Revenue Service work out his tax return, and is probably the biggest individual taxpayer in the country. Red recalls that Presley always marveled at the case of Joe Louis, the fighter who made millions of dollars and woke up one morning to find that not only was he flat broke, he owed the Internal Revenue Service a fortune. "That ain't going to happen to me, man," Presley would always say.

"You must understand that while a big thing was made of Elizabeth Taylor getting a million dollars, Elvis was getting that for most of the pictures he made," says Sonny. "That money was just piling up there in the damn bank account into millions. Elvis could not spend it fast enough." A lot of the spending sprees would follow a pill-taking spree. Says Red: "It's like a compulsion burning away inside of him"—as when Elvis began by buying a horse and ended up buying the ranch.

When the boys weren't at Rising Sun or Graceland, they hung out with their boss in Hollywood while he was making films. In 1966, Presley took his gang to

Los Angeles and rented a huge place on Rocca Place in Bel Air. Priscilla was living with him on and off between trips to Memphis. On one particular night, Sonny was driving Presley in his custom-made Rolls-Royce limousine.

"We were going back to Rocca Place and it was one of those beautiful nights," he says, "warm and clear. Suddenly out of nowhere Elvis says, 'This would be a great night to be driving a convertible.' Bang, that was it. Now, it was in his mind to buy a convertible there and then. He tells me to turn around and go over to the Hillcrest Motor Company, on Wilshire Boulevard and Beverly Hills. We get out and there is this beautiful solid black Cadillac convertible. Elvis had it in his mind that he wanted a baby blue one. The dealer didn't have one but he referred us to another dealer, Lou Ehlers, further down on Wilshire, near Fairfax. Elvis got out and walked to the sales office while I parked the car. When I parked the car, Elvis was coming out of the sales office, and he came up to me as I was passing this gleaming black Eldorado convertible.

"Elvis said to me, 'What do you think of that one, Sonny?' and I said, 'God almighty, that is beautiful, that is beautiful.' It was polished and gleaming in the night light, and I thought that was the one maybe he chose to buy. Then he walks over and hands me a set of keys and said, 'It's yours.' I backed away and said, 'No way, boss, no way. Oh, no, I don't want you to do that.' Elvis just kept on laughing and saying 'Come on, Sonny, I want to give it to you.' I told him—and I could hardly speak because I was getting emotional and there were tears in my eyes—I said, 'It seems like you're always giving things to us, we're always taking and never giving nothing back in return.'

"He said, 'You're giving when you don't know you're giving. I have always had reports about you, Sonny, how you always speak up for me when I'm not around, and you never put me down. So I want you to have it, man. You deserve it.'

"I ended up accepting it. It was a beautiful car. Elvis then canceled his baby blue convertible and got a solid black one instead. 'I guess a baby blue one would be nice, but a car should always be black or white.' Elvis had got out of the pink stage and he only wanted blacks or whites." All the boys agreed with him, which was just as well, because the next day all hell broke loose again.

He bought Red a black convertible Eldorado; Alan Fortas a white Cadillac convertible; Jerry Schilling a white Cadillac convertible; Larry Geller, the hairdresser, a white Cadillac convertible; Richard Davis, his valet, a white Cadillac convertible; Marty Lacker, who helped Joe Esposito as foreman of the gang, a four-door Cadillac sedan, and Joe Esposito—the only one who broke the black-white barrier—a maroon Cadillac convertible.

Presley paid cash for them, and the gift taxes, giving them out as if he were giving away autographs. The next day at Rocca Place, Sonny remembers, was chaos. "Everybody was talking about their cars. There were some tough guys up there, but I saw a tear of emotion in every one of those guys that next day. Now on this occasion I don't think it would be fair to say that Elvis gave out all those gifts because he was bombed on pills. It was a genuine, generous gesture, a beautiful gesture. I remember him saying 'Man, when we were all poor kids in Memphis, there wasn't one of us who didn't say that one day we would have a Cadillac convertible. It was our dream. Well, now we have our dream come true.' When I think back to that, I still can choke up, because he was really giving, man."

Before the Cadillacs were the motorcycles. And that meant *everybody* would go through the motorbike stage. He bought twelve in one order. The store was so astonished, they demanded a telephone number to call back to because they thought the order might have been a hoax. On top of the motorbikes, Presley also bought a customized Greyhound bus for all the gang.

All through this time, of course, Priscilla Beaulieu was not only growing up, she was growing into a mature woman, and one who was not satisfied with being Elvis Presley's girl friend. She wanted marriage. Her parents were calling Presley to ask politely if he intended to behave honorably in the situation. Col. Tom Parker wasn't too happy, either. So far, he had manipulated the press beautifully, but how long would it last? For everyone's sake, Colonel Tom wanted "his boy Elvis" and Priscilla man and wife.

Presley had a long string of romances with well-known and not-so-well-known actresses, and both Red and Sonny remember overhearing several heated scenes between Presley and Priscilla.

Red says. "They had fights, like any normal couple, but she had a mind of her own. She had suspicions that he was running around with other women, but she never really caught him in the act. She was not going to be made a fool of, I can tell you."

Sonny remembers a battle royal in the rented Bel Air home in Rocca Place. "It was about the same time that Elvis was buying us cars and things. I always got the feeling that in the early days, Priscilla didn't like us hanging around as much as we did. She never said anything, but I guess she had arguments along the line that he spent more time with the boys than with her. Anyway, this argument was a beauty. He was ranting and she was really screaming. We were about three bedrooms away, but you could hear furniture and things falling all over. Elvis comes out, and he is extremely calm for someone who has been ranting and raving. He said quietly, 'I just told her to pack all her stuff and get the fuck out.'

"At this time he is helping her pack, throwing her clothes out of the closet onto the floor. Well, she is all packed and he walks in and says to her, 'Now unpack, goddamn it, you are not going anywhere.' He told us later that 'women can get you by the balls, you know.'

"He could make a person feel very insecure with that sort of stuff; he did it with us all the time, making you think that you were not in as tight as you might have thought you were. . . . It was a reverse psychology thing."

Both Red and Sonny believe that to some degree Presley was keeping Priscilla off balance so she would get acclimatized to the treatment when they got married. There is no doubt in either man's mind that Presley intended right along to get married, although, like most men in his situation, he was in no great hurry.

The boys never really got close to Priscilla. Not that she was standoffish; she wasn't. She was extremely pleasant. But they respected her position, and also they didn't want to exaggerate their already noticeable presence to a woman who perhaps couldn't be blamed if she wanted more of Presley to herself. Besides, the boys were simply having too much fun.

"When Elvis first took over Graceland," says Red, "there was a ritual that every New Year and every July Fourth, he would put on these fireworks displays. Actually, they weren't so much displays as they were fireworks wars."

Presley would divide the boys up into two sides, dress them in gloves, football helmets and motorcycle helmets, set them about twenty yards from each other and let the fireworks fly. Red and Sonny marvel that nobody was ever seriously injured, because they would level arsenals of rockets and Roman candles at each other and blast away at point-blank range for hours.

"I've backed into burning rockets and had my ass burned half off," Red says with a chuckle. "I've seen Elvis bending over a giant rocket and the thing go off while he is leaning over it, nearly blowing his fool head off. Sonny carries a scar on his chest to this day where one of us tried to blow a rocket through him.

Roman candles would blow up in our hands. The house caught fire twice in these battles, and one time Sonny had to knock a wall down with a sledgehammer to get a hose to the fire."

Vernon Presley would look on with some misgivings, to put it mildly. "He would just gasp with horror at our antics," says Red, "but Elvis was just having fun. Whatever would happen, he would say, 'Give Daddy the bill,' and there would be poor old Vernon going white. Old Vernon can be pretty tight with a buck, whereas Elvis just never thought about the price of anything. It was hilarious to see Vernon clap his hands to his head when he saw the spending and the damage and the waste and say, 'Oh, Lordie.' He could be a very funny dude without trying."

On one particular fireworks night, when everybody, including Priscilla, was standing around the kitchen, Vernon was the star of the show. Red recalls that Presley had bought little explosive pellets. "They were things that you threw on the ground and they would explode. Or you would put them under someone's feet, and when they stamped on them, they would explode. Well anyway, Vernon comes into the kitchen, and there is a little bowl of these things sitting on the table."

Sonny continues: "Well, now these things, I guess, in all these different colors look a little like M & M candies. Anyway, Vernon is standing there and talking to us important like and reaches behind him. He was making some serious point, and he threw them in his mouth, thinking they were candies. Well, man, you should have seen it. He chomped down on these little bitty things, and they exploded in his mouth. Man, the look on his face. He didn't know what was happening to him. First this explosion inside his head, and there is smoke boiling out of his mouth. He could not speak; his lips had been numbed by the shock, and he still doesn't know what he did wrong to deserve all this.

"When we found he wasn't hurt bad, just in shock,

we died laughing. I mean, right to this day when I picture that scene I nearly collapse. Vernon used to tell that story and when he told it, it was even funnier. You know, that night he stood next to that bowl the entire evening trying to get someone else to fall for it, but nobody did."

The fireworks wars, like the fairground and the skating rink, were opportunities to play out teenage fantasies that Presley could never afford when he was younger. One such fantasy, according to Red, is the compulsion to knock something down or smash it to pieces. "I remember after we all moved out to Grace-land and to the farm across the Mississippi border, there was a nice, neat wooden house, three bedrooms, built into the northeast corner of Graceland. This is where his uncle Travis Smith, the gatekeeper, used to live. Well, as soon as Elvis got these trailers for everybody, he just got it into his mind that he was going to wipe the cottage off the face of the earth. There was no reason to, because it was a real nice house, but Elvis said it had to go."

The morning after the decision was made Presley mounted his small bulldozer, but it was obvious that it couldn't do the job, so he hired a full-size construction bulldozer. Red recalls: "I got in the little one and Elvis got atop of the big one. He put a football helmet on for protection. I remember this day because Vernon Presley was sitting on the porch in a rocking chair doz-ing off. Elvis starts up the bulldozer and yells out to Vernon, 'You better move, Daddy.' Vernon asks why and Elvis says, 'Because I'm going to knock the god-damn house down.' Once again, Vernon gives one of those looks like 'Oh, Lordie,' but he doesn't say any-thing; he knows too well for that now, so he just gets up and Elvis starts roaring away. We also lit the house and it was blazing like hell and he just bores into it, destroys it. At one time I was in the little bulldozer and he was in the big one, and I look behind and the sonof-abitch is pushing me into the burning house while I'm on this little bulldozer. He was laughing his ass off. He was having a great time.

"Anyway, in less than an hour we have just knocked the whole superstructure down to where it drops right into the basement and it's burning up a storm. As the thing is going up in smoke, we hear a fire engine, and the next thing, this fireman sticks his head over the fence and asks what in hell's name we think we're doing.

"Elvis looks up at him with a look on his face which says it was a damn fool question to ask and says, 'We're burning down a house.' And the guy says, 'How did you do that?' and Elvis says, 'With a damn match.' Now the fireman wants to know why Elvis hadn't informed the fire department about our little fire, and Elvis ends the argument by telling him, 'Fuck you.' That was the end of the house and the argument. He had satisfied his fantasy."

Dave Hebler recalls that Presley had told him many times of a similar fantasy: "He told me that one thing he would really like is to get one of those big cranes with a big wrecking ball and just demolish a giant building. He really wants the power to build and to destroy at his whim."

In Hollywood mansions, movie locations, Graceland and the big spread in Mississippi, Presley and the Memphis Mafia were acting out the childhood dreams that they had nurtured for years. Finally there was money, homes, horses, cars, tractors, fireworks and guns to make it all a reality. There were very few cross words, and everyone got along as one happy family. Presley did have his outbursts of temper and his eccentricities, but what superstar—then or now—did not? Looming on the horizon, however, was the inevitable marriage. Colonel Beaulieu and Colonel Parker were to get their way. For Red West, the marriage triggered the first real rift between him and Presley.

"It was between the movies *Clambake* and *Speedway*,

and I was living in Beverly Glen in Los Angeles," says Red. "I was doing stunts and fight scenes in the movies for Elvis when we were told about the wedding.

"As always in these things, there was a meeting, and I was called at my house and we were all told to get ready to go to Las Vegas for the wedding. We all flew down, together with Marty Lacker and Joe Esposito, who were handling the business side of movies for Elvis, Lamar, Charlie Hodge, Gene Smith, Richard Davis, Vernon and Dee.

"We all check into the Aladdin Hotel in Vegas. I brought my wife, Pat, along too. Anyway, we're sitting around waiting for the call from Joe Esposito, who was in touch with the Colonel, who was making the arrangements.

"I'm sitting in my room and there is nothing happening. No telephone calls, nothing. So I go down to Joe Esposito's room, knock on the door, and he opens the door and he is all dressed up in his tux. I ask Joe what's going on. How come nobody has told me what time we're going to the wedding? Now Joe looks like he has swallowed a frog, and he tells me, 'You all aren't going to the wedding. You're going to go to the reception. Marty and I will be there, but you will all be at the reception.'

"I blew my fucking stack. I just went ape. I didn't care who heard me. I was really pissed off. The man brings us all the way to Las Vegas, and then we are told that we are not invited to the wedding. I suspected Joe and the Colonel had fixed this up. And Elvis wasn't being thoughtful enough to make sure what is going on. Boy, was I mad! I went back to the room and told Pat, and she broke down and cried. It was the thought of it, man. I wasn't interested in going to a reception. I wanted to be there at the time 'E' was getting married. I thought we were that close. I thought we loved each other. I had tears in my eyes and I was very emotional. I just stayed in the damn room and heard about the marriage on television. They were married by a Supreme Court Justice in a room at the Aladdin. What a kick in the teeth! I didn't go near the reception.

"As it turned out, I just wanted to get straight back on a plane to Los Angeles. As a matter of fact, I didn't even have any money on me, so I had to borrow fifty bucks from a Memphis jeweler who had come down to lay on the ring. As it happened, the plane I got was the same flight that the rest of the wedding party caught. I didn't say two words to anybody. Vern and Dee were on the plane and we didn't even exchange a glance. As it turned out, I just ignored Elvis for a month or so. He had got on another plane owned and piloted by Danny Kaye, the comedian. They went to Palm Springs for their honeymoon. Joe Esposito and Marty Lacker were Elvis's best men. I have nothing against either of those guys, but right then I felt like decking them. I couldn't help feel there was something behind it. Somehow, I couldn't help feel there was some kind of a conspiracy behind the whole thing. I don't know who did it; all I know, I was very hurt. Sonny was in Los Angeles at the time working on a movie, and I know he felt it was a pretty lousy deal. You know, coming from the South and seeing as how I thought I was important to Elvis, it was a big thing in my life. It was like not getting invited to your brother's wedding. I was sullen for a few days, and I called Charlie Hodge at the hotel where they were all staying. Charlie had joined up with Elvis by now and I'm on the phone saying, 'Who organized the damn thing, what went on?' Anyway, Charlie don't know nothing, but Elvis is sitting there while I'm talking and he gets on the phone.

" 'What the hell's going on, boy?' He starts in like that, and I yell back at him, 'What the fuck you mean, boy?'

"We were at each other, and after a while we both calmed down and we agreed to cool it and talk again later. It was then that I did a stint working stunts on

Bob Conrad's television show *Wild, Wild West*. But it all blew over and we got together after that. I was back on the payroll. In those days, in 1967, I guess I was making about two hundred and fifty bucks a week with Elvis."

After leaving Palm Springs, Presley decided to go to the Bahamas to extend the honeymoon. He thought it would be like another Las Vegas, but when he got there he didn't like it. He was particularly disturbed at what he believed was the tense racial situation. So he went on to Hawaii with Priscilla and Joe Esposito and Jerry Schilling. Presley had wanted to go to Europe, but the Colonel dissuaded him, because he did not want to take the luster off Presley should he ever do a tour of Europe. So far, that has not happened.

While in Hawaii, they attended a big karate tournament organized by Ed Parker, with whom Dave Hebler worked in the art. In the competition was a young man who was born in the islands, the champion karate expert for his height. He was a handsome, smiling young man, quiet in his manner, who stood five foot eleven and weighed about one hundred seventy-five pounds. His name was Mike Stone. Presley met him and congratulated him on his fine performance at the exhibition.

After his marriage, Presley, while affectionate and attentive, did everything possible to keep Priscilla away from his immediate places of work. She would come on location from time to time during his movies, but the handsome young superstar had a lot of extracurricular activities to take care of. There was a romance, both light and heavy, on virtually every film that Presley made. "He would give the girls the cold shoulder whenever Priscilla was around," says Sonny, "and he gave Priscilla a lot of respect, but there is no doubt that Elvis wanted to have his cake and eat it, too.

"In the beginning of Las Vegas and the tours, often the wives would be along. For instance, in Vegas on, say, a four-week engagement, the wives would come down for the opening weekend and then every weekend until he closed. Perhaps, they would stay around relaxing for a few days after the close, too. Priscilla was there with the wives and girlfriends. They were around quite a bit. But toward the end of their marriage, 1971 to 1972, Elvis cut it down just so the wives and girlfriends were there at opening and closing. Then he cut it down to the opening, and there were times when he wouldn't bring Priscilla out at all.

"When Priscilla didn't come, neither did the other wives and girlfriends. No woman, no matter who she is married to, is going to take that. There were times when he wouldn't see her for maybe seven weeks. How can a marriage last through that? It was a strain on the other guys, too. Joe Esposito's marriage broke up. So did Jerry Schilling's. I'm not saying they wouldn't have broken up anyway, but that separation had to contribute to it.

"I know that in 1975 my wife, Judy, and I separated. It was my own damn fault for just neglecting her. Elvis used to say to us, 'You got to get away from your wives and kids now and then.' But none of us wanted to. Priscilla was gradually getting more and more annoyed. He kept her in a doll's house, an ivory tower. He didn't want her hanging around the movie locations, because he heard that Hal Wallis, the man who produced most of his movies, had said that he would offer her a movie contract anytime she wanted it."

Presley, according to the West boys, did not like that talk. He didn't want his wife to have any career; a woman's place was in the home looking after her man—when he was home. Sonny reports that Presley and the ones around him who weren't married took every opportunity to take advantage of their special position in the show-business hierarchy. "Oh, hell, man, before I got married, I was into all that running around with Elvis. We had girls coming out of our ears. It's not very hard when you say you work for Elvis. God, the offers I got from women were incredible. And sure I took advantage of it all. Priscilla knew Elvis was playing around, and she knew the boys were playing around also.

"I remember one time, in 1970, we had a bunch of girls down in his place in Palm Springs . . . After about three or four days of this carrying on together, we split to Las Vegas. Now Priscilla and one of the wives went down there for a few days a week or so later, and naturally, like all women, they go through the mail. First of all, there is a letter to Elvis saying 'Thanks for the great three days. It was great. Let's do it again sometime.' Well, there is a similar note left for me. Something like 'Let's do it again,' and it was signed 'Lizard Tongue.' Well, Priscilla got on the telephone and crawled all over Elvis, and she wanted to know who 'Lizard Tongue' was. There were so many girls around then, I'm damned if I remember who it was who was supposed to be 'Lizard Tongue.' Elvis was laughing his head off, but when Priscilla started to crawl over him, he got right back at her and turned it around where she was almost apologizing for calling him. He told her that she should be more intelligent to take anything like that seriously with all the crazy fan mail he gets. I don't really know whether she believed it.

"But what I do know is that after I got married she told the story back to my wife, Judy, and intimated that we were all screwing around when we were on tour. For quite a while that put a bit of a strain between Priscilla and me. I didn't want her causing that kind of trouble. Also Judy, my wife, was under pressure. Whenever a new girl friend or wife came into the crowd, a couple of the other women in the group were always putting them to the test. What they wanted to know was whether Judy loved me or was she just in the group to try and get to Elvis. I mean, Judy respected Elvis and everything, thought he was a great showman and a good guy, but that sort of stuff was ridiculous.

"When we were living in the same home as Elvis in Los Angeles on Monovale Road, there was quite a bit of tension between Priscilla and Judy. One day I'm with Elvis, I think we were at the doctor's together. Anyway, we get this call and they are at each other's throats. Priscilla is threatening to use karate on Judy, and Judy is yelling that she doesn't care, go ahead and try it. So we raced up there to calm them down. Elvis thought it was pretty funny. It was just a case of two women being in the same house. Later on, after Priscilla left Elvis, she sort of apologized for the way she acted toward Judy. We realized that Priscilla was under a lot of pressure too."

In January of 1972, Presley was halfway through his act at the Hilton International Hotel Showroom, when he took a break to introduce some members of the audience, among whom was a rich and respected record producer—let's call him Bill Heck (which is not his real name). With him, acting as bodyguard-companion, was a handsome, well-built Hawaiian. His name was Mike Stone. Presley remembered him from Ed Parker's tournament in Hawaii, where he and Priscilla had been on their honeymoon. Presley gave him a lavish introduction and said with a smile of affection, "This man is the world champion bad guy. He is one of the greatest karate talents in the world. There is nobody like him."

Later Heck and Mike Stone came backstage. In Presley's dressing room were Red West, Sonny, Lamar, Presley, Priscilla and a few members of the band. The record producer, says Sonny, "was a weasel. He kept on boasting that he had the baddest bodyguard in the world, and he is kind of trying to build himself up on Mike's reputation. He's telling everybody that Mike Stone is a real killer. Mike is sitting there very quiet, and you could see this sort of talk is embarrassing the hell out of him."

Everybody in the room was embarrassed. Red and

Sonny felt like throwing Heck through a wall. Presley finally cut off the conversation by saying with a smile, "Karate don't beat a gun, man."

Mike Stone smiled politely and agreed, "You're right."

After a while Mr. Heck seemed to be aware that he was not welcome and left. The boys and Presley cornered Mike and started to talk enthusiastically about karate. Presley mentioned that he wanted Priscilla to learn karate, and in a loose sort of way it was agreed that Mike would give Priscilla lessons at the studio of Chuck Norris, a well-known owner of a big chain of karate studios. Presley invited Stone up to the Hilton with some other karate experts, and they showed some films of a tournament in Japan.

Throughout all these meetings, Stone was the essence of quiet humility. Occasionally he talked to Priscilla, and within about three weeks she became his karate student. Once or twice Stone dropped by the house while he was giving her karate lessons, but, Red recalls, there was nothing in his behavior to suggest a romance. Sonny says that all the meetings seemed very innocent. "But," he adds philosophically, "apparently at one stage or the other the karate lessons got a bit out of hand."

For his part, Presley had every reason to trust Priscilla. She had never given him the slightest cause for suspicion. Once, when he was on location for a movie, Priscilla had been taking modern dance lessons from a male dance teacher. It was a completely innocent association, but somehow a private detective close to the Presley camp took it upon himself to report to a Presley attorney that Priscilla was leaving the dance instructor's home in the early hours of the morning. The attorney reported this to Joe Esposito, who in turn faithfully relayed the information to Presley.

The West boys recall that Presley exploded. "He crawled all over Joe," says Sonny, "although Joe had nothing to do with it. He told Joe to tell the lawyer to keep his nose out of his wife's affairs and stop spying on her." Both West boys recall that Presley was secure in his trust.

The first hint that romance was blooming between Priscilla and Mike Stone came to Red from the maids. "I just started hearing a lot of shit. Nothing straight out but they were kind of letting me know that they had seen Mike up at the house a lot more than we figured." Red was certain they were having a romance and even bet Joe Esposito one hundred dollars to back up his theory. He won the bet.

Sonny was the next to get the drift of what was going on between them. "Some time after she started taking lessons from Mike Stone, she went off to Chuck Norris's studio one afternoon for her usual lesson. Anyway, that afternoon, Elvis wanted her for something and told me to get hold of her. We called Chuck's studio and she wasn't there. We were told she went to a karate tournament. We rang the place where the tournament was held and she wasn't there either. I had a feeling that it was about to come out. I told Elvis we couldn't get hold of her because Chuck's line was busy. I was just playing for time. I didn't want to be the one to start any trouble. Anyway, a little later the red light goes on in the main room of the house at Monovale Road. That meant somebody was at the gate. I figured it was Priscilla, so I beat everyone out there so I could tell her what was going down, sort of prepare a story, I suppose. I got to the gate, poked my head inside the car window and said, 'Elvis has been trying to find you. We called Chuck Norris's place and there was no answer. Take it from there.' She didn't say anything to me, but she got the message. She went into the den and he said, 'Where you been, Nungan?' That was his nickname for her. She just said, 'Oh, I went to a karate tournament.' He didn't question her and that was it. I think she saw right then that us guys were pretty loyal to her and weren't about to go tattletaling. She knew that we understood what she had been going through. He wasn't spending any time with her at all."

To Priscilla's credit, she was not going to have a romance behind Presley's back. Soon after, it was evident to the boys that she was close to Mike Stone. They remember the night in Las Vegas when she finally told him that it was all over between them.

Red recalls: "We weren't there, of course, but it appears she told him between shows at the Hilton. Priscilla and the wives—my wife, Pat, was there—were having dinner at Leonardo's, the Italian restaurant at the Hilton. I was with 'E' up in his room. He just told me, 'Go down and get Priscilla.' I went down and told her Elvis wanted to see her. Whatever happened up there, Priscilla later told my wife, Pat, that he made love to her—very forcefully. He took her right on the spot when he knew another man was in the picture."

After the show, Presley gathered the Memphis Mafia around him—Red, Sonny, Lamar, Charlie Hodge, Joe Esposito. It was a summit meeting. He told them, "Well, another man has taken my wife." Everybody was quite shocked at his direct speech. There was silence in the room. Red thought back to a time when Priscilla had asked Presley that she be allowed to come to Las Vegas more often to be with him, and Presley had said to Red, "I wish she would find someone else to mess around with and quit bugging me."

With that thought in mind, he tried now to save Presley's face a little in front of the boys. He said, "Hell, man, ain't that what you wanted?"

Presley replied somberly, "Not that way, man, not that way." The meeting broke up quietly and Presley went to bed.

Both West boys believe it took a lot of courage for Priscilla to tell Presley that she was leaving him for another man when she could have cheated on Presley indefinitely without anybody giving her away. "She could have screwed around on him," says Sonny. "I remember one night I came back from Las Vegas unexpectedly and was at the house. She came in and was shocked to see me. I looked outside and Mike Stone was driving her Mercedes. Priscilla was a bit embarrassed and said, 'You remember Mike, don't you?' We shook hands. She knew that I knew she was going with Mike, and she knew I hadn't informed on her, so she was secure. If she had wanted, she could have kept up that double life as long as she liked. But she was up front about it. She didn't want to make a fool of Elvis. I liked her for that."

Actually, although Priscilla had told Presley she was leaving him and that another man was involved with her, she did not say who the man was.

Red remembers one time when he was talking to Presley about the problem of the split in his marriage. "He was sort of thinking of where he went wrong," says Red. "Her leaving him really shook him up, believe me. He was saying to me, 'Man, I tried to give her all the freedom I could. Sometimes a man and a woman have to have their own lives. I gave her all the time she wanted. I encouraged her to take those karate lessons from Mike Stone and everything.' "

It was then that Red looked quizzically at his boss. "Man," he said, "don't you know that Mike Stone is the guy she is seeing?"

Presley paled and was silent for a long moment. Then he said, "Goddamn." He was the last one to know.

Later that year, in 1972, they officially separated, and in 1973, after a generous settlement, they got a divorce in Santa Monica Court. Presley left the divorce proceedings with his arm around her.

Many people believe that Priscilla and Presley are still very much in love. Nobody knows except the parties involved. But, it just might be true.

# 18

If a lot of Hollywood celebrities are amazed at the incredibly accurate information the police seem to have about their various drug habits, Sonny West believes he learned the secret one night in the fall of 1970. He was sitting in a private room of a famous Hollywood bistro with Presley and a very well-known show-business celebrity. With them was John O'Grady, a veteran anti-drug cop for the Los Angeles Police Department who had set up his own private investigation firm. Presley first met him when he hired O'Grady to help investigate charges brought against him by a young woman who claimed the superstar had fathered her child. O'Grady helped gather the evidence that had the case, rightfully, thrown out of court.

The Hollywood celebrity will remain anonymous for reasons which will become obvious. In the course of having a few drinks, this celebrity showed Presley something that brought a shine of envy to the superstar's eyes. It was a Federal Narcotics Bureau badge.

Together with his entertaining, the celebrity was a full-fledged undercover agent for the Federal Narcotics Bureau. Presley would perhaps have gladly given away half his fortune to exchange places with the man.

A psychiatrist would have a field day examining Presley's pathological obsession with uniforms and badges of authority. If there is anyone who has more police, sheriff, marshall and detective badges than Presley, then Sonny West, Red West and Dave Hebler would sure like to meet him because they believe Presley is the champion collector of all time. "As soon as Elvis saw that badge," Sonny says, "he was both surprised and very impressed. His mind started working right away. He wanted one."

Presley got his trusted private-eye friend O'Grady to see if he could organize such a badge for him. O'Grady managed to set up a meeting between Presley and the Deputy Narcotics Director, John Finlator. Sonny and Presley were back at Graceland, when Presley did something unprecedented. Sonny says: "He dashed out of the house to the airport with no bodyguards, no companion, nobody, and hopped on a commercial flight. . . . Now I never knew him to do that."

He visited Deputy Director Finlator under the pseudonym of John Burroughs. Despite the cover name, he arrived resplendent in a purple suit and cloak, gold belt buckle and amber sunglasses. While Jerry Schilling waited for him in the Federal Building, Presley volunteered to Finlator all the help he could give in the anti-drug campaign and offered there and then to donate five thousand dollars to the Narcotics Bureau.

Finlator explained that the Bureau wasn't permitted to accept donations. Presley showed him some of his police badges from various law-enforcement departments and asked whether he could have one from the Narcotics Bureau. Finlator regretfully declined. It was impossible, he said. However, he would be more than glad to issue him an honorary badge. Presley quietly insisted that only the real thing would do, but Finlator stood firm. Presley said he understood, and the meeting broke up amicably, with Finlator thanking him for his interest in the anti-drug drive.

"But Elvis was bugged," Sonny recalls. "He wanted the real thing, and nothing was going to stop him getting it. This is a case where Elvis was very resourceful."

Dressed in full regalia and driving in a chauffeured limousine, Presley arrived at the main gates of the White House and handed a note to one of the security guards. What the note contained is not known.

"But suddenly," says Sonny, "I get a call in Memphis from Jerry Schilling in Washington, and he says, 'Sonny, come to Washington right away. Elvis wants you.' I didn't ask any questions. I just got on the first plane out. I caught a taxi straight to the Washington Hotel, where Jerry and Elvis were staying.

"I was just paying off the taxi and Jerry comes out of the entrance. 'Sonny, we got to go. We're going to see the president of the United States.'

"I look at him. God almighty, the president of the United States! Elvis was coming to pick us up in a limousine."

Sonny got the taxi driver to organize his luggage with the hotel, and he waited for Presley. Sonny, Jerry and Presley then went in a limousine driven by a man called Ben to the rear entrance of the White House, where they were met by a man Sonny recalls as Jeff and another gentleman who later became better known during the Watergate scandal, "Bud" Egil Krogh.

Presley went with Krogh into the White House, and Sonny and Jerry went with the aide, Jeff, into the Federal Building. Sonny and Jerry were mentioning the prospect of meeting up with President Nixon. They knew their boss was seeing him at this very moment. The aide good-naturedly warned them that it might not be possible to see the president. He was, the aide said, a very busy man.

"If it's possible for us to see the president, Elvis will fix it," Sonny said confidently. Minutes later there was a call in the room where Sonny and Jerry were waiting.

The aide picked up the telephone, then looked up and said, "I'll be damned. It's all fixed. He's going to see you." Sonny and Jerry walked on cloud nine across to the Oval Office.

Sonny relates: "When we got there we just stood outside the door in a kind of shock. I mean, the president of the United States. We could see him sitting at his desk signing something. It was just like a movie. Elvis almost had to push us through the door. President Nixon looked up and said, real friendly like, 'Hello there.' Elvis introduced us. I didn't know where I was. President Nixon slapped me on the shoulders and said to Elvis, referring to me and Jerry, 'You've got a couple of big ones here.' Someone took a picture of us all there, and I didn't even notice anybody had taken it."

Presley seemed very much at home in the Oval Office, and he said, "Now, the president has got something for ya'll."

President Nixon returned to his desk and presented Sonny and Jerry with key rings and cufflinks with the presidential seal emblazoned on them. Presley wasn't shy when it came to the president. He said, "You know, Mr. President, they've got wives."

And the president, on Presley's prompting, gave them each a brooch with the presidential seal on it for their wives. In a daze Sonny and Jerry and Presley then left the office, after warm handshakes.

Before Sonny and Jerry had gotten to the office, President Nixon assured Presley he would get his federal narcotics badge. Presley smiled triumphantly at Sonny and Jerry and said, "Who said something can't be done?"

Bud Krogh called Deputy Director Finlator and said, "I heard you turned Presley down."

Finlator replied good-naturedly, "I sure as hell did. Okay, I've been reversed."

The badge impressed Presley. It was the kind of present that money couldn't buy. And he even had occasion to use it. The incident had to do with someone I'll call Bill (which is not his real name), one of Presley's sometime go-fers. The boys gave him a nickname—let's say it was "Fetchum Bill"—which he got from running for take-out food at the Memphian Theater when Presley hired it to show movies. Early in 1973, Presley put him on the payroll. It was like a dream come true for Fetchum Bill, who loved to play with the big boys. He talked nonstop about his expertise with guns and would snoop around like Columbo, eyeing everyone as if they were potential assassins. He desperately wanted to be a tough guy. He was returned to Memphis with a promise that if he behaved himself, he could come on the next trip to Las Vegas. Red and Sonny were a bit apprehensive about his joining up.

On the next trip to Vegas the boys were all staying at the Hilton, and at the end of the engagement Presley gave everyone a bonus. Fetchum Bill was given five hundred dollars, and he promptly lost it gambling, but he moaned loud and long that somebody stole his bonus. As was always the case in matters like this, Presley held a meeting and decided, very generously, to give him another five hundred dollars. Shortly thereafter, Fetchum Bill was suspected of forging Elvis's name to some of Elvis's personal checks, and was told to return to Memphis.

"About this time," says Sonny, "there were several rings of Elvis's missing, and we suspected Bill. Suddenly Bill comes up with one of these rings, a nineteen-thousand-dollar, thirty-carat sapphire that had been given to Elvis by the Sahara Tahoe for creating an attendance record. He said he had found it in his brief-case. He said he put it there for safety and had forgotten about it. Elvis didn't care about this particular ring, but the missing ring he really wanted was this big karate ring he had. We looked all over but couldn't find it. We talked to Bill about it, and he said he didn't know anything about it. We looked everywhere. So Bill left."

The next day the boys found the karate ring next to the laundry chute, laid inside some pipes. The finger of suspicion was pointed at Bill.

Presley stewed on it all night and by the morning had built up a rage against Fetchum Bill. He wanted to know where he was. Somebody said that Fetchum was scheduled to leave for Memphis at eleven that morning. It was then ten. Sonny recalls: "Elvis flared. He jumped up and said, 'We're going out to the airport to get that sonofabitch right now.'" Presley, Red West and a security guard from the hotel raced downstairs and jumped into a hotel car. Sonny, who was still dressing, chased on after them in another hotel car.

When the Presley party hit Las Vegas airport, they saw a big jet about to take off. Presley thought that Fetchum Bill was on the plane.

Red recalls: "He raced out on the damn tarmac as the plane was taxiing for a takeoff. Elvis just ran right up to the cockpit, and he flashed his badge that President Nixon gave him."

A quizzical expression crossed the face of the pilot. He recognized that it was Presley standing in front of his plane, and he recognized the federal narcotics badge. The gangplank lowered. Presley raced on board and tore through the plane looking for Fetchum Bill, but he couldn't find him. He raced off the plane and waved the pilot on his way. It is safe to say that the pilot must have been somewhat mystified.

In the meantime, Sonny had arrived at the airport and he saw Fetchum in the lobby. "I got him out to the car," he says, and "went through his suitcase. There was nothing there except the .357 Magnum gun, which I relieved him of. Just then Elvis, Red and the security guard came up."

Looking back today, the boys laugh at the spectacle, because Presley flashed his badge at Fetchum Bill and said, "Bill, you have the right to remain silent . . . and . . . and all the rest of that shit." Then, says Sonny with a laugh, since "he could not remember all the words that cops use when they are reading prisoners their rights, he just said, 'Get the fuck in the car.'"

Presley and the security guard got in one car, and

Sonny and Red took Fetchum Bill in the other car. Sonny was in front driving, and Red sat in the back. Red's right hand was covered by a coat. "He thought I was pointing a gun at him," says Red.

Sonny remembers the first thing Fetchum said was, "I guess you guys are going to do a number on me . . . I think you're taking me out to the desert for a ride . . . I already called my daddy and told him what plane I was catching to Memphis. If anything happens to me, he'll know."

Sonny and Red told him to shut up. Sonny relates: "I think he was relieved when we got back to the hotel. . . . I felt sorry for him, really, but he was a pretty spineless dude."

When Sonny, Red and Fetchum Bill returned to the hotel, Presley was already in his suite steaming mad. Sonny and Red sat on either side of Bill. Red had a gun trained on him. Presley started screaming at Bill who was stupid enough to say something back to him. That triggered an even blacker rage in Presley.

After a while Elvis calmed down and then he came out talking quietly and calmly to Bill. "We all felt sorry for him," says Sonny. "Strangely enough, the guy who felt sorriest for him, after he got it out of his system, was Elvis. . . . He was talking about hiring him back, but we talked him out of it because we could see a lot of problems down the road with Bill."

Finally, Presley shook his head and said, "Go on, Fetchum, go back to Memphis. Nobody is going to bother you no more. Just keep your mouth shut." When last heard of, he was working in a gas station.

In one morning, the moods of Presley had changed from Kojak to James Cagney to Barry Fitzgerald—cop, avenger, father-confessor.

It is February, 1976, and Red West is summoned to Presley's bedroom in Graceland. He knocks, enters and is taken aback at a huge arsenal of guns lying on the floor. "The floor was just covered with automatic weap-

239

ons, pistols, rifles, rockets. There was every kind of weapon there except tanks and bazookas. I've never seen so much hardware in my life."

Presley gestured for Red to sit down. Then he handed him a list of names, some head-and-shoulder photographs, and also some police-file pictures. "These sons of bitches need to be wiped out," he told Red.

Red blinked in disbelief. The names and pictures that Presley had were of Memphis drug pushers. One was a well-known hoodlum who owned a pool room in a very rough area.

"He had it all planned," says Red incredulously. "He wanted myself and Dave Hebler and Dick Grob, the former cop, to go out and lure them, and he said he was going to kill them."

Dave Hebler chips in: "He was making the album *Elvis at Home,* and the way he figured it, he wanted to go out on this 'Death Wish' mission while the musicians were downstairs. He wanted to go out the back way from his room, make the hit, and then come back and do his album."

Red relates: "He couldn't have cared less about that album; he was into all this cop stuff. He reckoned if we sneaked out while the musicians were there, made the hit and returned, it would never be traced back to him."

Sonny recalls giving a word of caution. "Man, the whole thing was damn madness. I told Elvis he was getting into something very heavy.

"He said, 'Hell, the cops want them.'" He said that he particularly wanted the black guy who knocked his stepbrother Rickey Stanley down with a pool cue. "He said he wanted to kill this guy personally. The rest he said he would give them a break if they surrendered."

When Sonny continued to point out that he was getting into something beyond his capabilities, Presley gave him the cold shoulder. "He didn't like you giving him any negative reactions to any of his ideas," says Sonny.

Sonny, Red and Dave don't try to explain the inconsistency between Presley's wanting to conduct a one-man war against drugs on the one hand, and on the other persisting in consuming drugs himself.

"It really was a pathetic macho game," says Dave. "It was Batman and Robin time. The thing is that we all played these games when we were six, but Elvis is still playing them . . . and with real guns that go bang."

Presley does have strong ties with the narcotics division of the Memphis Police Department. "He has visions of bringing to life *The French Connection,* with him in the title role," Dave continues. "One night he tells me that a Memphis narc cop is taking us on a drug bust." Presley says he has to go in disguise. First he takes his .22 caliber Savage revolver. Then he puts on a jumpsuit. Then over the jumpsuit he dons a snowsuit. Over his face he puts on a ski mask that had holes for the mouth and eyes. On top of this, he puts on a hat. To cap off the vision of the masked marvel, he then sticks a cigar in his mouth.

"Jesus," says Dave, "you may not have noticed him before, but now he looks like a damn neon sign. It took an amazing amount of self-control to keep myself from laughing. It was, honestly, one of the funniest things I have ever seen. It was hysterical. The narc cop arrives and doesn't take any notice of this bizarre outfit. In Memphis, they are pretty used to this sort of stuff from Elvis. Anyway, I get in the back of the narc's car, and Elvis and the cop are in the front. I am cracking up, man. I can't hold it in any longer. I had to pretend I was laughing at something else. Anyway, apparently the drug bust had already gone down. So we go into the police station. The sight of Elvis was wild, man. It was like I had fallen down a well, and there is a rabbit and he invited me on a raid and suddenly I made it to Wonderland.

"Apparently the drug bust when it happened was pretty funny. They grab these guys and they make a break for it. One of the cops goes to fire a shotgun and it doesn't go off, and then the getaway car runs over a cop's foot. Just as well Elvis wasn't there. In that crazy outfit, I don't think I could have controlled myself.

"At the police station, we sat around shooting the breeze to these cops, and Elvis was baking in that outfit. It was like a sauna bath. He gives the two suspects his Dirty Harry look, and that's about all that happened."

Sonny relates: "At the time in Memphis, there was an undercover cop called the 'Candy Man.' I'm sure Elvis wanted to get himself a tag, a nickname like that. He wanted to be the masked marvel on these drug busts, and then he would brag to his friends that he was the guy all the newspapers were talking about. Very strange."

On a trip to Vail, Colorado, around the same time in 1976, Presley's imagination ran riot. Dave Hebler recalls that Presley had been on another car-buying spree. Joe Esposito was there with his girlfriend; so were Dick Grob, Linda Thompson and two local policemen, Jerry Kennedy and Ron Petrofesso. Presley had bought both the policemen cars, and he purchased a new Cadillac for Joe Esposito's girlfriend and a Cadillac Seville for Linda Thompson, one of the many gifts he continues to shower on his sometimes live-in girlfriend.

"The next day," says Dave, "I was with Elvis in his bedroom and we were talking. He had bought the cars the previous day in Denver. He then told me in very confidential tones the real reason he went to Denver. He looked all shook up and said that he had been on a drug raid with the Denver narcotics police. Then he told the story about what happened on this raid. He said that they had these drug runners trapped and surrounded. Elvis was sneaking up on this one guy who was crouched behind a bush holding a sawed-off shotgun . . . one of the bad guys. . . . He got real close when the guy heard him . . . pointed the shotgun at him. . . . Whereupon, Elvis, with all his skill and agility, brushed the weapon aside, threw a horrendous karate chop and broke his neck with the blow.

"When he told me this, I reacted with shock, like *wow*. A little later on he told the story again."

Red recalls: "He told it individually to each one of us, and it was different each time."

Sonny adds: "When he told it to me, the guy was lying in the bushes with a rifle. This time Elvis sneaked up on him, grabbed him by the head and the neck snapped."

When Red heard the story, he found himself believing it at first because Presley told it with such conviction. Dave later talked to Dick Grob, with whom he was rooming. Dick had been on the trip to Denver.

"I asked Dick what he did the night before with Elvis," Dave recounts. "He told me that they bought some cars, had a sandwich and came back. I asked him whether Elvis or he had been on a drug raid, and he looked at me like I was out of my skull."

The fantasy was bound to be exploded, because there were so many people with Presley at all times. Presley couldn't have really believed that Red, Sonny and Dave would not find out the truth. Red believes that Presley had gone beyond the point of recognizing reality. "We have pampered him so long by all of us saying 'Sure, Elvis, you're right, that's what happened,' that he really doesn't care what he tells you. I can't explain it, but he isn't living in the real world. He probably knows we didn't believe him, but he still persisted with the story. He persisted with the story even though he told it different each time."

Apart from wanting to be supercop, there is in Presley a compulsion—not altogether a bad trait, but often an immature one—to be protector of the weak and the poor, a Robin Hood figure. Dave, Sonny and Red all have stories to demonstrate this fantasy.

Sonny recalls: "It was 1975 and we are in his Cadillac. Elvis was driving. We were in Memphis. We were coming down Poplar toward the freeway, going back to Graceland. It was late afternoon. As we were coming down the street, a police car comes in the opposite direction, siren going and lights flashing. The cop car passes us and whips a left turn at the street behind us. As soon as Elvis sees this, he flipped a U-turn, drove up on the sidewalk, back off the sidewalk onto the street, and takes off after the police car. We had gone maybe a mile, and the police car was parked outside this gas station. We pull in behind this police car. Elvis gets out and asks the cops what came down. Apparently the gas station had been robbed. Elvis is in his element talking cop talk to these policemen. Well, he stands around, intrigued at what's happening. Suddenly a big crowd sees the cops and Elvis, so they are all crowding around. I was leaning against the car watching all this. Elvis is talking to the cops, and he is signing autographs.

"This guy comes up to Elvis and he wants to talk. He tells Elvis that his wife had just got out of the hospital. He says that two guys beat up his wife. He was really down, and he wants to get even with these guys. Was there any way, he asks, that Elvis could help him. To my utter amazement, Elvis says, 'Yeah, sure. Give me the information. Don't you worry about it, buddy, it will be taken care of.' Well, Elvis is writing down this information, names, details and stuff. He writes down the names of the guys who supposedly beat up on this woman. Elvis assures him not to worry about a thing. It will all be taken care of. He signs a few more autographs and he gets back into the car. I thought Elvis was just going through the motions to keep the guy happy. I didn't think Elvis would give it another thought. I was wrong. He gets Red and me up to his room. He tells us, 'I want you and Dave to go out and contact this motherfucker. Find out where he is.' He wants us to beat the shit out of this guy. Elvis gave us an address to go see this lady. Well, we figure we will go through the motions of this bullshit.

"With a lot of difficulty, we find this woman. She lived in a trailer not too far away. Her husband must have called her and told her that Elvis was going to fix things, because she was expecting us."

Red says the first thing he expected was to see a woman who had been badly beaten up, but "there wasn't a mark on her."

Dave picks up the story. "After talking to her, it was pretty obvious that this chick was balling the guy who supposedly beat her up, and she made up some story for her husband. It was all crap. So we went back and laid it on Elvis. But he was expecting us to play lone avengers. Frankly, I wouldn't beat up any guy for someone else."

Sonny remembers a similar case. In 1971 Elvis dispatched him to look after a man who allegedly had been bothering the girl friend of Billy Stanley, Presley's stepbrother.

"He had complained," says Sonny, "that this big guy was hassling Billy and his girl friend. Elvis wanted me to take care of the guy, whip up on him. I went out to this house with Elvis, Billy and Lamar. I took my gun off and handed it to Lamar. I didn't want no gun to drop out on the ground if things got physical. If it did, I figured I could handle the guy with my fists. But when I saw this guy, it was pitiful. He was big, two-hundred forty pounds, but he was a slob. This guy wasn't about to cause any trouble. As a matter of fact, his daddy came out, and when he heard what was going on, he told his son to get back inside. The father was a little guy, but you knew he owned his son and he was going to whip him. And the whole thing was very embarrassing. I shouldn't have even got into it. Ricky and Billy Stanley had an ego thing about being Elvis's stepbrother. They sort of put out the word that if you fuck with the Presley boys, there are guys around him that's going to kick your head in.

"But they used to blow up their troubles with other guys when they talked to Elvis. Then they would really strut. A lot of the troubles they got into, they brought it on themselves."

Red West puts his hand to his head when he remembers something he got into because of two of Presley's stepbrothers, Ricky and Billy Stanley: "Something apparently went on in a bar near the Memphis Airport with the brothers around 1970. Ricky and Billy told Elvis they had been slapped around by a motorcycle gang in this bar. We are all at Elvis's house describing what happened. I learned later what did happen was that Billy owed these guys some money and wouldn't pay it, and they slapped him around a little. Elvis gets the thing all blown up. These guys jumped on his stepbrothers and beat the hell out of them for nothing. Anyway, he said he wanted it taken care of.

"I called up Bill Wallace in Memphis, who is the world middleweight karate champion, a nice guy and a tough guy. We went with Jerry Schilling over to this house where these guys lived. These guys have guns and knives and chains and things, and there is Bill Wallace and Jerry Schilling. We didn't count the Stanley boys, who were with us.

"So I took my gun off, like Sonny, and leave it in the car. Myself, Jerry and Bill go up to the house. When I got in the house, I wish I hadn't taken my gun off. There were three guys inside. They were prepared, for some reason. One guy is sitting on a couch, another guy is sitting in a chair and there was a third guy in the kitchen.

"I started to question them about this thing, and I said that the three of them slapped him around and that Ricky was waiting outside, and Ricky would be glad to oblige them in a fight one at a time. Ricky never wanted to, but in front of us he said he would. Bill Wallace is in the middle of the room, and there is a kung fu movie on and he is watching this damn TV session. Besides the guy on the couch there is this big 30.06 deer-hunting rifle and I'm looking at it. The third guy comes in from the kitchen, a big dude, and I asked him whether he slapped Ricky around and he says, 'I might have.'

"He went back to the refrigerator. Now Jerry Schilling in this instance was a bit slow. He should have got by that 30.06 rifle. Suddenly I hear Jerry say, 'Wait a minute, Red.' Then I hear this sickening click. That 30.06 was pointing right at my stomach. He says, 'This is my house and I'll kill you.' For the first time in my life I thought fast. I said to the guy with the gun, 'Go ahead.' Then I noticed these small windows along the top of the den of the house, and I used one of the oldest tricks in the trade. Looking at the window, I said, 'Billy, if he moves, kill the motherfucker.' The guy looks up and I say to him, 'Billy's outside and he's got a .45 pointed right at your head. You just move and you're gone.'

"Of course, there was nobody out there. But that's when it got worse because this guy starts shaking. He's trying to get the shell out of the chamber, and I was scared he was going to kill somebody accidentally because he's shaking so much. I didn't feel too good with that thing pointing at my belly. If he had pulled that trigger, it would have blown a hole in me a mile wide. As he is flipping the shells out of the chamber, Jerry is watching him, making sure they are all gone. Then he grabs the gun and *whop,* he slaps the hell out of the guy.

"Bill Wallace later said to me, 'Goddamn, man, don't call me again on one of these deals.' He recognized we all might have got our ass blown off just because of some fool idea of Elvis's.

"Of course, we could have refused to go. It was our fault that we went. But we felt a bit embarrassed about it later because I had an idea these guys weren't at fault. There could have been a whole panic shooting there. I later made myself a promise that I wouldn't go out on a limb for the Stanley boys again. I figured we worked for Elvis and took care of him, but no more Stanley boys.

"I can see that gun pointing at my belly to this day. It was a damn fool thing to get into, but it just goes to show you how we would react to Elvis's orders. I always figured if he wanted to be the avenger, he should go out and do this stuff himself. It's too easy to get killed. And for what? Just because you are taking orders. No, sir."

# 19

Elvis Presley's most consuming ambition was to become a movie star—a real movie star. Sadly, by his own standards, the thirty-three movies he made between 1956 and 1972 never accomplished that ambition. He regards most of them as "Presley Travelogues": they all followed the same script but on a different location. However, although the critics reviled them, millions of fans relished them, and the money men reveled in them. No Presley movie was a financial disaster. Maybe one or two scraped in just over the bottom line, but the vast majority made staggering fortunes.

Toward the end of his frantic film-making period, during which he would sometimes churn out three a year, Presley resented not being taken seriously by Hollywood. His talent has never really been tapped, and Hollywood today is the poorer for it. Nobody really knows why his film career did not grow to more substantial proportions. Some close to Presley felt that Col. Tom Parker was reluctant to take any risks with Presley's image; others feel that Hollywood just didn't think he could handle the heavier stuff.

But if artistically the movies were a drag for Presley, they provided a launching pad for a lot of fun times for Presley and the Memphis Mafia. It was *G.I. Blues,* the first movie after his return from the service, that sparked the beginning of the Memphis Mafia as an entity.

It was April, 1960. Presley had just returned from the Fontainebleau Hotel where the Colonel had pulled off a staggering fee for him to appear on the "Timex Special" produced by and starring Frank Sinatra. Sonny West remembers: "He got one hundred twenty-five thousand dollars to sing two and a half songs. He sang 'Fame and Fortune' and 'Stuck On You,' and then his half a song was when he harmonized a number with Sinatra. That money was the most that anyone had ever paid for two and a half songs."

Whether by design or accident, the clan had started to gather in Memphis that month. Diamond Joe Esposito, the Chicago-born recruit Presley met in the army, was there. Presley put him on the payroll at sixty-five dollars a week to be his foreman. Ever-lovable Lamar Fike was there; he had been put on the payroll at thirty-five dollars a week. Gene Smith, Presley's cousin, was put on the payroll at thirty-five dollars, as was Sonny. They were to join Col. Tom Parker, Parker's assistant, Tom Diskin, and Freddie Bienstock, a producer for Hill and Range, on a special club car—hired for $2,500—that would take them to Hollywood. Red West was already there, working with Nick Adams on *The Rebel.* He was to work on location in *G.I. Blues* as stand-in and stuntman.

A huge crowd of well-wishers gathered at the Memphis station to bid farewell. Among them was Charlie Hodge, the rhythm guitarist, whom Presley had met on the boat to Germany.

Sonny remembers that Charlie Hodge looked forlorn. He had got very close to Presley, and this seemed like the last good-bye. "Charlie was standing on the platform and we were already on the back of the train," says Sonny. "He looked downcast and sad. Just before the train pulled out, it was evident to everybody that we were leaving Charlie behind."

Presley looked at Charlie and said, "Charlie, you sonofagun, what are you doing there? You want to come with us?"

Charlie replied in surprise, "What do you mean? I don't even have anything with me, no luggage, nothing."

Presley laughed and said, "C'mon, get your ass on here. We'll get your stuff shipped out there. Get on board." Charlie's face lit up and he jumped on board. The gang was complete. Everybody hugged everybody. In the years to come, others would join the group— Jerry Schilling, Alan Fortas, Cliff Gleaves, Richard Davis, Dick Grob, Marty Lacker. All of them at one time or another would have their flare-ups with Presley; some would leave, only to cool down and once again return to the fold. But on that April day in 1960, the charter members of the Memphis Mafia came together. Sonny recalls fondly: "I guess you could say we were a bunch of hicks. I had a crewcut and I had a tooth missing, which got knocked out in a fight. I was a toothless, crew-cut sonofabitch. There was a great warmth between us. No pettiness, just a bunch of young guys setting out for some excitement and going to conquer the world. It was fantastic, and the guy who was most fantastic was Elvis. I had quit my job in Memphis at the Ace Appliance store and I had traded my jeans and T-shirt uniform for some suits and shirts and ties that Elvis had given me. Man, we thought we were something."

The Colonel had wired ahead to all of the towns that the train was going to stop in. At each stop, the crowds were gigantic, frenzied. Presley would go to the platform at the back of the train and sign autographs while the Colonel dispensed pictures and Presley memorabilia. The fans grabbed at Presley's shoes, his legs, clutched his hands, tried to tear at his clothes, and pledged undying loyalty.

"The Colonel knew it would be good for Elvis to get back with the fans around him. Elvis loved it. He was being loved all over again. The two years away hadn't made anyone forget him. They loved him more. He had to take all the rings off his fingers, or the fans would have ripped his hands off. That was a great ride," says Sonny.

To Sonny West and the rest of the guys, Hollywood was all it was cracked up to be. "When we arrived," says Sonny, "it was all a bit of a dream. I remember we stayed in the Beverly Wilshire and in the lobby there was this shop. Myself and Gene went down there— and do you know they had a hairbrush selling for five hundred dollars? When I first saw it, I honestly thought the shop was selling for five hundred dollars and, God almighty, when I realized they were selling the brush for that price, I nearly died. I asked the lady about it and when she said that was the right price, I thought it must have belonged to Errol Flynn or some famous movie star.

"We really played the part. We would all dress in these dark suits and we would drive Elvis's maroon Cadillac convertible. We all wore shades and we would drive down Sunset Strip with the top down like we were millionaires. I'm sure if anybody had seen us, they wouldn't have believed we were boys from Memphis making thirty-five dollars a week. I started to let my crew cut grow out. I used to put that grease on it and tried to train it into a Tony Curtis hairstyle. Gene Smith, man, that guy was funny. He used to wear makeup. He thought all the movie stars wore makeup all the time. He had this stuff that would make him look real tanned. He was a very funny guy. His job was to look after Elvis's kit and his clothes, but if anyone asked him what he did, he would say, 'I don't do a goddamn thing. I'm Elvis Presley's cousin.' The thing is, we all played up this Memphis Mafia role, but we were young kids and who could blame us. We weren't doing nothing wrong except having a good time."

When they got to Paramount Studios, they were even more overawed. Names that they had seen on the local movie marquees were all over the place. They couldn't believe what they had fallen into.

Norman Taurog, the man behind the camera in a lot of Presley movies, won the respect, admiration and friendship of all the Memphis Mafia. Among all the movie people who came in contact with the Memphis boys, Taurog seemed to have a special understanding of them, their pranks and their dedication to Presley.

When Presley and the boys first met Juliet Prowse, who starred opposite Presley in *G.I. Blues,* she seemed to put them at arm's length. "She was a very cool lady," recalls Red. "She had that English-type accent and at first we all thought she was a bit standoffish. Actually, she was a pretty nice chick. But I guess at first when she saw all these wild men from Memphis, she probably thought, What the hell is this all about? Anyway, Elvis started to break down this coolness with his professional country-boy charm, real polite, real sincere."

"But," says Sonny, "we weren't too convinced about his sincerity when we heard him discuss the situation later."

At the time, Juliet, a sensational-looking dancer from South Africa, was going with Frank Sinatra. Many gossip columnists tipped that she would be his next wife. As pranking material, this was too much of a good thing for the boys to pass up. During breaks in shooting, Presley would always take Juliet into his dressing room—"Maybe he was showing her his karate chops," muses Red—and most of the boys would hang around outside. Red West would take the opportunity to bang on the door and yell, "Hey, Elvis, quick, here comes Frank! He's on the set." At first, Presley would open the door and peek outside to see if this was true.

At noon one day, the inevitable happened. Sure enough, weaving his way elegantly through the lights, cameras and wires came Frank Sinatra. As usual, he looked as if he had just stepped out of a tailor shop. He wore a flattop Panama hat with a colored bandanna around it, and he was heading toward the dressing room. Red nearly swallowed his Adam's apple. "Hey, Elvis, here comes Frank! I mean it, man, he's on the set!"

He banged on the door, but the only response he got from Presley was "Aw, Red, fuck you." Sonny remembers Sinatra as being very dapper and very cool. He walked directly to the dressing room. The Memphis boys held their breath. Sinatra knocked quietly on the door and Presley emerged, just as cool.

Sinatra stepped into the dressing room and remained there for about ten minutes, presumably passing the time of day. "Afterwards," recalls Sonny, "Elvis laughed about it. He said, 'Goddamn, man, the one time you guys banged on the door and there he was. It was Frank Sinatra.' " For some time during the filming and for a time afterwards, Presley dated Juliet Prowse. Nothing came of the wedding to Frank Sinatra. The boys remember that Elvis was dating Tuesday Weld at the same time. He was beginning to get the hang of how they did things in Hollywood.

The Memphis Mafia, although some of the press described them as go-fers or hangers-on, all had jobs to perform when they were around Presley. Joe Esposito was extremely efficient as a foreman, particularly on movies, where he would organize all the schedules, call sheets, and the scripting for Presley. Red would often help out with the music. He and Sonny worked stunts, and did stand-ins. Gene Smith looked after Presley's wardrobe as if it were his own. Lamar Fike would involve himself in transport, and Charlie Hodge would help out at odd jobs and on the music.

During *G.I. Blues,* Sonny's main task was to work as Presley's karate dummy. "He really started getting into it and he would like to show off this new art. I would act as the fall guy. That meant I would do the falling for his blows . . . and that meant anywhere, in a hotel room, dressing room, wooden floor or concrete floor. Man, there were days I ached. But I got to admit it was fun."

Karate in those days was a mystery art to the Memphis boys. Red and Sonny remember that Presley was in perfect physical condition. Sonny relates: "Hell, yes, man, he was doing it right. Beautiful condition. And, man, he was as handsome as you could imagine." Presley did a little karate in the fight scenes, Red remembers, and he was very impressive, which was certainly attributable to his fitness, although he wasn't slowed down any by the pills that he and the boys were popping.

Soon after *G.I. Blues,* Presley swung into *Flaming Star,* in which he played a half-breed Indian caught between the white settlers and the Kiowas in a bloody Indian uprising. Presley was like a one-man army, knocking people unconscious, shooting others and stabbing the rest. One of the Indians he stabbed was played by Red West. Hollywood was beginning to get an idea of what it was going to be like on a Presley movie. He might not win an Oscar, but he was going to have fun.

"Hell, man," says Red, "we were into everything. We were doing karate demonstrations all over the studio. Throwing each other around, busting boards with our hands, partying at night in the house he rented on Perugia Way. He was screwing himself silly, and when we weren't horseplaying on set, we were playing football in a little park at Beverly Glen."

Presley got the respect of the wranglers on that movie where he insisted on riding a maverick horse himself. If Producer Weisbart had developed an ulcer, it would've been understandable. Elvis's chances of injury were increased still further by the half-dozen games of football he played on the weekends. Red remembers meeting Robert Conrad, Ty Hardin, Ricky Nelson, Kent McCord, David Parks and Gary Lockwood on the football field, and also Pat Boone, who loved to play with the boys. "Whenever Pat came down to play, however," says Red, "his wife was always ten minutes behind him and she would drag his ass off the field. Shirley was her name. A sweet lady, but she always thought of something for Pat to do whenever he played with us. I don't think she was too keen on him playing with us, although he loved it. All these actors, a lot of them surprised me, especially Bob Conrad and Gary Lockwood. None of them was scared of getting their faces messed up. They were tough."

The Memphis Mafia expanded or contracted, depending on what "good ole boy" took Presley's fancy or who dropped in from Memphis. But at this stage something cast a pall over the boys: there was a thief in their midst. Some money was missing from Joe Esposito's room, and a diamond wristwatch was missing from Presley's jewel box. "It was a difficult time for me," says Sonny, "because I had been looking after his jewel box, and somehow I felt the finger of suspicion pointed at me. Elvis made it clear he couldn't tolerate a thief in his midst and I couldn't blame him. It was a bad scene, and at one stage I thought that Elvis was going to drop me from the crowd."

Through an ingenious idea of the Colonel's, the thief was discovered, and Sonny was relieved of any suspicion.

Meanwhile, thieves notwithstanding, the money was piling up in Presley's bank account. The *G.I. Blues* album was a million seller, and the singles from it broke all sales records.

But before Presley, or the Colonel, for that matter, had time to count their money, Presley was back before the cameras for his third movie in 1960, *Wild in the Country*. Glenn Tyler, played by Presley, gets into a fight with his drunken brother. The brother was Red West. "And once again, he knocks me on my ass," says Red with a laugh. "I ended up on my back in most of Elvis's movies. Can't remember when I did win a fight."

Presley sang "Lonely Man," "I Slipped I Stumbled I Fell," "Wild in the Country," and "In My Way."

Red West got knocked on his backside, Sonny West played a small part in the movie, and Presley and the Colonel made another fortune from the record releases as well as the movie fee.

The only unhappy note was that Elvis had some very ugly boils on his rear end during the filming. The movie was shot in the Napa wine-growing district, and Presley broke habit and got drunk twice, once to ease the pain of the boils and another time when he had to play a tipsy scene with Tuesday Weld. Both thought they would sacrifice a little sobriety for the sake of making the scene more realistic.

Hope Lange heard that Presley was suffering, and she appeared at his motel room one day. Sonny recalls that Presley was lying naked on his stomach with hot washclothes on his rear end and a sheet covering him. "She came in and said hi to him and wanted to know what was wrong. He told her, and damn if she didn't lift up the sheet and say, 'Where?' Elvis was as embarrassed as hell and grabbed for the sheet to cover himself.

"He yelled out 'Whoa, there!' He was still pretty shy about things like that, but it was obvious that Hope Lange was a grown woman who was not trying to sneak a peak. She was genuinely concerned. So he showed her his boils on his butt when he realized that she was concerned, and she looked and said, 'My goodness!' But it was funny to see his first reaction. He had a bit of wine in him and his inhibitions were gone. But he was still a country boy at heart."

At that time, Presley was going with a very pretty wardrobe girl called Nancy Sharp from St. Louis, Missouri. "This girl," says Sonny, "was very talented, very intelligent, and Elvis was so serious about her that he actually went to Missouri to meet her parents. Anyway, this leads up to the first time I ever saw Elvis pull a gun. We convinced Elvis to go to San Francisco for a break. We took the big white 1960 Cadillac he had bought, and he was sitting with Nancy in the back propped up on pillows. We're driving along the expressway and a car pulls up on the right side of us and there were a lot of young guys in it and they started giving us the finger. I don't think they saw Elvis. They were just doing it because we were driving a big fancy car. Anyway, Elvis tells me to catch up with them and I do. Suddenly he pulls down the rear window and he pulls out this derringer and points it right at the driver's head. I looked at it in shock. I didn't think he was going to shoot the guy, but it was a helluva shock. Anyway, those guys just zoomed off the next ramp. Elvis then said, 'That will teach that sonofabitch not to give anyone the finger because someone is driving a big car.'"

By 1961, when Presley went before the cameras to shoot *Blue Hawaii*, he had accomplished most men's dreams. He had a beautiful, fresh schoolgirl in Memphis named Priscilla Beaulieu, who was cut off from the action in Hollywood but was always waiting faithfully for him in Memphis. He was a millionaire, he traveled deluxe, he was surrounded by a group of the most dedicated men this side of the C.I.A., and had had more action with the ladies on movie locations and parties at his various houses than any four men could handle.

*Blue Hawaii* made buckets of money for everyone. The sound-track recording alone sold over six and a half million dollars worth of long-playing records. The title song was another million seller.

Sonny has special memories of *Blue Hawaii* for two reasons. He was involved in a drunken real-life comedy scene; and it led to a rupture between him and Presley. The movie itself was the first to become known as the "Presley-style beach movie." Again, a thin plot, exotic locations and a legion of Hollywood bit-part actresses in extravagant musical scenes. It was directed by Norman Taurog, which added to the fun because he indulged the Memphis Mafia in their roughhouse behavior.

"We were doing some shooting on an outer island in Kauai," says Sonny. "It was beautiful. We were all into the karate thing and Elvis and Red are breaking boards all over the beach with their hands. I don't think there was a piece of driftwood on that beach that wasn't cut in two. Anyway, there was not a great deal to do where we were. The meals were served in this big dining room, which was open on one side with a lagoon running almost alongside it. Across the sidewalk from the dining room, there was a bar. One night while Elvis and the boys were eating dinner, I skipped dinner and walked across to the bar. I started talking to a couple of girls, trying to promote them with my best country-boy act. In the end all I did was succeed in getting pretty drunk on too many Mai Tais. Man, they were dynamite!

"Anyway, I walked the girls back to their room and was walking back to the dining room-bar complex when I saw something that really grabbed me. There was this pretty little bridge across the lagoon. Now the bridge faced the open dining room. On this bridge there was a very attractive man and woman and they were singing the 'Hawaiian Wedding Song.' Well, this grabbed me, man. Just two lovers singing this song on a bridge in the middle of this beautiful island. I thought that was fantastic. So I walked up the bridge and I put my arms around both their shoulders, wanting to be a part of this wonderful scene. I sang along with them and they were beautiful singers. Now, as a singer, I'm a good football player. I can't sing worth a damn, but they went along with it and I'm just singing along in this beautiful scene."

What Sonny didn't know—was not capable of knowing because of his overconsumption of Mai Tais—was that the couple singing on the bridge were part of the floor show entertaining the diners. Oblivious to the screams of laughter from the diners, Sonny just kept on singing. Presley and all the boys were in stitches, realizing that he had crashed the floor show unwittingly. "I didn't remember too much about it," says Sonny. "I do remember that a lot of people came out laughing at me and this one woman who stormed up to me, mad as hell, and said, 'Young man, you have ruined my fifteenth wedding anniversary!' "

Despite Presley's amusement at the scene, he told Joe Esposito and Red West to keep Sonny away from his table. He didn't want anybody to know that the "Memphis Minstrel" was a member of his party. Red, under orders, gently took Sonny, singing merrily, to his bed. The next day, according to Sonny, the freeze set in from Presley. "He gave me the cold shoulder, and he is telling all the crew what I had done as if it was a big crime instead of something that was quite amusing. I started to think that he was a pretty phony bastard. On one hand he is laughing his head off and on the other he gives me the freeze. He was on my ass for the rest of the movie and sort of kept me at a distance."

The culmination came when the boys all got back to the mainland, at Presley's house on Perugia Way, the one that had been owned by the shah of Iran.

"One night we are up at the house," says Sonny, "and there is Tuesday Weld up there and this girl friend of hers called Kay. Well, Elvis was going with Tuesday, so I started to try to promote this Kay, a nice-looking girl. We had all been drinking a bit, so had Elvis. Alan Fortas was up at the house and so was Gene Smith. Tuesday and Elvis are on the couch and I am talking to this girl, Kay. Elvis leans over and kisses her and says, 'You're really cute.' Well, I knew that was the end of me trying to score with this chick, because whatever Elvis wants in the way of women, he gets, no matter if you're trying to score. He has Tuesday there and he wants this girl, too. Later on he comes over and really plants a kiss on her. So I go over to the corner of the room and start talking to Gene. I said something like 'If you had your choice, Gene, which girl would you go for?' And he says, 'Tuesday, man, she's beautiful,' and she was, really pretty."

Presley couldn't hear what Sonny said, but for some reason he got it into his head that Sonny was talking disparagingly about him. He stopped kissing and cuddling the girl and said, "What did you say, Sonny?" Sonny was mystified. He didn't know what Elvis was talking about. Again: "Goddamn it, you said something about me and I want to know what it was." Sonny flushed with embarrassment. He didn't know what to say. He didn't want to have to admit in front of the girls that he was discussing which girl was more attractive. Presley got up and walked over to Sonny, reached for a bottle of Coke, and said, "Tell me or I'll break your goddamn head open with this bottle."

Sonny stared long and hard at Presley. "You're not going to hit me with no bottle. I've had enough of this shit. . . . I quit!"

Presley got angrier. "You can't quit. I fire you." Sonny started angrily for the door. Presley walked in front of him and they started shouting at each other. "Then," said Sonny, "he drew back and punched me in the face. I didn't move. I didn't even feel the blow, but I could feel the tears of emotion coming out of my eyes, and I said quietly, 'I didn't think you could do that to me.' "

When Sonny went to his room and started to pack, Presley followed him, obviously repentant. Tuesday Weld came up to Sonny and apologized for bringing the girl to the house in the first place, since it caused the trouble and cost him his job. Presley asked Sonny if he had any money and handed him two hundred dollars. He added there would be more coming from his father, Vernon Presley. Now Presley seemed to have regretted what he had done, but it wasn't in him to apologize. He wanted to know where Sonny was going to live and what he was going to do. Sonny now feels that Presley didn't want him to go. He knew he had been in the wrong, victim of an insane temper made worse by booze. But Sonny was firm. "I told you, I quit and I'm getting out." Presley followed Sonny to his car with his luggage. It was a scene that was to typify Presley's behavior over the years: a blind rage, then striking out at someone he loves, followed immediately by regret. But there was never a word of apology. Perhaps he felt his apology came in the form of exotic gifts, and, of course, there were many of those.

Two weeks later, the studio shooting for *Blue Hawaii* was being finished and Sonny went over to the set at Paramount. The guards didn't know that he was no longer working for Presley, and they waved him through. As was the custom when Presley put someone in cold storage, the rest of the boys followed suit. They were cool to him. "I know about it because I must admit that when one of the other guys had a flare-up with Elvis, I did the same thing. If you're on the outer with Elvis then everybody puts you on the outer. Elvis came off the set and sort of slowed down when he came up to me." He gave me a big hello and Sonny replied, "Hi, boss, how you doing?" Presley motioned to Sonny to come into his portable dressing room. Joe Esposito was there, and Presley asked Joe for them to be left alone.

Presley looked at Sonny in the dressing-room mirror and started to laugh. "Sonny, you sonofabitch." Sonny started to laugh, too.

"Me, a sonofabitch?" he said. "It wouldn't have happened if you hadn't been drinking." They both broke up laughing.

Presley gave Sonny the opening to ask for his job back, but Sonny didn't bite. "What do you want to do, Sonny?"

Sonny replied, "Well, I was thinking of hanging around and trying to get some work in the movies but I know it's pretty hard."

Presley just said, "All right, okay." The next thing Sonny knew was that Presley had got him in the screen extras guild.

"There was a long list of people trying to get in the union, but Elvis, being who he was, just fixed it straightaway. He went out of his way to do a favor for me even though we had our flare-up. He didn't say he was sorry. But that was his way of apologizing, I guess."

Sonny stayed in Hollywood doing odd work on the movies while Presley and the Memphis Mafia, including Red West, took off for Florida to do the 1962 release, *Follow That Dream.* "It pretty much followed the same pattern," says Red. "Priscilla was in Memphis, Elvis dated his leading lady and I, as usual, ended up in the movie getting knocked on my ass."

With the shooting of *Kid Galahad* that same year, Sonny returned to the Memphis Mafia a full member in good standing. He acted as Presley's karate dummy during the filming, in Palm Springs. Red did some scenes in the boxing ring with Presley and took the usual falls. He also got a damaged eye when Presley poked a thumb in his face during one scene. It was the first time that Sonny and Red had met Charles Bronson, whom they liked, both for his quiet dignity and for the masterly performance he gave. "But," recalls Sonny, "Elvis just didn't go for him." Oddly enough, the rift between them was caused by Presley's incessant desire to impress everyone with his karate. Today Bronson is an accomplished karate expert, but the boys remember that in those days he wasn't too impressed with Presley's physical performances between takes.

Sonny recalls: "He was a very quiet kind of guy, a loner, and he just didn't think Elvis was that big a deal. Elvis hated this and he was always putting him down. He used to call him a muscle-bound smart aleck and a muscle-bound ape. Just never stopped putting him down, although I never heard Bronson knock Elvis." Watching the movie, however, one would suspect there was a tremendous rapport between the two, which the West boys attribute to Bronson's sterling professionalism.

Both Sonny and Red took a shine to Gig Young, too. Red relates: "He was a funny dude. He was married to Elizabeth Montgomery at the time and she was a real looker. Gig had a great sense of humor, just dry as a twig, very funny. I remember one time when Gig was having a few drinks and Elvis came up to him as he was looking at Elizabeth dancing in the hotel. Elvis said, 'Man, I have a new Rolls-Royce. I'll trade you for her.' Gig smiled quietly, looked up from his drink and said, 'Not bad, the Rolls-Royce is a newer model.' "

When things got quiet on the set, comic relief was provided by the latter-day P.T. Barnum, Col. Tom Parker.

Sonny recalls: "He had a thing where he would hypnotize me and get me to do crazy things. Now, I wasn't in a trance and I knew what I was doing, but I did them just the same, some really nutty things that always had people in stitches. I would just do whatever he told me. I was hypnotized.

"Now there was this director, Phil Karlson, who was very accomplished. He was directing *Kid Galahad,* and the Colonel just hypnotized me in front of the crew to go up and start abusing Karlson. I was an extra on the movie and what do extras know about directing? Well, under the Colonel's hypnosis, I knew a lot about directing. I went straight up to Mr. Karlson and started ranting and raving to him that this was the worst picture I had ever been associated with, that he was an incompetent director and the whole production was a disgrace.

"Well, Mr. Karlson looks at me long and hard. He hardly knew me, and here I am telling him he doesn't know what he is doing. He is looking at me like I've gone mad. His first assistant turns to the Colonel and says, 'Hey, who is this guy, who in the hell does he think he is?' Well, the crew, the Colonel and Elvis are dying laughing. Then the Colonel snaps me out of the hypnosis and I go about my work as quiet and polite as could be. Mr. Karlson really thought he had a nut case on his hands until he learned about the power of the Colonel's hypnosis."

Sonny and Red recall that the Colonel would often do mass hypnosis on the Memphis Mafia. "He would make us all get down on all fours and tell us that we were dogs. And he would have us barking and yelping like dogs and snapping at each other. The people who saw this performance were convinced all the Memphis boys were insane. Then on a command, he would tell us to attack one dog and that dog would be Lamar and we would be all over him, biting and yelping. I know it sounds kind of nutty but it was lots of crazy fun. That Colonel could be a very funny dude."

True to form, Presley dated his leading lady, Joan Blackman, Priscilla remained in Memphis and Red assumed his usual position in Elvis's movies . . . on his back. The sound track included the smash hits "King of the Whole Wide World," "This Is Living," "Home Is Where the Heart Is," and "I Got Lucky." The money continued to roll in.

As the money rolled in, however, so did the boredom. By 1962, Presley had made six movies in two years. Most of Hollywood's golden talent had not made that many in ten years. And it had become evident to Presley that he would never realize his ambition to become a true actor, in the real sense of the word. Around this time, after just shooting a scene, Presley was heard saying, "I must read the script one day."

Both Sonny and Red point out that Presley, like most talents, always needed a challenge. Red recalls: "He would always say to me, 'Why in the hell do they keep on giving me lousy scripts?' He would complain and complain, but the scripts never got better. The money got better, but the scripts didn't. The point is that I know how talented the man can be when he has a challenge. In the early days of his recording, he would cut an album in two nights, and that may be twelve or fourteen songs. He was fantastic. He really knew his stuff. Toward the end, when we were doing *Elvis at Home* in 1976, he couldn't give a damn. He would use any excuse to hold up recording or just goof off. By 1962, when the boredom set in, he started on those big spending sprees. He would get whacked out on uppers and then just spend a fortune to end the boredom."

Presley decided that if as an actor he wasn't going to be taken seriously, he would not be concerned about taking life too seriously, either. Sonny, Red and the boys would always be there to help cut up the boredom with their antics and pranks. The horseplay was the only thing that kept Presley in front of the camera. Sonny relates: "I wish we had a full-length documentary on the way we all carried on at these locations. It would be a heck of a comedy."

Predictably for a man of Presley's good looks, he was sought after not only by females, but also by males. Red and Sonny recall several instances in fight scenes, when there was a full-scale brawl involving a dozen or more people, Presley would whisper to the boys, "Man, somebody cover my back, there is someone grabbing my ass." As devoted a woman chaser as he was, Presley would run a hundred miles from a homosexual, which posed some difficulty because Hollywood is full of them.

Running away from them was one thing, but Sonny and Red recall a time in 1962 when a young man who had designs on Presley actually blew several scenes. Presley was making *Fun in Acapulco*, but he didn't go to Acapulco on location because of a Mexican newspaper story that wrongly quoted him as saying disparaging things about the Mexicans. To send him there was considered unsafe. In a scene shot in Hollywood on the Paramount lot, Presley emerges triumphantly from the sea. There were, Red says, "about six guys carrying him aloft on their shoulders in a sort of victory march. Now the cameras are rolling and every time the scene is halfway through, Elvis blows it because he is wiggling around." Finally Presley came over to the boys and said, "There is a fag in that bunch. Every time they pick me up, one of them six guys grabs me by the balls." "In the end," says Sonny, "Assistant Director Mickey Moore spotted the guy. He was mad at this guy blowing the scene. Mickey wanted to blow the guy off the set, but he kept his cool. He just told this fag quietly that there were too many people in the scene. We, of course, near died laughing. Elvis wasn't as amused. He was very upset at being handled in a most intimate way by this fag."

Despite his healthy appetite for girls, the West boys recall that there was one young actress of whom Presley was terrified. Sonny recalls: "He was doing a lot of screwing around, but this one chick, man, she really wanted a piece of him. Very persistent, she was. Anyway, we thought it was a bit of a joke, but Elvis very seriously said, 'Man, I don't want to be left in a room alone with her. I want you guys to hang around,' and he was serious. The girl looked like she was going to eat him alive."

*Kissing Cousins,* which followed *Fun in Acapulco,* was shot in the mountains outside Los Angeles. One of the mountains, Big Bear, was almost Presley's graveyard.

Presley had bought a luxury Winnebago mobile trailer. It was like a moving palace. After the shooting was completed, Presley, Joe Esposito and the personal hairdresser, Larry Geller, were driving down Big Bear. The road down was a narrow winding track with a sheer drop on one side. The trailer was curving slowly down the road, with Presley at the wheel, when the brakes gave out. As the Winnebago gathered speed, it almost crashed into the car ahead, which carried some members of the film crew. Presley frantically tooted his horn, but the trail was too narrow for him to pass, and the car had to accelerate madly to keep in front of the giant lumbering vehicle behind. Red recalls: "I wasn't in it at the time, but apparently it was really touch and go. Elvis had to use the gears to get to the bottom of Big Bear and I guess it was a miracle he didn't go over the side. He finally got to the bottom and kept running with the trailer until it just slowed to a stop." If Presley had not been the excellent driver he is, *Kissing Cousins* most surely would have been his last movie.

The next film, *Viva Las Vegas,* was when Presley met Ann-Margret. It wasn't long before he was seen in public many times with her, and the gossip columns churned out a raft of stories that Ann-Margret might be the next Mrs. Presley. Undoubtedly there was a special warmth between the two, and the West boys remember that she was always at the Presley house on Perugia Way in Hollywood. "She was a fantastic chick," says Sonny, "pretty but also very easygoing. She got on great with the guys and Elvis really dug her." The gossip-column items did very little to make Presley's life any easier with Priscilla Beaulieu, who was still closeted away in Memphis.

Despite Presley's obvious attraction to Ann-Margret, she was also the object of his professional jealousy. A member of the direction staff, a man who had worked with Ann-Margret in a previous movie and who dated her, was very much in love with her. He had a lot to do with the photography, and Sonny recalls that he was so smitten by Ann-Margret that he virtually cut Presley out of the camera angles. "He was shooting over Elvis's shoulder and getting close-ups of Ann-Margret. Now Ann-Margret had nothing to do with it. It wasn't her fault," says Sonny. "It's just that he was favoring her so much with the camera angles. He was trying to do anything to get her to like him."

Red recalls: "It was the first time I heard Elvis talk about camera angles, but after seeing the rushes he would complain bitterly to us that the sonofabitch was trying to cut him out of the picture. And he was right." It came to an end when Presley's complaint reached the ears of the Colonel. The big guns came in.

In *Viva Las Vegas,* Presley really came alive. Although the script was as unchallenging as all the others, he worked extremely well with Ann-Margret, both in singing and dancing. Undoubtedly they presented a special magic on screen. Sonny and Red had tiny parts, and Red wrote a song for the sound track, "If You Think I Don't Need You." Presley sang the Ray Charles hit, "What Did I Say," which was a top seller. The studio guitarist who did the sound track with Presley was a young man named Glen Campbell.

*Roustabout,* a 1964 release, was directed by John Rich, who, the West boys felt, had a decided intolerance for the antics of the Memphis Mafia. "Elvis didn't have much of a rapport with Mr. Rich, and somehow when he directed, the Memphis boys seemed to get the freeze from him," says Sonny. "It's not that he didn't like us, I just guess he thought we were not a necessary part of the movie-making. Elvis was convinced that Mr. Rich didn't have the right temperament to handle people like us." However, when Presley first met Barbara Stanwyck, he was the one who showed a lack of temperament.

"Elvis was a little bit late and Miss Stanwyck was already on the set waiting," recalls Sonny. "Now Mickey Moore, the assistant director, looked at his watch and commented on it." For some reason Presley thought it was the veteran actress Miss Stanwyck who had complained. He said, "I don't give a damn if the big star Barbara Stanwyck is waiting for me, I'll get here when I'm good and ready."

Miss Stanwyck, whom all the cast called Missy, did not take up the challenge and get offended. "She was a great lady," Sonny says, "and in the end a real rapport developed between her and Elvis."

By 1965, Presley was desperate to break the same-old-script mold, but Colonel Tom was just as determined not to fool around with his image. Ten years earlier, he had promised Presley he would be richer than his wildest dreams. The Colonel had kept his promise, but Presley had to pay the price. If he wanted to stay a millionaire, he had to go along with the Colonel's plans.

In his next movie, *Girl Happy,* Presley was relentless in his pursuit of Shelley Fabares, one of the romantic interests in the film. "He would be trying to promote her all day on location," says Sonny, "but she just wasn't interested. She was going with Lou Adler, the man who went on to become a big record producer. It was a blow to Elvis's ego that he couldn't get to her, but she was very faithful. When she did marry Lou a little later, Elvis said, 'She had to go and get married because she knew she wouldn't be able to go through another movie resisting me.' It really was an ego thing with him." Presley consoled himself for his failure to get Miss Fabares to go out with him by dating Mary Ann Mobley.

Next came *Tickle Me.* Presley's boredom now manifested itself in his buying ten motorbikes. While the boys had a ball, the neighbors of the Presley household on Perugia Way were outraged. The Memphis Mafia was one thing, but the Memphis Mafia as "Hell's Angels" was another. Presley took his motorbike affair seriously and dressed accordingly, decked out à la Marlon Brando complete with black leather, sunglasses and yachting cap.

The film had hardly cleared the cutting room when Presley was doing *Harum-Scarum,* in which he played a Rudolph Valentino-style movie star caught up in exotic Middle Eastern intrigue. Although his physical features bear little resemblance to the great Valentino, his manner and dash on screen capture all the excitement of a truly enchanting heartthrob. Red felt that in some scenes, despite corny scripting, Presley really excelled himself. "He proved to me beyond any doubt that he had that certain presence that could bring out emotions in the audience."

Presley was causing plenty of emotion in his off-screen life, as well. Priscilla Beaulieu had tired of her role as the captive princess of Graceland and was coming to Hollywood more and more and visiting the sites of Presley's movies, which made the star very uneasy. By the end of 1965 she had given notice to Presley that she was not going to spend the rest of her life imprisoned in a Memphis palace. She had moved into the Presley Hollywood headquarters, which were now at Rocca Place in Bel Air. The boys were witness to the Presley-Priscilla struggle of wills. Priscilla very much wanted to get married and Presley, while very much in love with her, was not prepared to sacrifice his enviable bachelor status.

While Elvis was mulling over his problems, Col. Tom Parker swept him into *Paradise Hawaiian Style*, a movie that placed Presley once again amid the exotic islands. If it was an attempt to recapture the success of *Blue Hawaii*, it failed—at least artistically, although the box office never complained. It was Mickey Moore's first shot at being director; he was disappointed when his star arrived on location terribly overweight. It was the first time Presley had ever had that problem. Despite the activity before the cameras and despite the handfuls of uppers he was taking to keep him going, Presley had just begun ever so slightly to have his first experience with downers—yellow jackets, Seconals. Although he took them sparingly, compared with later years, he would pop them occasionally and sleep for many hours on end. This perhaps was triggered by his depression about the standard of work he was being asked to do. In any case, combining the pills with an insane diet of banana-and-peanut-butter sandwiches fried in half an inch of melted butter did not help things.

By 1966, Presley, having lost any real interest in the movies he was doing, had started to get interested in philosophy, religion and books. During the filming of *Frankie and Johnny*, he broke with tradition by not dating his co-star Donna Douglas. Instead, Presley took a genuine intellectual interest in her. Sonny recalls: "She was quite religious and she talked a lot of sense. Elvis would talk to her and he started to get interested in books. He always was quite self-conscious over the fact that he was not well read. From about there on in he really started getting into books, all kinds, religion, the occult, the meaning of words, everything. So instead of dating, they just sort of talked books and religion."

At the same time that *Frankie and Johnny* was being shot, Robert Mitchum and Shirley MacLaine were making *See Saw*. Mitchum visited Presley on the set and offered him a starring role in a film property he owned called *Thunder Road*. He saw in Presley what apparently a lot of Hollywood film executives failed to see, and he thought Presley would develop into a first-class serious actor if he had meatier roles to play. Either the up-front money wasn't tasty enough for the Colonel, or he thought it would have broken too much with the Presley tradition. In any case, Presley passed up the chance. The movie was a big success.

In *Easy Come, Easy Go*, Presley hit back at Director John Rich. Sonny recalls the confrontation: "It was a thing that sort of started where Mr. Rich was trying to compete with Elvis and one of the actors, Pat Harrington, who Elvis really liked, for being the star of the set. Mr. Rich would tell jokes, stories and anecdotes and try to be funny, but we didn't think he was all that amusing. Elvis would tell a story and Pat Harrington would tell a story and it was hilarious. They were both born storytellers. The chemistry between Elvis and Rich didn't work.

"Well, one day, we had been fooling around and dying laughing and Elvis is in this scene and every time he looks at me or Red he bursts out laughing and blows the scene. Well, we cover our faces and try not to spoil things but again, Elvis just looks at us and again breaks up. Now Mr. Rich is getting mad and he yells out, 'Okay, all you guys off the set.' He was ordering us off the set. Elvis suddenly gets serious and says, 'Now, just a minute, just a minute. We're doing these movies because it's supposed to be fun, nothing more; now when they cease to be fun, then we'll cease to do them.'

"He was just addressing nobody in particular but it was actually directed at Mr. Rich. Elvis was mad. He wasn't going to be pushed around any more on these silly movies. Anyway, he won the point because we didn't get off the set." Presley was at the height of his car-buying spree and during that filming he gave Pat Harrington a maroon Cadillac, which totally blew his mind.

That was the last time Presley worked on a Hal Wallis production. Presley was grateful to Wallis for his generosity and the money that he made working for him. But one thing stuck in Presley's mind: *Blue Hawaii* grossed eleven million dollars. Presley believed it was that money that financed Hal Wallis's classic movie *Becket,* starring Peter O'Toole and Richard Burton. Presley felt he had been slighted; it was his movie that got that kind of money, yet he wasn't good enough to play in anything but beach and racing-car films.

By 1967, Presley had calmed down his womanizing. Priscilla was seen more and more in his company. By this time she was often on the set, so his style was considerably cramped women-wise. But the usual pranks and horseplay on location didn't stop. Red West remembers that there was so much playing around on *Clambake* that when *Stay Away Joe* began, "a memo came down from the MGM top office warning us about our behavior. We thought it was a bit silly for them to take us so seriously. We sure did cut up on *Clambake* but I don't think we held up production any. We didn't cost anybody any money." There were pie-throwings, firecracker fights, and water bombardments.

"In one scene," Red remembers, "Bill Bixby was before the cameras, which were rolling, and Elvis just walked right into the scene and hit him with a cream pie. Bill followed this up in another scene with something that really broke us up. There was a girl in this scene who had been a dancer. She wore a two-piece swimsuit. As the cameras were rolling, he simply undid her halter and her top fell off and these giant boobs fell out. The camera got it all.

"Up till that time, Arthur Nadel hadn't been hit. I think he felt a bit left out of it. So on the last day of shooting he came dressed in a raincoat and rain hat, virtually inviting us to hit him. We didn't. But that night as we had the end-of-movie party, he changed into a suit. After the party, he was going to a PTA meeting. Well, we all made a little speech about how we loved him and what a great guy he was to work with and what a great artist he was. Well, he gets choked up and begins to say thanks and that's when we hit him with a pie right in the face. At last he got the pie he wanted, but he was fully dressed."

At one stage, Col. Tom Parker must have sensed Presley's disaffection for the kind of work he was doing, although he was being miserable all the way to the bank. As a gesture, or perhaps as a gift of appreciation for Presley's fortitude in bearing the junk he was being served up, the Colonel gave him a black Lincoln limousine.

Presley squeezed out six more movies in the next two years before deciding he wanted to perform again in front of real live people.

"Into 1966, he started taking downers more heavily," says Sonny, "gradually at first. But he started heavy into them more and more as he got more and more bored. Around about that time, he fell very badly in the bathroom and hit his head. He got a concussion and he lost his equilibrium for a while. It was a real bad fall. He said he slipped. But he had been heavy into yellow jackets and Seconals. He was half asleep when he had that fall. He would go through periods where he would look after himself, and man, he would look like a Greek god. But then he would lapse back into popping the downers where the lapses got gradually closer and closer together. By the early seventies, the only thing that would keep him straight was if he had a challenge. Then he would be the old Elvis again. He needs a challenge more than anyone I know."

# 20

The sounds of frantic lovemaking could be heard coming from the bedroom of the mansion in Belagio Road, Bel Air. The bedboard was pounding against the wall, the man was whispering passionate words of love in the woman's ear, and the woman was moaning quietly in ecstasy. Suddenly the idyllic moment was fractured by the woman, who let out a blood-curdling scream. The scream was followed by the man's yelling out, "You little sonofabitch," which was followed by the sight of a squealing chimpanzee hurtling through the air.

Sonny West today gives a loud belly laugh when he recalls the incident. "It was Elvis's pet chimpanzee, called Scatter," says Sonny. The scene took place during the movie-making time, when Presley was doing anything to escape the boredom, at one of his many parties. One of the Memphis Mafia had let a pretty, young, and well-known songwriter into the bedroom used by Alan Fortas. Presley was quick to pick up on the opportunity for a prank. Sonny and Alan were dispatched upstairs to follow the couple with Scatter the chimp. "Scatter was led through the doorway where this couple were getting it on," recalls Sonny. "They were too swept away in what they were doing to notice. Now old Scatter is very interested in watching two humans do what animals do. He started to get excited. He jumped on the bed and started leaping up and down screaming 'Woooo, woooo, woooo.' That poor gal on the bed, she damn near died. She thought she was being attacked by a strange creature. Of course the guy on the bed knew what we were doing. Man, he threw that monkey ten feet. But I don't think they finished getting it on with each other. The poor girl was near dead with shock."

Between 1963 and 1965, the chimpanzee was very much a part of the Memphis Mafia. Presley had a strong affection for him. Scatter was originally on a Memphis television station owned by Captain Bill Killebrew. "Alan Fortas saw him," Sonny recalls, "and told Elvis about Scatter and Elvis bought him for a couple of hundred bucks. He was a funny little dude. He learned how to dress himself and we had these little suits and ties for him." He learned to do a lot of other things, with Presley's patient training. He was most adept at walking up to a girl, lifting up her dress, and looking up. He also had a dreadful habit of molesting himself in front of ladies, particulary when he had a few drinks.

"Man," says Sonny, "old Scatter was a damn alcoholic. Never stopped drinking. He would get drunk and start going crazy, doing flips all over the house and yelling like a madman."

One day when he had had too much to drink, he completely ruined the entire telephone system in the house. It took the telephone repairman three days to fix it. Presley had another little prank, which never really endeared him to his more conservative neighbors. He would have Alan Fortas dress the chimp in his Sunday best and then put him in the back seat of the Rolls-Royce while Alan drove it. A chauffeur-driven rock 'n' roll singer was bad enough, but a chauffeur-driven monkey? Disgraceful!

Scatter, like most of the members of the Belagio Road household, liked women. "He would chase them into the bathroom and try and get a peek at them," says Sonny. "He would run after them and try to grab them. You would swear he was like some horny old guy, chasing a piece of ass. He also loved to wrestle with this pint-size stripper who used to come up to the house. They would put on these wrestling acts and she wasn't much bigger than Scatter, but it looked funnier than hell because it looked like they were getting it on and Elvis would just die laughing. In the end Elvis built him an air-conditioned cage in Memphis. He died there."

A fair question that perhaps every Presley fan has asked himself or herself is: "What is a sex symbol's attitude toward sex?" In Presley's case the answer is interesting. In his early life, Presley was ruled by shyness and obviously that spilled over into his sex life. He never, in his early years, approved of any of the boys' dating married women. Although he never made an issue out of it, he also didn't approve of his father, Vernon, going with Dee, although they later married. Incidentally, Presley did not attend the ceremony. But over the years, his earlier strict principles wore off.

Sonny recalls: "After Elvis punched me for moving in on the girl I was trying to promote, I was always careful about the kind of girls I brought up to the house. I was always damn sure that before I brought any girl around he already had a real good-looking one at his side, because he would move in on you."

Red adds: "I only used to bring ugly ones around before I got married, so he wouldn't pick up on them."

In later years he was so intent on trying to win any girl he came in contact with that he once gave Jerry Schilling a sleeping pill to knock him out while he took off with his girlfriend. "We knew he did that," says Sonny, "and we kept it from Jerry Schilling because Jerry at the time would have got mad and maybe done something physical with Elvis. When he broke up with the girl, he found out about it and was still mad. I remember him saying 'The sonofabitch doing a thing like that to someone who was supposed to be his friend.' There were other times that he even dated the wife of one of his relatives."

By Memphis standards perhaps, Presley had some pretty wild sexual ideas. But in fairness, comparing him with the jaded crowd in Hollywood and Las Vegas, he really did nothing outrageous. He is, however, according to Red West, an inveterate peeker. "Most men are," says Red, "let's face it. We all like a little harmless turn-on now and then. When he took over the house on Perugia Way, he had two big mirrors installed. They weren't ordinary mirrors. They were one-way mirrors, where you could see from one side into a room but the person couldn't see you looking in. We had one of the mirrors in a closet that looked into a bedroom. Now whenever any guy was making out with a chick in this bedroom Elvis and all of us would rush in and see the action. He took a lot of girls into that closet, and some of the names of the girls who used to be there digging the action would surprise you. We even had a gospel group up there and although they were supposedly religious, it sure didn't stop them getting in there in the closet and taking in the action. There was another mirror in the dressing room of the pool house that he had installed and he could watch the girls getting undressed when they were changing to go into the pool. Now, to be fair, even though he was the one who had it installed, all of us, all of the boys, there was none of us innocent, although you don't like to admit it."

The house in Perugia Way, which had become the headquarters for Presley partying, was the scene of a bizarre LSD trip. It was the end of 1964, when the entertainment world in Hollywood started to hear about this weird, so-called creative drug. Presley was fascinated with it, although he was wary about taking it. Enter the two test pilots, Red West and Sonny West.

"He told me that a lot of people were saying that you could create and write songs under its influence," says Red. "He didn't want to take it himself, so he got us to do it. He wanted to observe its effects." Sonny remembers that Presley, Charlie Hodge and Larry Geller were in Presley's bedroom in Perugia Way when the two of them took the drug.

Presley was going to take them through the trip by reading, page by page, a book on the subject by Timothy Leary, the dropout professor of the LSD generation. Sonny recalls: "Us, like idiots, went along with it as being guinea pigs, although it never turned out to be a bad trip. But I never did it again. And I think back what might have happened if we had tripped out. There were guns all over the bedroom and we could have grabbed them and gone nuts."

"I was sitting there with my guitar," says Red, "trying to write a song, bombed out of my skull. . . . Don't think I did much song-writing. I was going in and out of the trip. One moment I was sane, the next moment I was crazier than a loon. I saw the figures on the wall move as if they were little people." Sonny looked at himself in the bathroom mirror and saw himself as a wolfman. "I looked at this sonofabitch in the mirror looking back at me and all I could see was this wolf and I was going 'Wooooo, woooooo.' "

Presley, in the meantime, was exhorting them both to get closer to God, to see if they could see a light that was God. "I was in the bathroom taking a leak," says Sonny, "and I had my eyes closed and I could see this light and I'm thinking I'm seeing the light of God which Elvis was talking about. Then I opened my eyes and I realized I was looking straight into the ceiling light. Apparently Elvis thought we were going to see God and he kept on urging us to try and get closer. There were some very weird feelings. Red and

I would say the same thing simultaneously like we knew what each other was going to say.

"Then I started to feel hemmed in by the room so I went outside in the garden. There were a lot of people in the den, but Elvis didn't want us to go near the rest of the crowd. So Larry Geller takes me outside. There is a dog out there, which belonged to Elvis and Priscilla. His name was Baba, and I started talking to him. He took one look at me, this big collie, and he leaped into the ivy patch. I leaped in after him and I was rolling around in the ivy. I grabbed a piece of ivy and held it up to the sun and what terrified me was that I could see the veins in the ivy leaf pulsating until it died. I had this dreadful feeling about killing something that was living. I tried to replant it. Then I saw my own hands and they looked like they had turned to transparent cellophane and all my veins and muscles had turned to green fibers. It was as if I could see through my skin and now my veins were the same as that plant I had killed. Larry Geller, who was a pretty intelligent dude, talked me all through it."

Meanwhile, Red was back with Presley trying to compose the great American song. "I was bombed out of my skull. I don't know what I did, but Sonny said I had more movements than a third-base umpire."

Both boys finished their trip inside eight hours. "We would never touch it again, man," says Sonny. Red agrees: "It was too weird, although I didn't have any bad after-effects. But I still get flashbacks like I was on the trip." After the trip, Presley, according to the boys, got the courage to take the drug himself, or so he told Red and Sonny. "The point was," says Red, "we were the tests. That was the kind of influence he had over us. I would never do that again for anybody."

Sonny remembers that in the early days Presley would never have anything to do with sexual orgies or "scenes" that were so popular in Hollywood then, as they are now. Sonny relates: "I remember about 1964, two of the guys in the gang had promoted this real wild-looking chick. Well, they both got her into bed. We were all up there at the time and we knew what they were doing, no big deal. Anyway, Elvis hears this noise going on in the bedroom and he walks in. He apparently didn't see the girl because these guys were all over her. He got the shock of his life, he said later, because when he didn't see the girl, he thought two of his faithful friends were making it together, and Elvis don't like fags, man. He was shouting obscenities at them at the thought they were doing it with each other. They showed him the girl they were screwing and she wanted him to get into the act. She tried to kiss Elvis and he wouldn't have any part of it because she was with these two other guys. In those days, he couldn't stand the idea that another man would ball a chick he wanted to screw. The poor girl, she ended up crying because Elvis's refusal to kiss her made her feel cheap and she really cried. I felt sorry for her."

Both boys recall that Presley's objection to going to bed with anyone whom anyone else had touched stuck with him. "The reason why he never wanted to screw a married broad," says Red, "was that he always felt they would leave his bed and go to another man. I suppose it was an ego thing. Also he had a thing about if a woman he was screwing had a baby. Something in him just turned him off when he learned a woman had had a baby. It's quite a strange hang-up." But as Presley was exposed more and more to the "action" in Hollywood and Las Vegas, he gradually changed.

The year 1968 was about the time that video-tape recorders started to come out. As they were a new gadget, Presley got one immediately. "Of course, Elvis didn't actually use them for taping football games and home movies," says Red. "He would videotape himself in bed with chicks. I don't mean he did it sneaky, without them knowing. They knew what was going on because he would set it up in the bedroom. Now, that ain't all that big a deal in Hollywood because a lot of stars with money do that sort of thing.

"It's funny, when Elvis gets the urge to do something, he wants to do it straightaway. I remember one time we were driving back from L.A. to Memphis and we were in Oklahoma City, Oklahoma. Suddenly he tells us we're going to stop there and book into a motel. Okay, we said, but we didn't know why. Well, he had his video tape machine with him. He gets on the telephone to a chick in L.A. and tells her to catch the first flight out and she did. She stayed over one night just so Elvis could get a bit of action with her on his machine."

Despite it all, Presley was still relatively backward by Hollywood standards. There are many well-known stars who make a point of showing their action to their friends, but Presley wouldn't. "He was self-conscious about being naked in front of someone," says Red. "I remember he and another guy around this time picked up some chicks in Palm Springs and took them back to the house. There were some guys skinny-dipping and one of the chicks took her clothes off and dived in the pool. The one Elvis was with, he told her he didn't want her to strip naked, didn't want all the guys seeing what she had. Now, Elvis just had a towel wrapped around him and he wasn't going to go in naked. I came up behind him and whipped the towel from him and he was standing naked there in front of this girl. He got so embarrassed he dived into the pool to hide his nakedness. He just was a guy that didn't like being seen naked. He had an ego about getting any girl he wanted but he wasn't a show-off stud like lots of guys are."

Presley does have some very personal likes and dislikes about the women he takes to bed. Sonny relates: "He doesn't like them too big. He likes them very petite and feminine. He does not like big chicks with big bosoms. He is not a boob man, he is an ass and leg man. He likes them about five foot four, five foot five, and there is one thing that really turns him off and that is chicks with big feet.

"He would tell us that he could be in bed with a chick and he would roll over and see those big, wide soles and oh, man, he just couldn't get out of that bed fast enough. He really likes them feminine."

Up until the time when he lost Priscilla, Presley would always boast that he would never pay money to get a girl. Red recalls: "That was pretty much the truth, but after Priscilla left him, he just couldn't be without a girl, not necessarily for sex, but he would have to have them. He would take up with one and he would have another waiting in another room for him if the first one didn't work out." In the Hilton Hotel in Las Vegas, there were always men working at the hotel who would tip off Joe Esposito if there was any fresh talent around. "If Joe thought they were sharp," says Red, "he would introduce himself to them and then introduce them to Elvis. There were times when there were three or four of them waiting for Elvis that had been tipped to Joe by some of the waiters or headwaiter," says Sonny.

One of Presley's big kicks, according to the West boys, was to hire two hookers to make it with each other. "Once again," says Sonny, "he didn't want any big dyke broads, they had to be pretty and feminine."

Red relates: "If he had a girl in his room, he would give her a sleeping pill and get the two broads in another part of the suite. He would get charged up watching this and make a dead run to his bedroom and make it with his girl."

Gradually, Presley was more and more a mark for the girls who were "takers." In 1970, Col. Tom Parker was negotiating with MGM to make the movie, *Elvis— That's the Way It Is*, which was a documentary of sorts of Presley's performances, rehearsals and attitude to his craft. Jim Aubrey, then head of MGM, went to Las Vegas and met with Presley and the boys. Sonny recalls that he met Aubrey in Presley's dressing room in Las Vegas. "He had this very beautiful chick with him who had just been in a big movie. Let's just call her Shirley (which is not her real name). Anyway, she walks in wearing this black floor-length sheath dress. She was very vampy looking, great eyes.

"Elvis was quite taken with her and he is making eyes at her when Jim Aubrey was there. Mr. Aubrey was a supercool kind of guy, a pretty attractive man. He could see that Elvis was trying to make out with her. He couldn't give a damn, he had so many chicks. Anyway, Elvis takes her on a tour of his wardrobe, showing her all his different outfits and things. She was out there staying with Jim Aubrey but Elvis got her telephone number. Anyway, he had her flown back into Las Vegas. He was bragging about how while he was talking to Mr. Aubrey, his mind was working on how he could get this girl, not that Aubrey would have given it a second thought."

Red remembers Presley was with her from time to time for about eighteen months to two years. Sonny relates: "There were lots of girls who Elvis was very generous to, but most of them just wanted to be with him. Now he was seeing that girl Sheila Ryan for a while. Now with Sheila, who was a beautiful lady, he had to force gifts on her. She didn't want a whole lot of presents and gifts. He had to really force things on her. She wanted nothing from him. But this one, brother, she promoted a 250 coupe Mercedes out of him. She knew he was very generous and he probably would have given her a car anyway, but she hinted about how much she loved the car and everything and he took the hint and got her a beautiful new maroon Mercedes coupe with tan upholstery. Of course, she was working on him heavy. She also used to go downtown to this very classy boutique in Las Vegas called Suzie Creamcheese and she would buy all these gowns."

The boys saw a gradual degeneration of Presley's health, as he seemed more and more locked into taking masses of pills. He was fascinated with pills for every kind of function. "He even told us," says Sonny, "that there was a special new chlorophyll pill, which would eliminate body odor. And he also talked about special pills that would give you a sun tan and change the pigment of his skin, although I don't know whether he took them or not. But he thought a pill could fix anything. This is when he started losing Priscilla, right in there around 1971. He was taking these painkillers like Percodan that would just knock him for a loop. Also Demerol and very, very strong stuff. He started that thing of staying up for hours on end and then going to bed for days at a time."

Red remembers that it was at this time he discovered he had a serious case of glaucoma. "We were doing a session, a recording session in Nashville. His eyes really started to irritate him. Then he called us all in for a meeting after he had seen this doctor and announced what he had. It was really a close call because Dr. Nichopoulos had to call in a specialist from Memphis, Dr. David Myers. It was so close that Dr. Myers hardly had any time left. He gave him this shot in the eye without an anesthetic. There was no time to fool around. Elvis said give him the shot. He could take the pain. The thing was he had so much Percodan in him, he wouldn't have felt it if you had put a knife through him. He was in that hospital in Nashville and we all were called in and he made us look through this special machine into his eyes. He went through the whole detail. I mention the eye thing because he had the girl we call Shirley with him during all this. He had a two-bedroom suite.

"Elvis found out that she had once been married and had a child, and when he found out that she had given birth to a child . . . he dropped her. It was a turn-off."

## 21

It's a frightening, haunting picture. He sits in a courtroom guarded by policemen. There is no room for the public. The courtroom is packed with reporters from every part of the globe. The man in the prisoner's box is a seedy, weedy little guy who never made an imprint on the world until now. And there he is smirking and the smirk says "I assassinated Elvis Presley." It is a vision that is forever with Elvis Presley. And he has even told the West boys what he wants done if ever it happens. "Look, the FBI and the cops have a job to do. They have to arrest the guy. But if it ever does happen, I want you guys to get him first. I want you to get him before the cops do. And when you find him, I want you to pop his eyeballs out with your thumbs. I want you to rip his tongue out. I want you to tear him to pieces. I don't want no sonofabitch smirking in court that he killed Elvis Presley."

If he had an unwarranted paranoia in the past about his personal safety when he lived in virtual seclusion while making his movies, it all changed in August, 1969. That was when the fear became justified because Presley was a constant target for death threats and extortion plots. It was in 1969 that the decision was made that Presley would go before a live showroom audience, his first appearance in nine years. And it was then that Red West and Sonny West—no longer expected to be stunt men, stand-ins and faithful members of the Memphis Mafia—became bodyguards for real.

There are several possible reasons for Presley's returning to live audiences: his hatred of the movies he was expected to churn out like popcorn; a genuine need to feel waves of love coming from real people; Col. Tom Parker's realizing that the movie rainbow had dulled and that the new pot of gold was to be found in live concerts. Whatever the reason, Colonel Parker maintained his reputation for faultless timing and showmanship because the change in gear worked perfectly for Presley's bank account, even if it did introduce a whole new set of personal problems.

The location for Presley's reentry into live entertainment was to be the International Hotel, the sixty-million-dollar extravaganza that would have looked out of place in any town but Las Vegas. "It was the challenge he needed," says Red West, "and he really went at it. There were plenty of doubts about him making his comeback to live shows. Everyone was asking had he lost his touch, could he still carry a live show, would the Las Vegas crowd go for him? In the back of everyone's mind was the first time he had performed in Las Vegas at the Frontier Hotel in 1956. The Las Vegas customer just wasn't ready for him. He was ripping up the kids, but the crowd was too old for him. Of course, the Colonel made the big decision and he wasn't wrong."

Sonny remembers that Presley really got himself in shape, both physically and mentally for his Las Vegas opening. Barbra Streisand had opened the showroom and Presley was to follow her. Streisand was not an easy act to follow. She was a known quantity as far as audience appeal was concerned. She had just won an Oscar and her numbers were topping hit parades everywhere. Presley, despite his name, had been away from the center ring for nine years. Big performers have flopped before in Las Vegas.

No matter what sort of show he might have turned in, however, the financial side was assured from the moment the booking office opened. It was an avalanche. Not just from America. There were charter flights winging their way from Britain, Australia, Japan. The Presley fans just refused to let the performance be a flop. And, of course, it was a sensation.

Sonny West remembers: "Man, he looked great before he went on. He was nervous, sure, but he had rehearsed and rehearsed. He was trim as a twenty-one-year-old. He looked fantastic."

The Sweet Inspirations, a fast-moving black quartet, warmed up the audience for him, and the atmosphere in the showroom, which seats twenty-five hundred, was hard to describe, but there was definitely electricity bouncing off the walls. He burst onto the stage singing "Blue Suede Shoes," and none of the first part of the number could be heard. As one mass, the crowd jumped to its feet and exploded with ear-splitting applause. It seemed weirdly out of character for a showroom. A baseball stadium, a fight arena, the coliseum of another era, yes, but not a gilded showroom that served rare steaks and French wines. The love affair picked up where it had left off. The women were a little stouter and the lights danced off gray hair. The men were fatter in the middle and thinner on top, but the love affair was raging again. He continued to paralyze them with "I Got a Woman," "Heartbreak Hotel," "Love Me Tender," "Hound Dog," and "I Can't Stop Loving You." He also sang "Suspicious Minds," one of his all-time personal favorites. Elvis Presley had never been away, as far as that crowd was concerned. He had simply been preparing for this night.

"That night," says Sonny, "he was popping with natural energy, not energy from some damn pill, but pure Elvis Presley, physical, emotional and mental. He was popping like a new instrument." The scene after the show remains indelible in Sonny's mind. "It was one of the most beautifully emotional things I had ever seen between two men. The Colonel came down after the show into the dressing room. He just said, 'Where is he?' The Colonel, that old man, had tears in his eyes. His face was twisted in emotion. I had never seen him like that before. I was with Joe Esposito and we pointed inside. Elvis came out. The Colonel took one step forward and so did Elvis. There were no words. They just put their arms around each other in a big hug. The Colonel had his back to me and I knew it was a private thing where we shouldn't hang around. We excused ourselves. But the Colonel's body was shaking with emotion. I left there with a big lump in my throat. It was a beautiful moment."

The Colonel extracted a massive five-year contract from the International Hotel. They paid a staggering price for him, but they had no complaints, because he was a guaranteed sellout. "He did a lot of great shows in Las Vegas," says Sonny.

The challenge stayed with him for a year, more than a year. He would prime himself for Las Vegas. Both he and the Colonel loved the town, loved the atmosphere. This was show business at its best and they were both made for it. But, like everything else with Presley, the challenge eventually left him. And then he would get up there on stage and sing the same songs, show after show. The same show was okay when he was touring the country, but not in Las Vegas. The Colonel pleaded with him to get new songs. But even when he did, he wouldn't bother to learn them properly.

Sonny recalls: "There were times when he had a guy named Kenny Hicks actually lying under the plexiglass stage of the hotel in Las Vegas with idiot cards with the words to the songs."

"There were even times," says Red, "I heard him announce to the audience that this was a new song he was singing and he didn't know the words so he would actually read them off a piece of paper. I was amazed the audience stood for it. I'm also amazed that it never got into the newspapers. But he would just get up there and read the lyrics to a song. It was the same old thing. He was getting bored again and when he got bored that was when he was impossible to be around. He would be taking all his stuff and be wired all the time and he would have us going where we wouldn't get three hours' sleep in three days."

To give Presley his due, the pressures on him began to mount. With public exposure came the waterfall of nut mail. A lot of it was dismissed as the ramblings of people who just wanted to write threatening notes. A lot of it was not. "We tried to keep most of it away from Elvis," says Red West, "but there was a lot of serious stuff coming down that he had to know about."

One threat was serious enough for the FBI to involve itself. Sonny and Jerry Schilling were working the show in 1970 when a call came from a man who had taken the time and trouble to know how to get his message through. It was an extortion attempt—the caller said there was a madman intent on killing Presley for fifty thousand dollars. He would give the name to Presley. Red was in Memphis at the time and Presley put in an emergency call for him to get to Las Vegas immediately. "I arrived there," says Red, "and Elvis just stumbled into my arms and hugged me. There was no doubt that he was taking this very seriously. So were we."

And so were the FBI when a menu arrived addressed to Presley. The menu was for his Las Vegas appearance and had a photograph of Presley on the front. Someone had scribbled out the face and drawn a gun pointed to his heart. At the bottom of the menu, carefully written backward, were the words "Guess who, and where?" The FBI tested it for fingerprints but found none; they were convinced it was the work of a badly twisted mind.

"Nothing came of it," says Red, "but that engagement we had Sonny and Jerry Schilling in the musicians' pit with their guns ready. I was cruising the audience, so were the security guards at the hotel and the plainclothesmen of the FBI. As a matter of fact, one very suspicious guy I hassled turned out to be a Fed."

Another time, in 1972, when Presley was halfway through the act, a tip came from the maitre d', who'd told Joe Esposito that there was thought to be a crazed woman in the audience who had a gun and was going to shoot Presley.

Sonny recalls: "When we got the message, Red and I stood up in front on the stage as a block to Elvis. Elvis moved to the back of the stage and sang in a sideways stance to make himself a smaller target." As the show came closer to the finale, Sonny and Red moved together almost obliterating Presley from view. Red says that by the time the curtain came down, they stood right in front of him so that if there was a bullet, it had to hit them first.

"Damn," Sonny remembers, "that curtain took about twenty seconds to come down but it felt like an hour." Red adds: "Man, I know I was shaking. I was ready to hear that pop of a gun and feel a doggone bullet go right through my heart. And I was thinking about my wife and kids. I was scared."

By this time, Presley was paying Red and Sonny $425 a week, and today both of them feel a little stupid when they admit that they were willing to stop a bullet for that. "If anyone was going to hurt him," Dave Hebler says, "they would have had to kill us to get to him. That was the relationship."

The West boys recall that Presley, instead of showing real gratitude for their willingness to take a bullet for him, would boast to anyone who cared to listen, "If a guy gets up with a knife, they take the knife for me. If it's a gun, they take the bullet for me. That's the kind of loyalty I can get."

While some of the hairy, scary stuff was happening, however, Presley and the West boys had not lost their devilish, perhaps a little wild, sense of humor.

Red chuckles at one memory. "There was a group that had joined Elvis," he says, "called J. D. Sumner and the Stamps Quartet. It was a very good gospel group led by J. D. Sumner, who must have the lowest bass voice in the world. Anyway, it was in 1972, when we're getting a lot of these threats, and they were very nervous about this. To break the monotony and have a little fun, Elvis, Sonny and myself decided on a bit of a practical joke."

The joke was to tell J. D. Sumner and his group that there was a madman in the hotel with a gun who was trying to kill Presley. To set the prank up to perfection, Elvis, Sonny and Red recruited three of the security guards to be in on it with them.

"We decided," says Red, "to act out a fake gun-fight with an assassin. The assassin would be hidden, of course, because he was Sonny. Sonny and I load our guns with blanks and the security guards empty their guns, which, as it turned out, was a good idea for a reason that will become obvious. So I prime J. D. and his boys about what's happening and I tell them very earnestly to be very careful because there is a madman loose. Well we are up in the suite and J. D. is checking inside doors and his boys are pretty nervous about what's coming down." Sonny was there and he left the suite with the excuse that he was going to check out the rest of the hotel. Left in the suite were J. D. Sumner, the Stamps Quartet, who were talking to Presley near the bar, and the two security guards.

"I leave by the front door," says Sonny, "put on a black pigskin jacket and then return with my gun loaded with blanks through the back entrance to the suite while the crowd inside are talking about this madman."

Then the sinister black-clad arm of Sonny reaches around a corner and he shouts, "You son of a bitch!" And he starts firing away . . . *bang, bang, bang!* Red dashes to the hallway, gun blazing, and then yells "Oh!" He staggers back into the suite "dead." The next fusillade of shots cuts down the security guards who were in on the prank. They're all "dead" and it's a mass slaughter.

Panic and terror seize J. D. and his group. Donny Sumner, J. D.'s nephew, ran from one side of the suite to the other in two giant steps and hurdled the bar to an accompaniment of smashing glasses. J. D. Sumner bravely threw himself across Presley. Ed Enoch, J. D.'s son-in-law, dove behind a piano and yelled: "Give me a gun, give me a gun!" Bill Baize, a very religious member of the group, dove under a table and recited every prayer he knew.

"I then doubled back behind and through the kitchen, near the bar," says Sonny, the "assassin." The guns had fallen silent. J. D. then slowly raises himself from Presley's prone form. Just as J. D.'s head pokes over the level of the bar, Sonny fires again. "I fired like I was shooting at his head from about ten or twelve feet away, and the wad from the blank hits him in the head." J. D. yelled out "Goddamn," which is understandable even for a gospel singer. Donny Sumner, who is behind the bar, sees Sonny's pigskin-coated hand poking around the corner, although he can't see his face. In a desperate move he picks up a big can of tomato juice, grabs Sonny's hand and slings his missile around the corner hoping it will connect with the assassin. "His hand slipped off mine and the can missed me and crashed against the wall," according to Sonny, who then wheeled around the corner pointing the gun at Donny Sumner. "You're a dead sonofabitch," he said.

Donny's face registered shock. "Sonny, oh my God!" He thought Sonny had flipped and was the killer. Ed Enoch by this time had reached for one of the "dead" security guard's guns and was pulling the trigger, which produced nothing but dull clicks. Donny Sumner was slumped on the floor in a near faint.

Presley had been laughing convulsively through it all. J. D. Sumner had felt it as he was sprawled across him but thought Presley was in a convulsion of fear.

"It pretty much ended there," says Sonny, "but we all thought Donny Sumner was out of it. It was a long while before the blood started circulating in his face. We had to fix him a drink." The night ended in an uproar of hilarity as the story was retold. All agreed that J. D. and his boys had performed admirably under fire. That night Sonny and Red could have got an Oscar.

While the bodyguards of the Memphis Mafia were always sensitive to death threats and the safety of their boss, the concert audiences in Vegas and particularly on tour were another source of worry. It was feared that someone in the audience would get killed. Red West, from the early days on the road with Presley, was used to the hysteria. But after Presley's comeback, it was even more horrific. "I swear," says Red, "I don't know how someone hasn't been killed at some of these shows. There have been a lot of people hurt but it's a miracle somebody hasn't been killed." Dave Hebler is just as incredulous.

Sonny West relates: "People in these crowds aren't people any more. They become absolute animals. They are ordinary honest men and housewives and stuff and yet when they get in that crowd when Elvis is up there, they become wild, wild animals."

Dave Hebler, when he first started, knew that the security work would be tough. "It's not a matter of duking a guy out. Any idiot can do that. You have to use minimum force to keep things cool without letting any madman get up and hurt Elvis. When I first started, I was amazed to see respectable grown ladies take their pants off in a class showroom like the International Hotel in Las Vegas, take their pants off, show everything and wave their panties at him and throw them on the stage. Anyway you look at it, it's pretty disgusting for a grown woman to behave that way, but Elvis just does it to them. There are no plants in the audience to do it for publicity. It happens." But it was in towns where they played a convention center or an auditorium that held ten to twelve thousand people that the real problems started.

Dave recounts a situation that once got out of hand in the Omni Hall in Atlanta, Georgia. "It's an amphitheater set-up. There is a high stage about ten feet off the ground. But two feet away from the stage, there is a section of seats that slope upwards. There is a ten-foot drop onto a concrete floor between the stage and where the seating begins. Well, Elvis has reached the part of his act where he throws out about fifty scarfs into the audience. I look out into the audience and I just go cold. The crowd has gone berserk and is charging the stage. The cops in Atlanta were great, but they couldn't stop this charge. But worst of all was where I was on the edge of the stage trying to stop people leaping over the railing and jumping the two feet onto the stage, because if they missed they would have gone straight down onto the concrete. Of course that's what happened. First this girl takes a running leap down from the stairs, over the rail. There are dozens of people crushed against the railing and I'm terrified a little kid is going to get crushed to death. As it happened, that tragedy was never far off, and it was only quick work by the cops and Red and Sonny and me that stopped a tragedy. But on this night, this chick comes flying over the rail. I catch her, a two hundred-pound broad. I'm holding her with one arm and a cop underneath is climbing up to stop her. Eventually he loses his footing and they both go down, *whap*, bodies on concrete. Then another girl comes over and she goes down. God, it was sickening. In the end three broads came over there. The cops and the girls were carted off."

Meanwhile on the other side, a scarf flutters around a girl's neck. Red recalls: "It looped around her neck and a pair of maniacs grabbed both ends. Well, they would not let go. This girl is choking to death and the sons of bitches would not let go. I see it and the girl is going down. She is dying, man. I got across there and there was no hope of trying to battle with them. These two broads who were pulling at each end had a death grip. I whipped out a knife and cut it before it was too late. Then the broads were fighting over the shreds of scarf. It was scary."

In Hampton Roads, Virginia, Red remembers that the crowd completely swamped thirty policemen. "Those cops there were getting badly hurt. There is no way thirty police can really control a mad rush of three hundred or four hundred people. They just crushed these guys against the stage. Knocked the hell out of them. They pulled Charlie Hodge off the stage and passed him over their heads like baggage. When they decided he was too small a fish, they threw him back like a javelin. In San Diego, the situation got very ugly mainly because there was no regular police on duty."

"The San Diego Police Department don't let their men moonlight like most towns," says Dave. "So we have to have rent-a-cops. They aren't trained and they either overreact or do nothing at all. Well, hell broke loose and people are going down everywhere. This one girl just kicked the hell out of two of them, booted them in the groin and down they went.

"In Springfield, Massachusetts, when the cops started telling everyone to sit down, Elvis really blew it. He said, 'Don't take any notice of the cops. We're here to have fun. If you want to scream and jump around that's what we're here for.' Well, I come from up that way and I knew that was the wrong thing to say because in this convention center, which held about eighteen thousand people, about one thousand of them just charged the stage. Man, the cops didn't have a chance. Once again I saw a broad do something awful to these two cops, kicked them in the groin. There are cops falling like flies. I'll never know how we got out of there alive."

Red, Sonny and Dave got most annoyed at mothers who held their two-year-old and three-year-old children up to get a scarf. The kids would be terrified. They didn't want a scarf. Their mothers did and they risked their children's lives to get one. All the boys have rescued children from under the feet of stampeding mobs.

Dave recalls: "The worst thing is when someone wheels some poor unfortunate up to the stage in a wheelchair. They tell you that they are dying of leukemia and only have three weeks to live. You have to get them out of there because when the riot starts they will only have about a minute to live. One incident that sticks out in my mind was this woman yelling for a scarf. I'm trying to calm her down and ease her out of the way of getting crushed to death and she yells at me, 'But my daughter has got emphysema, don't you understand? She has emphysema.' That blew my mind."

Presley encourages the pandemonium. Sonny says that Presley told him, "When they stop attacking me, I'm dead." When an audience is quiet and polite, he will go to any lengths to get their juices going.

Red West remembers the time Presley actually "bought" an audience. It happened in North Carolina, in 1973.

"He was in the dressing room," says Red, "and he told me that the audience wasn't worth a damn. They weren't responding, which wasn't really true. This was pretty much a rural audience and they were very enthusiastic but they were polite. There were no riots, which he had been getting used to. When he would come across a quiet audience, he would often chew them out. He would tell them, 'You are allowed to clap, you know,' or he would say, 'This is where the audience usually applauds.' But he wasn't turned on by this audience at all. Well, after the first show he decided to get a requests box going. The audience would write their requests and he would sing them. He thought that might goose them a little, but once again, no riots.

"Okay, so he gets Joe Esposito to get in touch with a Memphis jeweler, Lowell Hayes, who was a good friend of ours, and he tells him to bring up some rings. He even gets Lowell to fly back to Memphis and get more than the first load of rings he got. Well, Lowell comes racing back with all these rings. Now I can't remember exactly but there is in excess of thirty thousand dollars' worth of rings. There was one, which I know was worth eighteen thousand dollars, and plenty of others worth five thousand dollars."

Presley came out on stage and introduced J. D. Sumner of the Stamps. Sumner's left hand is what he calls "Elvis Presley's hand"—it is festooned with rings and jewelry Presley has given him. The boys guess that gifts to Sumner total in excess of one hundred thousand dollars in jewelry alone. Presley came out on stage and, as was often his habit, he said over the mike, "J. D., hold up your right hand and show them your jewels," which J. D. always dutifully does. Then he said, "Hold up my hand," and then J. D. held up his "Elvis Presley" hand with all the gifts on it. Then Presley bent down and took off a very expensive ring and handed it to a man in the first row. The audience snapped. Then a woman came down, and he repeated the process. Then another, and another ring came off the hand. He then gave rings to each member of the band. Whoever was there got one.

"The audience just went crazy," says Red. "These weren't dress rings, these were real diamonds and sapphires and stuff like that. On that night he gave away maybe thirty-five thousand dollars' worth of rings. It was insanity, but he got what he wanted and when he wanted it. And what he wanted were those waves of love from the audience—at any price."

With a smile Red recalls that watching this lavish gift-giving from the wings was Vernon Presley, who had an expression on his face approximating the reaction to a bad pain. "Old Vernon would look like he was going to die whenever Elvis started that gift-giving business. We used to crack up when we would see him get that look on his face and he would clap his hands to his head."

While Presley could be capable of some of the wildest gimmicks to turn an audience on, he could also, when under the influence of the wrong kind of "medication," be capable of saying outrageous things to an audience.

In Greensboro, North Carolina, the audience-buying performance, Presley was ad-libbing to the audience in his introductions. When Presley is feeling good, his sense of humor is sometimes as keen as the most accomplished comic's. This was a night when it decidedly was not. One of his featured singers was a very talented, pretty soprano named Kathy Westmoreland. In the recent past, he had taken to introducing Kathy with the aside, "This is Kathy Westmoreland. . . . She doesn't care where she gets her fun." And then he would introduce the Sweet Inspirations, a talented group of black female singers who had been with him from his first opening night in Las Vegas—then as a quartet but now a trio—with another aside, "Their breath smells like they have been eating catfish," an apparent but very unfunny reference to the fact that they ate soul food.

After two or three instances when Presley made his

reference to Kathy Westmoreland, Red remembers that she very politely mentioned to Joe Esposito that she wished he would stop introducing her in this way because she was getting obscene telephone calls. Very diplomatically, Joe mentioned this to Presley. Neither Kathy nor the Inspirations appreciated the introductions.

On the Greensboro night Red recalls that Presley got up and said, "This is Kathy Westmoreland, our soprano singer who doesn't like the way I introduce her . . . and if she doesn't like it, she can get the hell off the stage."

Dave Hebler remembers that "there was a shock in the audience. You could have heard a pin drop. Damn, it was so damn embarrassing just to hear it, I wanted to dive into a big hole. First Estelle of the Inspirations starts to cry, then Sylvia, another of the group, starts to cry. They both walk off the stage in tears. Then Kathy gets up, very distraught, and walks off. The audience just doesn't know what to do. It was mass embarrassment. The only one of the girls to stay on stage was Myrna Smith of the Inspirations, who was going with Jerry Schilling. Myrna is stuck there, the only one left, and Elvis makes this big thing of going over to her and taking off a diamond ring from his finger and gives it to her. Poor Myrna, she nearly died from embarrassment. This was supposed to be a gesture toward her because she stayed on. She gave it back to him after the show but he refused to take it."

Presley got through the act using J. D. Sumner and his quartet to sing back-up for the numbers that the Inspirations would have done. After the show, Presley was insane with rage. "We get in the car to go to the motel," Dave says. "In the car is Red, me, Dick Grob, Joe Esposito, Elvis, and he had this blond-haired girl friend from Georgia. The scene is maniacal. We're all talking at once to calm him down, get the thing straightened out. But, I promise you, he had gone completely off his head with rage. He couldn't take the fact that someone would stand on a principle and go against the great Elvis Presley."

Presley was vitriolic. Turning to Joe Esposito, he said, "Joe, get me another nigger group." Then he switched his wrath to Jerry Schilling, who was going with Myrna Smith. As Dave points out, Jerry Schilling was not around, or there most certainly would have been blood flowing.

Finally Presley consented to having Kathy Westmoreland and the Inspirations finish the tour, although he was going to fire them after the trip. A little bit of sanity came from a member of Colonel Parker's office, who told all the girls not to worry. Their jobs would be secure. He told everyone, "Look, Elvis is just too lazy to break in another group. Your jobs are secure." He was right, and they are still with him today, although whether they remain out of loyalty or because it suits their career is open to question.

Red West, bodyguard, was also an accomplished songwriter and as such was much closer to Presley musically than any of the other boys. Between 1969 and 1976, Red acted as a conductor for Presley. The King of Rock 'n' Roll could have afforded the best music technicians in the world but he relied heavily on Red's musical skill. Because Presley can't read music he would count on Red to cue him in with the lyrics. It is ironic perhaps that Red, who during the years when he was close to Presley spent so much time swinging punches, was to some degree the musical "brains" behind many of Presley's best recordings. It went even further than that. The millions of teenagers who rocked to some of Presley's most gigantic hits didn't realize that a quiet, slow-talking bodyguard was the genius behind the music. "Elvis just asked me to pick out the music," says Red. "There would be ten or twelve musical spots on each film. Now there would be anything up to twenty songs competing for each spot. Elvis just handed that job over to me. I was flattered, and I guess I did a pretty good job because those records sold millions and millions."

By 1970, Red could see the first subtle signs of Presley's professional decline. "Elvis really started getting lazy," he says. "He still had his skill, his instinct, but . . . he started getting into all the heavy stuff he was taking. Anyway, I first noticed it when we were doing a recording session at RCA Victor in Nashville. I just sensed that he didn't want to do the recording session and I was right. There were three numbers he had to do, 'If Every Day Was Like Christmas,' a song I wrote for him, and there was 'Indescribably Blue' and 'I'll Remember You.'" Presley began to pull the first in a long line of nonappearances at recording sessions. He told Red he was sick, which Red took with a pinch of salt. "Red," said Presley, "you go down and cut the tracks. You sing with the orchestra. I'll dub it in later on." Red West is a man who is rarely frightened of anything, but he was suddenly scared to death.

Presley holed up in a motel while Red went to RCA Victor's famous "Music Row." The boyhood buddy and general factotum all at once had millions of dollars riding on his shoulders. He was to sing exactly as Presley would. Behind him were Jake Hess and the Imperial Quartet as the back-up group. Every musician in the band behind Red was the top man in his field in Nashville, which meant tops in the country. Red admits that at the time he was taking some of Presley's prescribed "medicine"—amphetamines. "I was high and I was nervous," he says, "but these guys made me feel really at ease. And, good Lord, I pulled it off." He did the three singles in seven hours, approximately the time it would have taken Presley. Felton Jarvis, Presley's record producer, came over to Red at the end of the session and said, "Man, you did a helluva job. I appreciate what you have done, because there was a helluva lot of money going down the drain if somebody had not done something." Of course, two months later Presley went back and dubbed in the voice. But Red had to sing in the exact key that he thought Presley would sing in, and with the identical timing. "If Every Day Was Like Christmas," the song that Red wrote, and "I'll Remember You" each sold almost two million discs—which wasn't a bad day's work for a guy who was supposed to be just a body-guard.

Typical of Red West's musical vision had to do with a now famous song with which Presley scored a big hit, "The Green Green Grass of Home." Red had heard the song in 1966 on a Jerry Lee Lewis album, and he took it to Presley. "Man, this is a heck of a num-ber," Red told him. "Why don't you give it a try." Country music had not yet reached the popularity of today. Presley listened but halfway through he said, "No, man, it's too country." In 1970, driving back from Los Angeles in the Presley Greyhound bus, the group heard Tom Jones's rendition of it on the radio. Presley turned up the volume. "Man, that's a helluva song," he said. Red raised his eyebrows. When the group got into the range of WHQB, the Memphis radio station, Presley stopped the bus and asked Marty Lacker to telephone the station's top disc jockey, and his old school friend, George Klein, and ask him to play the tune. About every fifty miles, Presley repeated this; suddenly he had a passion for the song. When they got to Memphis, he told Marty Lacker to get the Tom Jones album, which Presley played until it almost wore out. In early 1976, when Presley did his album *Elvis At Home,* "Green Green Grass of Home" was Presley's first choice. "Hell, that was the tune I recommended to you four years ago," Red told him. Presley looked up and said, "It sure sounded different then." Needless to say, it became yet another Presley hit.

Red recalls such anecdotes with something close to regret: "Look, Elvis never forced me to be a body-guard but the way it turned out, that was how I was regarded. I remember one guy calling me a pistolero. Well, I regret that. Music has been my life and I sometimes think that if I hadn't fallen for the demands of Elvis wanting me to look after him and had done my own thing in music, I might have been wrestling with a music score in a studio rather than with some half-drunk or mad gal who was trying to throw her panties at Elvis."

In the 1973–74 period, Red, Sonny and Dave saw just how incredibly Presley could dive from absolute heights, physically and emotionally, to the rock bottom. It is a tribute to this man's phenomenal constitution and his gigantic talent that in 1973 he could in one year perform one of the most memorable engagements of his life—the "Satellite Television Special," watched by more people in the world than man's landing on the moon—and degenerate into a screaming emotional wreck.

The separation and subsequent divorce from Priscilla played heavily on Presley's mind. Similar traumas have shattered stronger men. But it ushered into his life and the lives of the Memphis Mafia an incredible yo-yo behavior pattern. Sonny recalls that the satellite special, seen by a billion people throughout the world, was a crowning glory for Presley's talent and for the Colonel's. After all, if successful promotion is gauged by the size of the audience, the satellite special had to be the greatest show on earth in the history of show business—or any other business. "Man, we were going through tough times," says Sonny. "Elvis's diet was going mad. He would eat whole gigantic cakes all by himself. He would get mad at us after he ate the stuff, and if we hid it from him he would get mad again. He was very fat and he had a lot of problems with his stomach, which just quit working. His body wasn't working. The pills were doing all the work, and yet when that television special came up, he dropped down to one hundred sixty-five pounds, thin as a rake and more handsome than ten movie stars."

But after it was over, it was back to Las Vegas and on tour, doing the same old stuff. "There was a time right in there," says Sonny, "when I thought I would have a nervous breakdown. Joe Esposito was being run ragged too. It was the same old thing. Even if he had a girl with him he would wake us up and we would have to go to his bedroom and talk to him until he dropped off. But he was so wired with so much stuff in him we would get a call an hour later. I was taking sleeping tablets and Valium to knock myself out. When he and Joe had a flare-up, Elvis picked up an ashtray and threatened to smash Joe's head in with it. Then when he went on stage, he was doing all this talking and fooling around with the audience. They paid their money to hear him sing and perform, not give his philosophies on life."

During one such period, Presley and the Colonel came perilously close to a parting of the ways. The Colonel had always been concerned about Presley's health and his physical condition.

When Presley suddenly got enamored of a particular singing group, which he wanted to sign for $100,000 a year, Sonny recalls that the Colonel pointed out that their worth to the entourage was only $50,000. "Elvis was insistent. One night he was really out of it. He called me into his suite in the International Hotel and he had made up a damned contract on toilet paper to give this group, which I won't mention, one hundred thousand dollars. Now, the Colonel knew what they were worth. They were good but not one hundred thousand dollars good. The old man is never wrong. So he brings me in and wants me to witness the signing of a contract for one hundred thousand. I refused to do it. He got mad as hell at me, but I knew he wasn't functioning properly at the time. That started a little friction."

Next came an incident where a chef at the hotel was fired. Presley had become close to this chef and he was annoyed about the firing, so much so that he took his complaint to the audience. Red recalls: "He got up there on stage and started putting down the management of the hotel that was employing him. It was madness. He told the audience that the hotel wouldn't fire the chef as long as he was working there."

The Colonel was furious. He had swung a very lucrative contract from the International Hotel and had done everything to stick by his part of the bargain. The International Hotel, in turn, had been very good to the Colonel and Presley. It was a sound business relationship. According to Sonny, the Colonel exploded: "You can't tell them how to run their business. What right have you got to say a thing like that on stage?" Presley and the Colonel locked horns. They blew up at each other and disappeared into Presley's suite. The Colonel emerged with the words "Okay, I'll call a press conference in the morning and say I'm leaving."

According to Red West, Presley replied, "I'll call a press conference tonight."

"Actually what happened is the Colonel stayed up and worked out all the money that was due to him," says Red. "I didn't see the figures, but it was like a million due him for this and a million for that. Elvis showed Vernon the figures. Vernon was ready for the Colonel to leave, but then after looking at the figures, things seemed to quiet down."

Apart from the trouble over his marriage break-up and friction with the Colonel, Presley's throat was in bad shape. Doctors were using suction devices to clear it of congestion. There was a fear that Presley might be developing pneumonia. The strength of the Memphis Mafia was weakened by the departure of Joe Esposito and Jerry Schilling on a trip to Europe.

Sonny seemed to be sleeping about an hour a day. "I tell you," says Sonny, "I was going nuts looking after him with his actions." Two weeks after the blowup between Presley and the Colonel, Sonny West was at his wit's end. "I talked to a doctor friend of mine who had given Elvis a shot. I got his assurance that it would knock him out for at least five or six hours. I got him to give me a shot too. Damnit, an hour after, at about eight o'clock in the morning, Elvis wakes me and wants me to come to his room. God almighty, I couldn't believe it. I go into his room and he is awake. I don't know how he did it, because I had the same shot as he did and I was wasted." Presley looked at Sonny and said, "I've been thinking. We're going to have to call that old sonofabitch because he ain't going to call us."

Sonny replied, "Who?"

Presley said only two words: "The Colonel."

Sonny got onto the Colonel, who commented that he was slurring his words. "I've just taken a shot and Elvis woke me," Sonny told him. "He wants to speak to you." Sonny did not stay there during the conversation, but he believes Presley apologized. He recalls there had been a lot of speculation among the boys whether the break would be final. Some thought the relationship was at its breaking point. Others thought that Jerry Weintraub, the manager of Frank Sinatra and John Denver, would be the man to fill the Colonel's shoes, but Sonny thought otherwise. "No, Elvis would never listen to Jerry, as good a manager as he is. And that's why deep down he doesn't like the Colonel, because he has to listen to him. He knows what the Colonel has done for him. They are the two greatest at what they do. It was meant that they were to come together no matter how much friction. The two of them are like an immovable object meeting an irresistible force."

The split was over. After the nightmare in Las Vegas that Sonny went through, Presley had some idea how far he had pushed him. Soon after he bought Sonny a gleaming Eldorado.

By this time, it was an accepted fact that Presley's emotional and physical state fluctuated like the stock exchange. In 1974, Sonny, who had been doing advance work with the Colonel, had not seen Presley for about a month. He had always been in the city ahead of the tour, finalizing security details and taking care of the general logistics of the Presley caravan. Dave remembers that Sonny finally saw Presley in College Park, Maryland: "Sonny got an awful shock to see the condition he was in. He was so torn up physically and emotionally, the tears just came to Sonny's eyes."

That day, Red West, Sonny West and Dave Hebler went into a room in a motel in College Park, Maryland, and said a prayer to God to put their boss back on the right track.

"That's right, we all prayed together," says Dave. "And I promise you, I'm not a particularly religious person, but that's how we felt about the man."

If money meant nothing to Presley during his first years as a millionaire, by 1974 it was treated with more contempt than ever. At one stage during 1974 and 1975, he bought and owned no less than five airplanes. Not even Howard Hughes or Aristotle Onassis had five personal planes. He bought a Jet Commander, a Falcon, a Jetstar, a Gulfstream and the granddaddy of them all, a Convair 880. The West boys and Dave Hebler don't pretend to know how much it all costs. There are accountants right now who probably still don't. Presley made no attempt to use the planes in any businesslike manner. He could have leased them when he wasn't using them and at least got some of his investment back, but there were times when he actually paid to lease another plane because it was more convenient.

At one stage he was amused by a news report that singer John Denver had given his manager, Jerry Weintraub, a Rolls-Royce that reputedly cost $40,000. Presley laughed and said, "I'll show that sonofabitch. I'm going to give my manager a million-dollar airplane." The million-dollar plane was the Gulfstream. Col. Tom Parker, in his infinite wisdom, refused the gift.

Dave Hebler cracks that Dick Grob, one of the

faithful bodyguards who had once been a U.S. Air Force pilot in Korea, could have flown cover for the flotilla of planes. At one stage there were five pilots on his payroll.

It was, says Red West, very similar to Elvis's earlier buying binges. "You know, he started off buying that horse for Priscilla and ended up buying a farm with trucks, horses and trailers for everyone. He bought one plane, then went overboard and bought five of them. Old Elvis never did things by half measures."

Sonny remembers that when Presley got into the plane-buying spree, he was commuting between Memphis and Dallas, where the planes were purchased, as if he were going down to the local pizza parlor. He was particularly bent on trying to impress Priscilla, even after their break-up, with his acquisition of planes. "He was very proud, and rightly so, of his Convair, and flew Priscilla into Dallas for a personal inspection of the plane," says Sonny. "He seemed very anxious to have Priscilla use the plane any time she wanted it. It was almost as if he was saying to her 'Look what you left—here is a man who has his own airliner.' "

The bizarre pattern of Presley's behavior seemed doubly erratic after the 1973 divorce from Priscilla. Dave Hebler remembers a day in 1975 when Presley suddenly slapped him on the back and said, "I'm going to buy you and Joe [Esposito] a Maserati each." Dave and Joe flatly refused the offer. As it turned out, there were no Maseratis in Memphis, but Presley was in a gift-giving mood, so he piled into a car and headed down to Shilling Motors in Memphis, where he proceeded to buy no less than nine Lincoln Mark IVs.

"It was madness," says Dave. "He bought cars for all of us, but it got crazier the next day." It appears that Presley found out that the salesman should have offered him a discount by virtue of the mass purchase. "He got it in his head that the salesman had screwed him," says Dave, "so he called us all together and told us that we were going to take the cars back. He didn't want to take the cars from us. He just wanted to take them back and buy Cadillacs instead. Well, as it worked out, we took back seven of them. Can you imagine the salesman's reaction when we all drove up in seven Lincolns with mileage on the clock and said, 'Take them back'? The guy almost had a heart attack. Well, it was resolved and we ended up going to another Lincoln dealer, and he also bought some Cadillacs that day, although I can't remember how many. What I do remember however, was this black couple were at the Cadillac dealers, Madison Cadillac, it was. Anyway, he sees this lady looking at a Cadillac Seville and he strikes up a conversation with her and idly asks, 'Do you like that car?' She replied, 'Oh, yes, it's very nice.' Presley said, 'Fine, pick one out. I'm going to buy one for you.' The lady looked like she was going to faint, but she did pick one out and he did buy it for her."

When the story hit the wire services, an announcer in Vail, Colorado, reported the story. He signed off the report with a one-liner: "Elvis, if you're listening, I could use a car myself." Presley got Red to call the announcer and then he got on the telephone.

"What color do you like?" Presley asked casually. Predictably the announcer thought it was one of his friends putting him on.

"Aw, come on, who is this?"

"No, I'm serious. This is Elvis Presley. I want to buy you a car." The next day the announcer was driving a new Cadillac, paid for by Presley.

"A lot of people think he does those things for publicity, but he doesn't," says Red. "When he gives, he really gives. It's a genuine gift and he doesn't announce it."

Sonny and Red remember that Presley read a story about a black woman in Memphis who was badly crippled. Completely unannounced, he bought her the most expensive wheelchair available. "Man," says

Sonny, "that woman's face was a picture when he just walked into this old rundown house and he got us to unload this expensive wheelchair. It was a beautiful gesture and Elvis was very capable of doing those things. And yet, he would turn around and spoil it all by some thoughtless gesture."

His gift-giving usually ran to cars or jewelry, but he is also a very generous giver of cash to the various Catholic, Protestant and Jewish charities in Memphis. "Which," says Red, "is something I could never work out. Elvis would often tell us that Catholics were the demon referred to in the closing section of the Bible. And although he hired Jews and had many Jewish friends, he was convinced that Jews were out to take over the world. Marty Lacker, who worked for him, was Jewish, and Elvis would always say, 'Well, Marty is one of the good Jews.' But deep down Elvis is very prejudiced and he made no secret about it in his talks to us."

One person whom he was intent on giving a gift to was none other than Vice-President Spiro Agnew. Sonny recalls: "The Vice-President was staying in Palm Springs when Elvis was there. Anyway, he set up a meeting with him. We all went to the house he was staying at and Elvis had bought a gold inlaid .357 Magnum revolver. It cost about two thousand dollars. Anyway, he goes into the house to present the gun to him and stayed talking to him for about half an hour." Curiously, in the light of other events, Vice-President Agnew demurred on the gift of the gun, saying that as an elected official, he could not accept a gift. When Agnew was forced from office, Sonny recalls telling Presley that Mr. Agnew could now accept the gift. Presley replied, "No, screw him, he got caught as a crook."

Presley is particularly generous to his female friends. The West boys estimate that Presley has given girl friend Linda Thompson over a quarter of a million dollars in jewelry alone. Presley met Linda in 1972, soon after his break-up with Priscilla. A friend of Presley's, George Klein, a former Memphis disc jockey, introduced them. Linda impressed the boys as extremely religious when they first met her. "She would never curse or use bad language," says Sonny. "I remember that instead of cursing she used to substitute the word *hullo,* which we all thought was kind of cute. It took a heck of a lot of work for Elvis to get her to move in with him. She just didn't think it was right. But she finally gave in."

The West boys remember, however, that Linda was not shy about receiving gifts from Presley. "I would say," comments Sonny, "that she has more dresses and clothes than Elizabeth Taylor. Whenever she travels she has many suitcases with her. She must be one of the country's best-dressed women. Man, I have known her to go into Georgio's in Los Angeles and buy a dozen dresses, and that is one very expensive store. Also in Las Vegas, she would shop at Suzie Creamcheese and buy a dress in every color. Her jewelry is something else again. Elvis has given her at least a quarter of a million dollars in jewelry, and that is a modest estimate. He has also bought her family a house in Memphis and he has got her a beautiful apartment in Los Angeles."

Linda appears to have a particularly tolerant attitude toward Presley, according to the West boys and Dave Hebler. "The average girl couldn't take Elvis's lifestyle," says Red, "particularly now when he stays in his room for a week and two weeks at a time without coming out. Linda doesn't seem to mind. That kind of life didn't appeal to Priscilla, but Linda seems to take it in her stride."

She also has a tolerance for other women in Presley's life. In 1974, Presley was introduced by Joe Esposito to Sheila Ryan, an incredibly pretty girl from Chicago who is now married to James Caan. "He often would alternate taking them on tour with him," Sonny recalls. "One time he would take Linda, then the next time he would take Sheila. If ever Linda made a fuss about him alternating her with another girl, I would always hear Elvis tell her over the telephone, 'Woman, take that knife out of my damn back.' I really think Linda wants to get married to Elvis and you can't blame her for wanting marriage, but I don't think Elvis will ever make the step."

When Presley was dating a beauty queen from Georgia, Dave Hebler recalls that a photographer went to shoot a picture of him sitting with his new girl friend in the back seat of his car. The driver started to drive off, thinking that Presley didn't want a picture taken of him with a new girl. But Presley told him, "Let him take the picture. I don't mind if they use it. Linda thinks she is married to me."

While still dating Linda, the boys remember that Presley introduced Sheila Ryan to a Las Vegas audience as his girl friend and asked her to show off her new diamond ring. That was not all. In the audience was his ex-wife, Priscilla. "It was weird," Red recounts. "He had Priscilla and Sheila sitting in a booth next to one another."

Presley introduced Sheila as his "new girl friend," then introduced Priscilla and added, "We get along fine. There is no trouble." Then he turned to the band and said, "But Mike Stone ain't got no balls. Mike Stone ain't got no balls. Mike Stone is a stud, my ass."

Dave Hebler was incredulous. "There were people in the audience who heard it. It was a wild thing to say but Elvis couldn't help make the crack. Of course, Mike Stone is one hell of a good-looking guy and Elvis knows it. But saying that, my jaw dropped open. Poor Priscilla and Sheila seemed very embarrassed, but they both handled it with lots of class. Priscilla said at the time that she should have known better than attend the show. God, it was embarrassing!"

Mike Stone became an obsession with Presley, understandable, perhaps, under the circumstances. Red recalls with a laugh: "We made damn sure that the television show 'The Streets of San Francisco' was never on when Elvis was around. Karl Malden plays the part of Mike Stone, a detective, and I promise you, Elvis was very likely to blow a television set out with his gun if it had come on the screen."

"There was an incident on stage in Las Vegas," says Sonny. "It was the night of the eighteenth of February. Elvis was half through his act at the International Hotel and suddenly this guy from a group sitting down front jumps up on the stage. He had this coat draped over his arm and we didn't know what was going on. We thought it could have been a gun inside. Anyway, he comes running toward Elvis on stage from the left side. Red grabs him in a headlock and drags him off to the security guards. Meanwhile, one of the guy's friends leaps up on the stage. J.D. Sumner sort of tapped him on the shoulder and told him to sit down. This guy draws back his fist to hit J.D. and then we all get up there on the stage and it's like a big brawl. One guy goes smashing back from the stage into a table and there is glasses and stuff breaking. Anyway, we got the place cleared of the guys. Elvis, meanwhile, is leaping around the stage kicking the air with karate kicks. He didn't touch anyone. He was just kicking the air. It all calms down and Elvis tells the audience that he should have broken their goddamn necks. The audience cheered and it was over. But after the show, Elvis got us and said that the guys who caused the trouble had been sent by Mike Stone to break up his act. The man who drew back his fist to hit J.D. Sumner had tape across his fist, and Elvis was convinced that he was a karate expert sent by Mike. And that's when he asked us to hit Mike Stone. He was absolutely convinced that Mike was planning to do him in, which was ridiculous. Frankly, I don't think Mike gave Elvis a second thought."

The West boys and Dave Hebler saw a steady decline in Presley, both physically and emotionally, over the past three years. He had severe problems with a twisted colon, and his weight seemed to go up and down like a yo-yo. He lost all interest in the physical aspects of karate. The boys remember that when they would work out at it, Presley would go through the initial meditation called for during a proper karate workout and then lose interest and sit around eating and watching the others work out.

Despite his ballooning weight and a double chin, Presley is still convinced of his good looks. "He believes," says Sonny, "that he has a face like King David. He is quite vain, although he doesn't look after himself. When he goes on stage, he often wears one of those elastic-type girdles to keep his stomach in. He wears lifts in his shoes to make him look taller. He even wears lifts in his slippers around the house." Once again, the problem is simply boredom. Presley has nothing to interest him. Regrettably, the one challenge that the boys believe could have changed Presley's life was not taken.

Sonny recalls that in 1975 Barbra Streisand and her boy friend, Jon Peters, visited Presley in his dressing room in Las Vegas. "She came in and congratulated him on his show," says Sonny. They talked at length, and in the course of the conversation, Miss Streisand announced that she was producing the remake of *A Star Is Born,* which she eventually starred in with Kris Kristofferson. Miss Streisand's original choice, however, was Presley.

"She wanted him to play the part," said Red, "and I tell you what, it was a damn tragedy that he didn't, because Elvis would have been great in the part of the washed up superstar who gives his career to his girl friend. Now they were very serious about the offer. I remember they both were joking about each other's weight. Elvis was very keen to do it. You could see the interest in his face. It was going to be a real challenge. How it broke down, I believe, was because the money wasn't right.

"I believe that the Colonel wanted a million up front and Streisand wanted him to go on a percentage deal. Anyway, it fell through, which was a damn shame. I think the Colonel said after, 'We don't need Streisand.' And then Elvis started talking himself out of wanting to do it. You know, he said that it wouldn't have been his picture, that it would have been all Barbra's picture."

After the discussion with Miss Streisand, Presley must have been concerned about his appearance, because he got cosmetic surgery. "He had it done at the Mid-South Hospital in Memphis, Tennessee," said Sonny. "He had it done in 1975 because I got the bill. He went into the hospital under my name and it came up on my Blue Cross-Blue Shield card. The hospital pointed out that Blue Cross does not cover cosmetic surgery. After he had it done, he brought me into his room and asked if I noticed any difference. Actually, I didn't until he told me. He had his eyes done and there is a thin little scar around his ears where he had his face tightened. You can hardly notice it. After he got it done, he tried to talk me into having it done, but I wasn't interested."

Presley's behavior seemed to reach a peak of unpredictability in 1975. "I remember," says Dave, "in Las Vegas that just the tiniest incident would set him off. One time a guy took a picture of him in a gun shop in Las Vegas. Sheila Ryan was with us at the time. We asked the photographer not to take a shot with him holding a gun. Anyway, the guy got a bit aggressive but we forgot about it. Elvis, when he got back to the hotel. . . . He screamed and yelled like a madman about one guy backing down all us karate experts. I remember Sheila ran from her room with her hands to her head crying."

Dave remembers that in Tahoe at one hotel Presley had bombed himself with so many pills that he couldn't walk. "It was scary," says Dave, "because he was on the roof and we were trying to get him to get some sun. But, man, he almost tumbled off the roof, he was so far out of it. He almost fell over the side. I had to carry him away."

When the brother of a police friend died in Denver, Presley flew in to sing at the funeral service. He also paid for a colossal floral tribute. He then attended the funeral dressed in a police captain's uniform with specially tailored flared pants. He also wore the police captain's uniform to a recording session in Memphis.

The boys remember that by January, 1976, Presley seemed to be having more and more flashes of uncontrollable temper. Sonny relates: "He took us to Vail, Colorado, for what he said was going to be a dream vacation. Well, it was a nightmare. He was heavy into pills. On January 8, it was his birthday. We drove up to Vail in a bus and we congratulated him on his forty-first birthday that night. Well, Linda got a cake, but we were staying in another condominium, so we didn't know she was going to present it to him. Well, she did and he called a big meeting complaining about none of the bodyguards being there. He was like a spoiled kid."

Then Dave Hebler was involved in an argument with another member of the group who accused the bodyguards of not doing their jobs. Dave argued back that the security was the tightest part of the whole Presley organization. Presley flared at Dave, "I'm not going to have any more of this bullying bullshit. It's going to stop or someone is going to die."

"It really got black," says Red, "he was flashing at everyone. He had a lot of stuff in him." It reached a dramatic climax when Presley decided to move into a condominum occupied by Jerry Schilling. Presley decided at three in the morning he wanted to move out of his quarters and into Jerry Schilling's. He woke Schilling up and ordered him to move. Schilling protested that a move could wait until the morning.

Presley recruited Red to go over to the Schilling quarters. Schilling was angry and made it abundantly clear to Presley. "The next thing," says Red, "he tells me to beat up Jerry. I managed to cool that kind of talk down. Well, I thought I did. Then I see him putting a bullet into a gun and cocking it . . . It was getting very hairy. Elvis really wasn't himself."

During the same trip, Dave recalls that Susan Ford, the daughter of President Ford, was in Vail. "Her girl friend was going to throw a party for her and wanted to get Elvis along as a surprise. The security guys came over and tried to organize but Elvis wouldn't do it. He said he would be quite willing to meet her if she came to his chalet but he wouldn't go to a party. He was trying to make it like he was more important than the president's daughter."

More and more, say the West boys, Presley seemed to lose interest in everything about him. "He would only talk about his jewelry, cars, and wardrobe," says Sonny. "He didn't seem to have any other conversation. Other stars would come backstage and all he could talk about was his possessions. He wasn't interested in other performers. In fact, he didn't like other performers. He would always have something catty to say about them. If they came to his dressing room to see him, he would keep them waiting for an hour on end before he would make his entrance." Red continues: "I remember Jimmy Dean, a nice guy, was waiting for him one night. Elvis came out of his bedroom after keeping Jimmy out there for an hour. Jimmy greeted Elvis with a big hullo and said jokingly, 'I'm out to rip a yard from your ass, keeping me waiting.' And Elvis whipped out his .22 revolver and stuck it under Jimmy's chin and said, 'And I ought to blow your head off for talking to me like that.' Jimmy smiled and laughed it off, but he was embarrassed by Elvis doing that."

The boys report that Presley does not like to be around other performers unless he is in charge. "We used to see a lot of Tom Jones in Las Vegas and he was a real gentleman," says Sonny. "We would go to his shows and Elvis always would say something to knock him. Tom wears very tight pants and Elvis would always say, 'He sticks a damn sock down his pants.' He would comment on Tom's singing, and during a performance, when he was in the audience, he would sing the songs along with Tom, making out that he could sing the high notes, which he couldn't."

"Unless he is the center of attention," says Sonny, "he just isn't interested. His ego is just out of control . . . and it's a pity because he wasn't like that way back. . . . It hurts to see someone you love change so very much."

# Epilogue

It was the morning of July 13, 1976, and Sonny West was at his dentist's office in Memphis. Red West was at the office of a private investigator discussing a lawsuit that had been brought against Presley. Dave Hebler was at the pool of the travel lodge near the Memphis Airport. "Judy, my wife, called me," says Sonny, "and told me that Vernon Presley had called the travel lodge and wanted to talk to me about an important matter. I called Mr. Presley from the dentist's office. He was at Graceland. He said that he would like to see me in person. I told him I was a grown man and could handle anything he could tell me on the telephone."

Vernon Presley's voice lowered and he said, "Well, things haven't been going too well, and, well, we're going to have to cut back on expenses and we're going to have to let some people go."

Sonny felt a chill creep into his body. "Oh, I see, and I guess I'm one of the ones that is going to be let go."

Vernon Presley said, "Yes, I'm afraid so. There will be others, too, unfortunately." Sonny asked who they were, but Vernon declined to answer, adding that he would prefer to tell them himself.

In a daze, Sonny drove back to the hotel and watched morosely out of his hotel room as his young son Bryan and his beautiful wife played outside by the pool. He wondered how he was going to break the news to her. Sonny called Dave and told him the news. Dave answered that he had been summoned to see Vernon Presley also. It looked like he was going to get the chop too, which materialized about an hour later. Red called Sonny's room soon after. His voice was flat. "I've been fired, man." That completed the firing of Sonny, Red and Dave.

Vernon Presley told all of them it was for economic reasons, but the boys believe the execution came as a whim of Elvis Presley's. "But what pissed us off," said Red, "after all those years I had been with him, he never took the time to tell me himself. He just cut out and left it to his father to do. It was cold, man."

It was not so much the loss of the job that hurt the boys. "It was," says Sonny, "that we believed Elvis loved us, really loved us. We knew he behaved pretty wildly and we knew he could have a bad temper, but we believed that underneath it all, he loved us and we loved him and we were part of the family. That's what hurts."

Red West had been offered fortunes in the past to write a book about Presley but had always declined. "Even when we had our blowups, I would never have considered it. We were like brothers, man. But in the end, it just worked out that we meant nothing to him."

Dave Hebler, when he got over the shock of being fired, said he was relieved. "At last I could get on with my own life and not have it tied to the whims and moods of another human. But frankly, the worst part of it all was telling my mother, Willy. She, like many other mothers, believed that Elvis was God-fearing and a Christian—a wonderful non-drinking non-smoking person. She's the one who will get a shock out of reading this, and for that I'm sorry."

All three, despite their obvious bitterness about the firing and their realization that Presley felt nothing for them, pray and hope that Presley will read the book and come to a realization that his life is leading him on a path to disaster.

"He will read," Sonny says, "and he will get hopping mad at us because he knows that every word is the truth and we will take a lie-detector test to prove it.

But just maybe it will do some good . . . if he can realize what he is doing to himself."

Under the circumstances, it would have been near impossible for a man like Presley, given his background, to come through life without his stability's being threatened. Dirt-poor kids don't grow up in a tiny shack town and become millionaires before they are twenty-one every day of the week. Presley was a classic case of too much too soon.

Red feels that if his mother had lived, it would have brought a direction to Presley's life that he seems so badly to miss. Had he stayed married to Priscilla, the same thing might have happened.

Presley, one of the world's most glamorous males, today is a very lonely man. "It's kind of sad," says Red. "All that money, all the homes and all the comfort, and yet Elvis doesn't know if he has a friend in the world. He doesn't know if the people who hang around him are there because of the money or because of him. I loved him . . . but now he hasn't got me."

Three months after the firing, a man called the boys asking if they would put off writing the book about Presley. The boys refused. The next day, Red called Graceland and spoke to Charlie Hodge, who told him that Presley was "screwed up."

At seven the next morning, a slurry-voiced Presley called Red West at his motel in Hollywood. The conversation went like this:

PRESLEY: How you doing, man?
RED: I just woke up.
PRESLEY: I was just on one of those singing binges. . . . I got a coupla new guitars and singing my ass off . . . watching little kids marvel. I'm by myself. Linda is in L.A. She's changing apartments. We had that apartment, the people found I was in back of it and raised the rent double. She got another one right down the

street. . . . Charlie [Hodge] told me about the talk you all had. I guess I do owe an explanation.

RED: I wish you had come to me and told me.

PRESLEY: You don't do things like that cause that's my daddy's business.

RED: No, it's not.

PRESLEY: I was getting a lot of excess pressure . . . you know that racketball thing? [a business he went into] . . . Two courts for a million three hundred thousand dollars. My understanding was that we were going to just use my name. And that's all and that was the contract I signed. I did it as a favor for Dr. Nick [Nichopoulos] and Joe [Esposito]. I'm just trying to tell some of the things that led up to it. . . . I was wrong about Hebler. Just a bad thing on my part. He was very undermining and sneaky. He hated all you guys and everybody else and I kept hearing this shit. It just burned into my ear . . . and those goddamn lawsuits, you know how them lawyers are. There were six lawsuits in two years. I don't know whether you heard it, but they were trying to prove us insane. . . . I'm talking about some influential people who were checking psychiatrist reports. . . . They were trying to prove us insane . . . the whole bunch.

RED: I could not believe it. You had left town. Your daddy called us and talked about cutting down expenses and giving us one week's notice. They give Chinese coolies two weeks.

PRESLEY: I didn't know anything about it. The one week thing.

RED: The bottom fell out. I got a little hurt at first.

PRESLEY: Well, I can see that. You know my damn voice is so low, I make J.D. Sumner sound like a tenor. My damn fingers are blistered. I'm not operating on but one cylinder. Well, you know what happened was a combination of a whole lot of things that piled up on me. . . . It was like a fuse burning. And maybe I did lose sight of a whole lot of things. Especially you, your family and everything.

RED: It was cold, man.

PRESLEY: I love Pat [Red's wife]. You got a good family and everything.

RED: Maybe sometimes I overprotected you. You have problems.

PRESLEY: Well, you know what it is. It's like that old guy said in *Cool Hand Luke,* a failure to communicate.

RED: We sure didn't communicate in the last year or so.

PRESLEY: Like I said, it was just a series of things. If I could lay them out to you one by one, I could show you the reasons of the separatisms. . . . My daddy was sick . . . nearly dead . . . My family is strung all over the face of the United States. It's the goddamn lawyers and lawsuits making a mountain out of the mole hill.

RED: We had some rough times. Everyone was after our ass.

PRESLEY: That's what I mean. One gets away with it or thinks they do. What they try to do is establish a pattern of insanity and violence. Like me shooting out that lamp up there.

RED: Where was that?

PRESLEY: Up in the Hilton Hotel with a .22 target pistol.

RED: Well, we're known as the Wild Bunch.

PRESLEY: Yeah, the good old days are still a fact.

RED: But the fun left.

PRESLEY: The fun ceased to exist. I couldn't pinpoint it. I couldn't pin it down. . . . Goddamn racketball courts. Two courts for half a million dollars each.

RED: That's too much.

PRESLEY: What the fuck, man . . . poor old Joe had his mother hock her house to get the money. That's what he had to do. Well, I pulled out of it. . . . It started off kinda innocent. I was told one thing, like I wouldn't have to put up a dime. Wouldn't be any money or nothing. Well, that was the contract I signed. I talked to Daddy about it just after he came out of the hospital. We talked over a period of time. If it will help Joe and Nick, they could use my name because I couldn't benefit nothing from it. I talked to my attorneys yesterday about the racketball. What would happen is that we would be out and they would start hitting me for ten thousand, one thousand. Well, I thought, are you guys putting up that kind of money? They came on tour pretending being interested in numerology books. . . . It all falls into place now. It amounted that they wanted eighty thousand dollars. I said for what? They said for a secretary.

RED: Goddamn, those secretaries, they got a union or something?

PRESLEY: I said how in the hell is a secretary going to cost eighty thousand dollars. I didn't want to crush their dreams. I tried to hang on in there with them, you know. They had all these cards and shit printed up . . . chairman of the board. It started off Presley Center Courts and they change it to Elvis Presley Center Courts without even asking me.

RED: But old Red was doing his job.

PRESLEY: I wasn't using that as an example. I was just telling you. What started out as a friendship and favor and they turned it into a million-three-hundred-thousand-dollar project. Do you realize how long it would take to realize a profit? These contractors are cold-blooded businessmen. I'm in the process of getting out of it. You know I don't even care that much for racketball. . . .

RED: I guess all that pressure led up to our demise. It was a shock. We were broke. I sold my house. Hated to do that.

PRESLEY: You sold your house?

RED: Oh, yeah, I sold my house, hated to do that. It was a bad time by all.

PRESLEY: Well, I guess there never is any really good times. It was bad for me, too. I hadn't been out of the hospital long enough to start rolling. My daddy, I almost lost him. He's my daddy, regardless of anything.

RED: I understand, but if I had just heard from you, it would have been easier to take.

PRESLEY: Well, in doing business and things of that nature, I don't do that.

RED: You mean about firing us and everything?

PRESLEY: Yeah, I had to go to Palm Springs, analyze and weigh . . . goddamn racketball courts. I'm still seeing little fuzzy balls. But Charlie was saying . . . Charlie talked to you and you thought I was on the line. I was over at Daddy's house going through these figures. If I wanted to hear something, I wouldn't do that. I would go another way.

RED: You know how paranoid everybody gets.

PRESLEY: Oh, sure, like looking over your shoulder and not knowing who the hell it is regardless of what. How's Pat and the kids and things?

RED: Just hanging on until I get something going.

PRESLEY: I was very disillusioned about Hebler. He faked me off something terrible.

RED: What did he do?

PRESLEY: He would say little things to me, who he hated. Ed Parker told me, keep him at arms length. This went on over a period of two years.

RED: I don't know what you're talking about.

PRESLEY: It's hard to explain. I don't think he liked anybody in this group. I think I'd become a dollar sign to him. In the process he lost sight of Elvis. That can easily happen. It happened, man. I'd become an object, not a person. I'm not that sign, I'm not that image, I'm myself. You're so wrong on one thing and don't get paranoid. I'm talking to you as a friend on a private line and there is no soul here. I'm not fucked up by no means. On the contrary, I've never been in better condition in my life.

RED: You had been pretty fucked up. That's what I was talking about.

PRESLEY: Well, I went through a divorce, you know,

you were there. That wedding thing [referring to Red's complaint that he was not invited to his wedding to Priscilla], I had nothing to do with that. That was railroaded through. I didn't even know who was there in that little old room the size of a bathroom with a Supreme Court Justice. It was in there over and done so quick I didn't realize I was married. I could see it back then, but that wasn't my doing. I had nothing to do with . . . you know. All of a sudden I was getting married. When you go through that you keep your mind on one thing.

RED: Let's get to the last couple, three years. Let's face it, you haven't enjoyed yourself.

PRESLEY: I enjoy my work.

RED: I know that, but what about the rest of the time?

PRESLEY: We had a pretty good time in Vail.

RED: We had a ball in Vail.

PRESLEY: I know I did.

RED: We were always worried about you. We were worried about you. Taking a few things.

PRESLEY: You worried about me so much that you turned around and tried to hurt me. You see, I know what that is.

RED: Well, that's after you hurt me. . . . You hurt me and my family very bad. . . . You left us out in the cold, so let's not talk about me hurting you.

PRESLEY: Things went on that you didn't know about.

RED: All I know I was left out in the cold.

PRESLEY: All I know there was friction created in the group, the vibes were so bad, people were scared to move and everything, so who knows what the hell they were hearing and being told. I just know it got to be very, very tense. A situation where it could have been fun and a relaxed-type thing something went wrong, and that on top of the racketball thing and everything else and all the personal things. It was a fact we did have to cut down on expenses.

RED: You gotta do what you have to do. You could

have cut down someone else. I thought I was important to the organization, and I'm glad I found out that I wasn't. I still got a little life left. I'm going to enjoy it.

PRESLEY: Oh, yeah. . . . It's just an unfortunate situation. It's just now that it's started to get back on its feet. My daddy has lost down to one hundred sixty-five pounds. . . . I think he's back up to one hundred seventy-eight now. That just shocked and scared me to death. Because you know how I feel 'cause you know how you felt about your daddy. Suspicion was cast on this group. . . . I couldn't figure out the source though. Just like that song we did, "We Can't Go On Together," with suspicious minds. Maybe I did act abruptly . . . first one to admit it . . . without thinking. You know Sonny was never around. I got nothing against Sonny. Hebler tried to bully his way through everything with scare tactics with some of these young guys. They would ask questions like . . . and they never could get a straight answer. . . . They were turned down . . . at every corner. I just felt I should talk to you and let you see my side of it.

RED: I appreciate that. That's what I wish we had done at the very first. Maybe I could have understood it a little better. What's done is done. I wish you all the luck and I hope you stay right where you are for forty more years.

PRESLEY: I'm working on it.

RED: You got to get healthy, Elvis, you haven't been healthy for a while.

PRESLEY: Oh, yes, I am. I just had an absolute physical, head to toe, in the last three weeks. One of those things that is required by Lloyds of London. That thing I had, that lower intestinal blockage corrected itself. I went on a weird liquid diet. That big intestine down there has to have bulk . . . went on a diet . . . twenty days of diet . . . and I heard that was another mistake. . . . Turns out that large intestine had nothing to work with, so as a result it stopped working. I keep hearing that shit about being fat and middle-aged.

RED: No, no, you ate a lot, but you weren't fat, you could tell there was something else wrong, something was wrong inside. When I tried to talk to you about it, you'd get mad, you wouldn't listen. We were worried about it.

PRESLEY: You know, I thought I told y'all it was the lower intestine. I supposed to undergo surgery and take part of it out. That was psyching me out because I didn't know what it was.

RED: Well, I'm glad it's all straightened out. I really am.

PRESLEY: It's been straightened out a long time. It's just a failure to communicate. What we have is a failure to communicate. Like that song Roy Hamilton did, "Understanding Solves All Problems."

RED: We didn't have much understanding there.

PRESLEY: I don't know whether it was you and I as much as it was coming from someone else . . . you know, negative vibes.

RED: I'm not into the psychic thing.

PRESLEY: I'm not either, but I do know we are constantly sending and receiving . . . all the time. I could feel the negative things but I couldn't exactly pinpoint what it was. I just reached a boiling point, hoped that you would understand it. It was a temporary thing. That was what it was, I didn't feel I could communicate with anybody. I felt terribly alone, you know, like that number eight. The thing that says they're intensely alone at heart. For this reason they feel that they feel lonely but in reality they have warm hearts toward the oppressed. But they hide their feelings in life but do what they please. Well, I'm a number eight person and so are you.

RED: It's been lonely, man, I can tell you.

PRESLEY: Well, I can see it. Maybe I was absent and listening too fast. It bugged me when you were talking to Charlie and said I was all fucked up. I'm not. I got a daughter and a life. What profiteth a man if he gains the world and loses his own soul? I love to sing . . . since I was two years old. We were sitting here playing the guitar and singing some songs, "Love Is a Many Splendored Thing," and me and Charlie talked about that harmony part, missing that harmony part.

RED: Well, what can I say, I miss singing it.

PRESLEY: Well, look, you take care of yourself and your family, and if you need me for anything, I would be more than happy to help out.

RED: Appreciate it.

PRESLEY: I mean it. I don't give a goddamn and that ain't got a goddamn thing to do with articles or no publications or none of that shit . . . that I've heard. I've just heard rumors . . . bits and pieces. I don't know nothing. I was on tour and thing . . . I have never sat down with anybody and had it laid out to me. I just know that you as a person and Pat, if there is anything I can do, any way of getting a job, anything else, let me know. I'm still here, son.

RED: I appreciate that and I will tell Pat what you said because she was hurt and the kids were hurt.

PRESLEY: All of us were hurt. It's like that song "Desada Deraida," listen to the dull and the ignorant because they too have a story to tell, and then Hank Williams wrote, "You never walked in that man's shoes and saw things through his eyes." After analyzing the blamed thing, I can see it, I can see it clearly. That's why I saying, anything I can do at all. Worried about the book? I don't think so, not on my part. You do whatever you have to do. I just want you and Pat to know I'm still here.